HUNTING AND TEACHING

In East Africa

To Matt,

Good to see you all grown up & with such a nice family. I hope you enjoy the book.

Dan McNickle 8/04

DAN McNICKLE

© Copyright 2004 Dan McNickle. All rights reserved.

No part of this publication may be reproduced, stored in a retrieval system, or transmitted, in any form or by any means, electronic, mechanical, photocopying, recording, or otherwise, without the written prior permission of the author.

Printed in Victoria, Canada

Note for Librarians: a cataloguing record for this book that includes Dewey Classification and US Library of Congress numbers is available from the National Library of Canada. The complete cataloguing record can be obtained from the National Library's online database at: www.nlc-bnc.ca/amicus/index-e.html

ISBN 1-4120-1935-4

TRAFFORD

This book was published on-demand in cooperation with Trafford Publishing.
On-demand publishing is a unique process and service of making a book available for retail sale to the public taking advantage of on-demand manufacturing and Internet marketing. On-demand publishing includes promotions, retail sales, manufacturing, order fulfilment, accounting and collecting royalties on behalf of the author.

Suite 6E, 2333 Government St., Victoria, B.C. V8T 4P4, CANADA
Phone   250-383-6864   Toll-free   1-888-232-4444 (Canada & US)
Fax   250-383-6804   E-mail   sales@trafford.com
Web site www.trafford.com   TRAFFORD PUBLISHING IS A DIVISION OF TRAFFORD HOLDINGS LTD.
Trafford Catalogue #03-2313   www.trafford.com/robots/03-2313.html

10   9   8   7   6   5   4   3

Table of Contents

Maps v
Chapter –

1	SettingSail.	1
2	Columbia & N.Y.C.	4
3	Into Africa	7
4	Moshi and Kili	10
5	Malangali	14
6	Pre-Hunting	21
7	The Election	24
8	First Safaris	30
9	A Death in the Family	34
10	Life in Malangali	36
11	The Schools	43
12	Malangali School	46
13	Malangali Students	50
14	First Elephants	58
15	Mkwawa	68
16	Got Snakes?	73
17	Dar	81
18	Central Province	85
19	Rhodesia	89
20	Daily Life	96
21	Scouting	102
22	Rujewa	105
23	Hasan	109
24	Sports Day	113
25	Third Elephant	116
26	3500 Miles to Malangali	121
27	Scotty's Camp	128
28	Back	131
29	Bro Arrives	135
30	Travels with Dave	142

31	Zanzibar	147
32	Dave's Elephant	151
33	Back to School	156
34	Lake Rukwa, One Last Time	158
35	The Rain Forest, Again	162
36	Leaving Home	165
37	Going Home	169
38	NU	176
39	Arusha	178
40	Serengeti to Tsavo	184
41	Kwa Kuchinja	191
42	Mombasa	200
43	Safaris with Hal	203
44	Socialism	216
45	AR 384/66	219
46	Oldoinyo Lengai	227
47	A Hunt with the Professionals	231
48	Last Hunt, Last Elephant	235
49	Another One Bites the Dust	239
FAQ		242
FTQ		252
Appendix A		256
Appendix B		259
Glossary		261

Maps

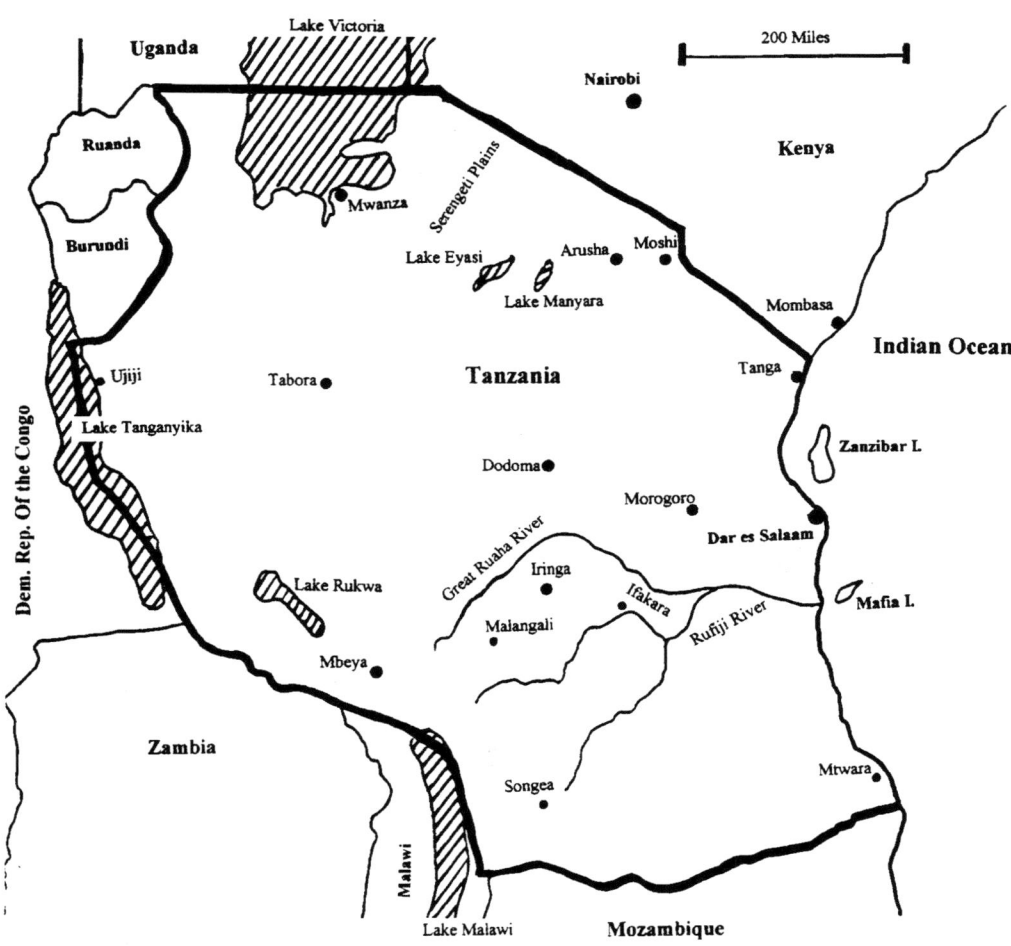

Maps

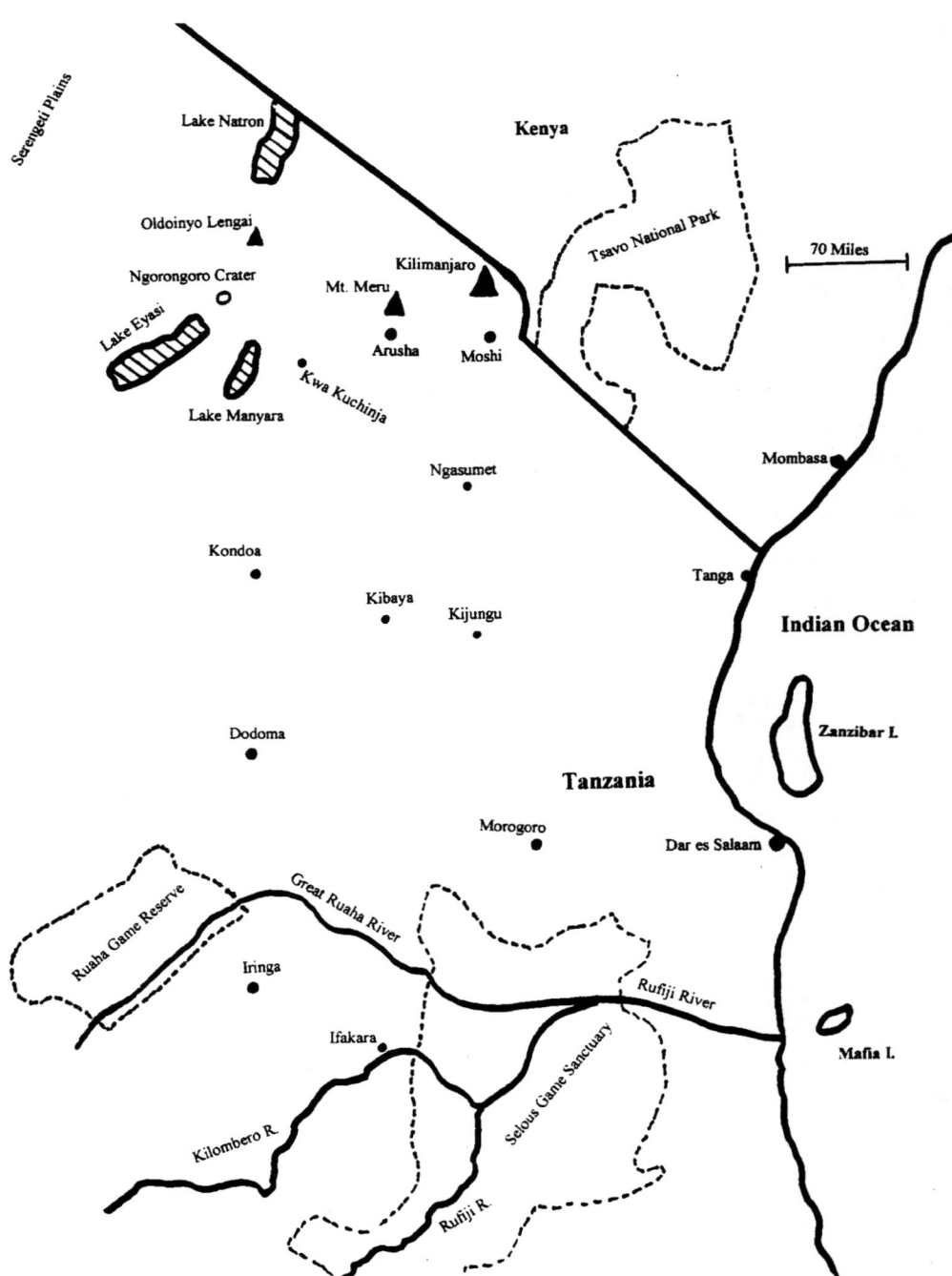

Maps

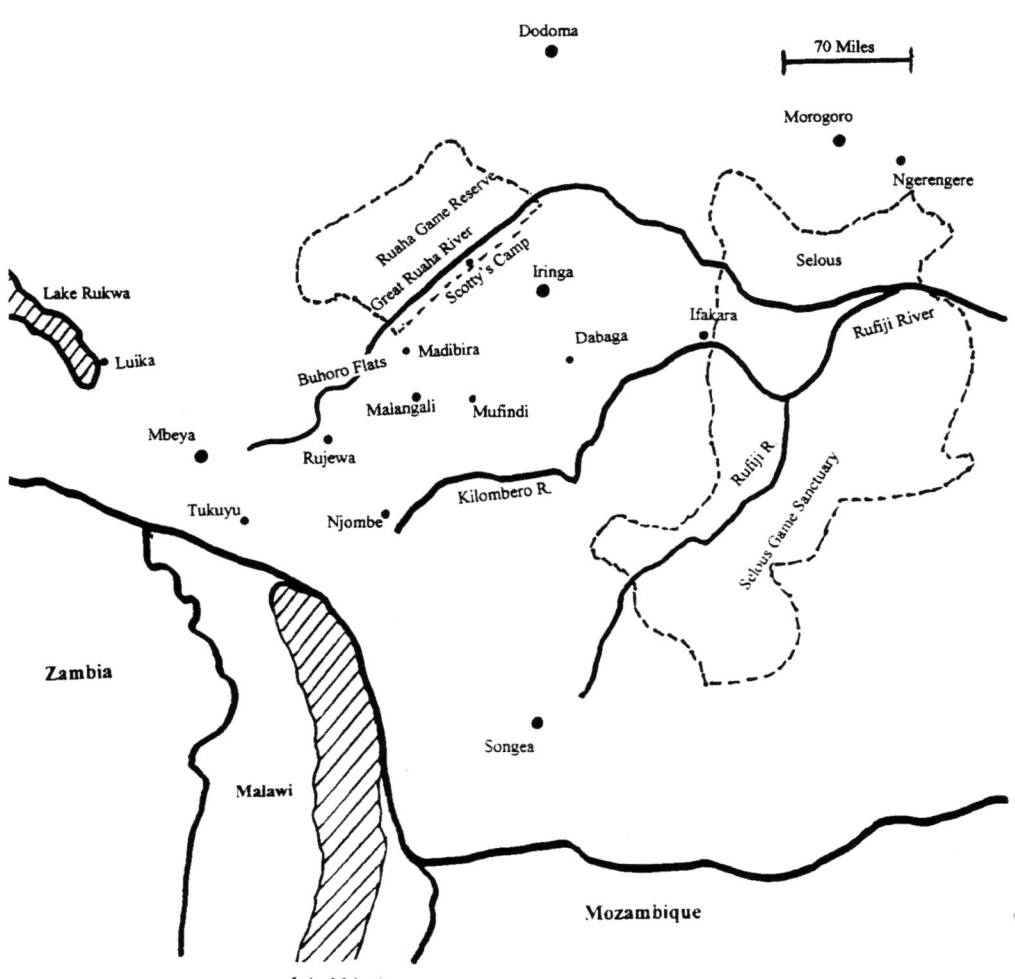

CHAPTER 1

Setting Sail

There was this phone call. It was the spring of 1962. The vice-principal came to my room and took over, while I headed for the office; excited, apprehensive, nervous, hopeful. I had a feeling this call was to be the gateway to a great adventure. The adventure of my life. And so it was.

Growing up I had become fascinated with two areas of the world: Russia and Africa. Russia because of her great writers and epic history; Africa because of the mystery, the fauna, and most of all, the possibilities.

At my junior high school in Parkland, just south of Tacoma, the library contained a good selection of books on Africa, mostly adventure and hunting. I read them all. I grew up with guns and hunting. My father, Arthur Wood McNickle, had been a marine in the 1920's. He was a good marksman and my brother Dave and I quickly and eagerly picked up on his interests in the outdoors, nature, hunting and fishing. Pop taught us the ethics of hunting. You made sure of your target. To kill a doe in buck season would have been a cardinal sin. You hunted on foot. Road hunters were an abomination. Gun safety and shooting accuracy were essential, and we were instructed early and often on the finer points of each. I got my first buck when 12 years old.

Franklin Pierce High School had a rifle team and we competed with other high school teams from Everett to Aberdeen, and a number of points in between. My senior year I was the best shot in the league. I also joined a men's team and our competitions were held one night a week at the range situated above the aquarium at the Point Defiance Zoo. These activities were all indoors. We shot .22 caliber rifles at targets 50 feet distant, with the bulls-eye the size of the bullet. The entire black, the 6 through 10 rings, was about one and one quarter inches across, with the 5 ring out in the white. There were ten targets on one sheet, one shot to each target. A perfect score was 100. We used iron sights at school, but could use iron or scope in the adult league. I had a model 52 Winchester with a peep sight in the rear and an aperture up front. With the men, I sometimes used my coach's rifle with its twenty-power scope. I always shot with both eyes open, though that took some getting used to when one

Hunting and Teaching in East Africa

view was being magnified twenty times. With such a scope you could see your heartbeats translated to the target. You could see your hits. You learned it was essential to ignore the pattern generated by your pulsing veins, and squeeze the trigger. If you tried to time the rhythm of the pattern, you invariably threw a nine, or worse.

I also shot outdoors, .30 caliber, in the summer with the Tacoma Sportsman's Club. We usually shot the national match course: offhand at 200 yards, sitting at 300 yards, and prone at 600 yards. We also had a sitting rapid fire at 200 yards, and a prone rapid fire at 300 yards. Nobody wore earplugs. You learned to concentrate and not let the blasts on either side upset your aim.

As I was walking down the long, quiet hall to the office, my recent past pushed into my thoughts. College at the University of Puget Sound. A history major more or less by default. What do you do with a history major? I hadn't really thought it through, but a person had to turn a college degree into something practical, namely a job. I didn't really want to teach American urchins, but I knew there were lots of opportunities overseas.

One of my education professors knew of both my distaste and desire, and handed me a bulletin from Columbia University, about teaching in East Africa. Before long I was heading back from the interview at Reed College, disconsolate. The representative from Columbia was very British, and he and I did not hit it off at all. So I took a teaching position at Sunnyside Junior High School in Sunnyside, Washington, for $4,700 per year. That spring, 1962, I again made the trek to Reed College and had a great interview. I think it helped that I had matured, or aged, during that first year of teaching. I was elated.

As I picked up the phone the caller identified himself and asked if I would accept an appointment to the Teachers for East Africa program. It was Columbia.

When I called my mother there was a long silent pause at my momentous news. She had gone with me to both interviews, but had evidently consoled herself with the notion that it would come to nothing. Now she was abruptly jerked from that comfortable invention and faced with the prospect of her first born disappearing into the abyss that was the Dark Continent. The continent of snakes, fierce animals, and primitive, unpredictable peoples. The continent of dread diseases, some with names and others not even in the lexicon.

We were a poor family, in retrospect, though we kids didn't see it that way at the time. Our hard working parents always managed to provide for us, but the depression weighed heavily on them. My father met Bessie Hamer, from Hoquiam, at a dance when he was stationed with the marines at the naval yard in Bremerton. They were married during the depression and I came along in January of 1938, followed fifteen months later by David, and seven years later by Judy. My mother had excellent secretarial skills, taking shorthand faster than a person could talk, and she typed accurately at over one hundred words a minute on those old manuals. Pop had schooled himself. He never finished high school, as mom had, but he learned various

Setting Sail

trades and skills: mechanic, welder, boilermaker, machinist, and operating engineer. By the 1950's, they had provided us three kids with a secure home on five acres south of Tacoma. Life was good.

And here this damned kid wants to run off to Africa, of all places. Finally, mom's voice came over the phone in the form of a question: "You aren't really going to do this, are you?" She wasn't awfully happy with the answer.

CHAPTER 2

Columbia & N.Y.C.

New York City is a marvelous and exciting place. I wouldn't want to live there, but next to London, it is my favorite big city. Neither compares favorably with Seattle, however, and I much preferred Malangali and Arusha to all of the above.

In New York one cannot help but become a tourist. There is a lot to see, and during my six weeks at Columbia I got around pretty well. I had a friend and former high school classmate who was living in New York City at the time, Ardene Brown, a nurse. She took me in tow to the usual tourist haunts, but three events stand out.

The Metropolitan Art Museum held many of the most precious creations of man. There were works by Rembrandt, Van Gogh, Rubens, Goya, and Monet, to mention a few. The paintings were not behind glass, or even fenced off. You could have walked up and touched them, if you dared. I went there often, but kept my hands to myself.

I took in a few ball games with Ardene, the Yankees and Mets. The subway dives under the East River to get to the Bronx, where seventy-five cents got you a seat in the center field bleachers at Yankee Stadium. This was the no-shirt section. We were there for a doubleheader and I watched the games some of the time, but the locals were more interesting. One middle-aged man stretched out on his back on the wooden bench, eyes closed, shirt off, radio on. He listened to the game, but didn't look. Another fan watched the Yanks, but listened to the Mets, and another was listening to the Phillies. One man came fully outfitted: picnic basket with snacks and three thermos bottles, a clamp-on chair with cushion and backrest, and of course a radio. Then there was the fellow with the strap on binoculars, leaving his hands free to attend to his radio and snacks. Nearby, an elderly gentleman talked to himself all through the ball game, and a young black man with a San Francisco baseball cap stood through the whole first game talking steadily and rapidly to a silent, bent eared friend. Oh, and the Yanks broke even that day.

One evening I subwayed to the north end of Manhattan with Ardene to attend a party. We took the Seventh Avenue line, but had to change over to the Eighth Avenue line on the way. I headed back toward Columbia about one in the morning, without my guide. Mistake. I examined the subway map, saw that the Eighth Avenue route would deliver me to the east side of Columbia, so decided there was no need to switch. When I got off and worked my way to the surface, I was in Harlem. Harlem in the 60's was not the Harlem of the 40's or 90's. Racial tensions were throbbing in the black community. As I walked at pace toward Columbia, I came upon three somewhat startled men standing on the corner visiting. I figured the best plan of action was to approach and ask directions. So, acting like a lost and stupid, fully qualified in this case, white boy, I asked and they pointed, slightly shaking their heads: "That way man."

Shortly, I entered Morningside Park, a green stretch between Harlem and Columbia. It was very quiet, with shadows everywhere. The only noise was that created by me crunching the broken glass strewn along the blacktop path. I had a Smith & Wesson .44 magnum back at home, and tried my best to will it into my hands. That didn't work, but fortunately my legs kept working and I eventually found myself at the top of the trail, staring at a locked iron gate. This gate was eight to ten feet tall, and on the other side stood one of New York's finest. He knew I was there, but didn't acknowledge my presence with so much as a glance. In my stupid mode again, I asked directions. He cocked his hand and pointed, but said nothing. I then inquired as to how I might arrive at said sanctuary. He uttered one word: "fly." Well, I wasn't going to retrace even one step, so I took his advice, clambered over the gate, said thanks to the startled flatfoot, and with considerable relief, scurried towards my safe and cozy burrow.

Most of the time I was in New York was not spent in such pleasant activities, but was spent in class. The three countries of East Africa were gaining independence from the Crown. They wanted to expand their secondary schools, but were loath to have the British in charge. After all, the idea was to get out from under the old colonial power, not be further enmeshed. They approached the United States Agency for International Development, and A.I.D. contracted Columbia University. Thus, the Teachers for East Africa Program was born. From 1961 through 1967, 461 teachers were selected for the program, and of these, 405 completed their tour of twenty-one to twenty-four months. A few would serve two tours, while others had their assignments terminated, or they resigned early, unable to cope with the magnitude of the physical and cultural challenges Africa would impose.

A.I.D. financed the program and Columbia ran it. T.E.A. was a wonderful program. We had none of the baggage of the Peace Corps: we weren't top heavy with administration, we weren't junior ambassadors, we didn't carry the 'made in America' label, and we weren't saddled with a bunch of demeaning personal restrictions. We were teachers, professionals, being sent to do a job. That is not to say we were not idealistic. Certainly there was an abundance of that, and no small amount of romanticism also. We saw ourselves going into Africa at a most important historical juncture, hoping we could play a constructive role in a successful transition from colony to country.

Our classes were centered around anthropology, history, and Swahili. We also had guest speakers with East African experience who gave us some of the flavor of living there, and some useful tidbits of information. What side of the road do you drive on? Why, the best side of course. The steering wheel was on the right side of the car, so you drove on the left side of the road, generally, and certainly when other vehicles were about. But out in the country, you weaved the best course you could. Concerning anything mechanical, you had to be specific. One of our British guests told of asking a local gas station attendant to put a patch on his flat tire. That is just what the man did, without reference to the puncture. A rather disconcerting but emphatic piece of advice was to the effect that if you hit an African with your vehicle, you should not stop. Get to the nearest police station and report the matter, but: Do Not Stop.

Our classes were full of useful stuff, but we were all anxious to know our destinations: which country; which school? In mid-July I learned I would be posted to Tanganyika. Perfect. Tanganyika was the largest and the least developed of the three countries. Even the name, Tanganyika, had a rhythm and ring to it. A week later my name appeared next to Malangali Secondary School. Malangali was a small village in the Southern Highlands. On the map it appeared to be out in the middle of nowhere. It was all I could do to control myself and not do cartwheels down the hall. Not dignified old chap.

As our last week at Columbia approached, my parents came to visit, see New York, and see me off. Columbia offered them a room for $9 a night; same building and same floor that I was on. They had the days to themselves and gallivanted all over the city. Occasionally Ardene would get time to go with them, but mostly they got around on their own. They found most New Yorkers friendly and helpful, as did I. Seems these folks were not living down to their reputation.

Shortly after my parents arrived, one of the administrative people pulled me aside and said he could get my posting changed to a less isolated school. Perhaps he misread my parents' visit. They were the only parents there, but I enjoyed their presence immensely. We went to plays and dinners in the evenings, and on the weekend I spent my time with them. But, this was not evidence of a lack of confidence or independence, on my part. We were just close. I felt my parents had got me to this point, I was grateful, and I was certainly willing to share some of the experience with them. To the administrator's surprise, I was adamant about going to Malangali; and I did, and I loved it.

August 11, 1962 was set as our departure date. I boarded the plane along with the other 113 people in my group, my dad beaming with pride, as was my mother. Whatever lay ahead, her time at Columbia reassured her that I was in good hands, and Africa was probably not going to devour me.

CHAPTER 3

Into Africa

Sitting in the Standard Bank in Moshi, I composed my first letter home from Tanganyika. I was here to cash a salary advance of 1200/-, or $171; seven shillings to the dollar, at that time.[1] We were to spend two weeks here for orientation before departing for our schools.

The trip over had been interesting and, at least in Chad, educational. Our first leg got us to Paris. We lit in one airport and took a bus across town to another. From what we could see on this one-hour transit, Paris was nothing like New York City. New York is vertical, Paris is horizontal, like a sprawling village. My most enduring impression was of the ubiquitous bicycles on the narrow streets, many with a tiny, one cylinder engine mounted on the front fender, connected by chain to a sprocket on the front wheel. These motors were about the size of a half-gallon jug. I guessed they were an aid for going uphill.

From Paris we hopped over the lake to Tripoli. After the Atlantic Ocean, the Mediterranean Sea didn't seem like much. Tripoli was hot. There was a pop machine at the airport: Pepsi, fifty cents a bottle, five times the cost in the U.S. We were only there long enough to top up the fuel tanks for the trans-Sahara flight. Our plane had two propellers on each long flexible wing. The wings were so flexible it looked like they were slowly flapping, as if to hurry the motors along over this vast expanse of sand. I grabbed a window seat. I was amazed at the extent and emptiness of the great desert. Hours droning over the Sahara at night and only occasionally a cluster of lights to be seen, a small oasis glowing like a bright star in a black sky.

Fort Lamy, now N'Djamena, was a bit of a shock. We touched down there at one in the morning: one hundred degrees and one hundred percent humidity. As soon as we stepped from the coolness of the plane our clothes were soaking with sweat. Fort Lamy was not really a city, it was one very large sauna. I am sure I was not the only one with a fleeting concern that East Africa might be similar.

Fort Lamy is near a swamp called Lake Chad. This isn't your neighborhood swamp. Lake Chad varies in size dramatically, from season to season, year to year. In October, at the end of the rainy season, the lake's surface can cover 10,000 square miles, and yet by May it will be a third that size. At a maximum depth of thirty-three feet, with most of it being between ten and twenty, it is a vast shallow basin. 1962 was a peak year for the lake, so at the time we were there it was somewhat larger than New Jersey.

As we entered the airport, we were aggressively inundated by craftsmen hawking their wares. All but one of our group heeded the pilot's advice and politely declined their offerings. There is always at least one sucker. Anyway, as I was the only person showing any inclination to purchase, I was soon surrounded by ten to twelve serious salesmen. They wore Muslim dress, had light brown skin, black flashing eyes, and daggers tucked into their robes. They knew only the operative English necessary: numbers to five, and the American word for money, dalla. The action commenced with one man offering me two pair of leather sandals for five dalla. Another man pushed through and priced two pair at four dalla. An altercation ensued with the first fellow knocking the sandals out of the other's hands, twice, and cursing him roundly. I was sorry my virgin ears couldn't decode Arabic. There was a large, black policeman standing nearby and he would occasionally cover the scene with a bored glance. I could tell he had French training. No blood, no problem. Eventually I paid five dalla for three pair from the cursed one.

Next I bought a large cow horn carved in the shape of a bird, an angry looking bird in a huff, feathers ruffled. I christened the bird on the spot: Clare Boothe, after the acid tongued wife of Henry Luce, founder and owner of Time Magazine.

A python skin wallet also found its way into my hoard, but the grand prize was two of those daggers. One in particular was very well executed. The blade was straight, seven inches long, and double edged with a needle sharp point. Lines had been engraved close along the edges of the blade, and what looked like stylized stork legs and feet, eight pair on each side of the blade, were also etched into the surface. The handle was covered with the white belly skin of a snake, with a leather pattern woven in. The butt of the handle housed a flat triangular piece of metal, not sharp, but ideally shaped to gouge out an eye, or so I fancied. The sheath was even more intricate, covered in the same white snakeskin, with more leather embroidery, a leather nub at the end, and a two-inch strip of leather near the top. A leather loop at the top of the back was just the right size to fit snugly on your forearm, thus concealing the weapon under your sleeve or robe, handle at the ready.

Experts do not always know what they think they know, much less what you think they know. In this case the pilot was just dead wrong. There was nothing like these mementos in East Africa, and as a bonus, I had a great time at the center of that little whirlwind.

Our next to last stop was Nairobi, capital of Kenya. The name comes from the Kikuyu words for cold water: "Enkare Nairobi." Nairobi was originally the site of a water hole, but when it developed as a rail head and trading center, the population grew to around 250,000[2] by the time of independence, December 12, 1963.

My impression of the physical Nairobi from the air was that it could have been any medium size American city, say Omaha or Denver. Once we got on the ground, my first impression was that it was very cool. Enough to induce shivering. Nairobi is

Into Africa

located in the highlands, about a mile above sea level. June through August, the temperatures can dip into the forties Fahrenheit, giving it a very pleasant climate for the Wazungu, or Europeans, and in fact the upland area was locally called the White Highlands.

Here our group split up, some staying in Nairobi to be posted throughout Kenya, some flew on to Entebbe, Uganda, and those of us bound for Tanganyika boarded a two prop DC-3, or gooney bird, for the flight to Moshi.

Tanganyika would be my home four of the next five years.

---

[1] In 2001, the official exchange rate was 850/- per dollar. The black market rate would vary.

[2] In Africa, all statistics are a 50/50 proposition: half educated guess and half, plucked out of the blue invention. Numbers that have to do with static situations, like elevations and distances, are often accurate.

CHAPTER 4

Moshi and Kili

As our gooney bird circled into the Moshi airport, we could see Hemingway's 'Snows of Kilimanjaro'. This massive, dormant volcano reaches to 19,340 feet, give or take a couple hundred, depending on whose numbers you accepted. Ki-**li**-ma N-**ja**-ro, just three degrees south of the equator, was first exposed to European eyes when the German missionary/explorer, John Rebmann, visited Uchagga in 1848. His report of finding a mountain with a permanent snowcap so close to the equator, was greeted with scientific skepticism by the experts of the day in Europe. Rebmann states that the Suahili people of the coast called it Kilimanjaro, or mountain of greatness. Also, he said it might mean mountain of caravans: Kilima, mountain, Jaro, caravans; a beacon for travelers visible for miles. In any case, the meaning isn't exactly clear. In Kiswahili,[3] kilima does mean hill, and mlima denotes a mountain.

The Kiswahili peoples had no word for snow and used baridi (cold), to describe the white stuff, although some Swahili thought it was silver. But the Wachagga, who lived on and around the southern slopes, called the main peak Kibo, or snow, and knew that when warmed, snow turned to water. The lesser peak, seven miles distant across the saddle from Kibo, is Mawenzi. Soaring to 16,900 feet, Mawenzi is the third highest peak in Africa, after Kibo and Mount Kenya, at 17,058 feet. For those who scale mountains, Mawenzi is much more challenging than Kibo, which is more of a stroll if you are in hiking condition and don't get too sick from the altitude.

To the Masai, the mountain is the House of God, Ngaje Ngai. I figured I was too young to enter the House of God, so never came down with the urge to climb up there. I did top Oldonyo Lengai, but that volcano was just a bump on the topography, though an active bump.

Moshi, which means smoke, was a pretty little town of perhaps 8,000-10,000 people, nestled up against the mountain like a cub snuggling mom's belly and gaining nourishment from one of her many teats. The slopes get abundant and reliable rainfall, mother's milk in Africa, and the area is also blessed with rich volcanic soil and a benign climate.

Moshi and Kili

Around the turn of the century, the Roman Catholic Mission at Kilema introduced coffee to the area. The Fathers shared their plants with the Chagga and by l9l6 some 14,000 trees were owned by Chagga growers. The crop proved so successful that in l925 the Chagga formed the Kilimanjaro Native Coffee Planters Association, "to protect and promote the interests of the native coffee growers on the mountain side."[4] By l933 this organization had evolved into the present day Kilimanjaro Native Cooperative Union or K.N.C.U. Coffee became the mainstay of Chagga prosperity and development, and it is coffee that fueled Chagga admittance into the cash economy and thus the modern world.

We were put up at the K.N.C.U. Hotel, where we had single rooms, a communal bathroom, and excellent food, including home made ice cream. Before scattering to our schools, we had two weeks of additional orientation, and acclimatization. Classes and sundowners (colonial for evening parties) were held at the hotel, but we also visited secondary schools in the area and did a little touring and hiking. At one of these schools, American pride took a humiliating beating. We played a game of softball against a team of African students coached by a teacher from Harvard. We scored ten runs, but our Ivy League infield leaked like a sieve and the locals put twelve runs on the board. The Harvard chap beamed like a proud papa. To reward this traitor, some of us were considering warming some tar and plucking some chickens.

In the evenings and on weekends we had plenty of time to explore the town. I decided to work on my negotiating skills at one of the curio stands and wore the vendor down from 20/- to 12/-, for a Masai mask carved in ebony. I was pretty pleased with my prowess, when Gloria Lindsey, a black American in our group, comes by and in no time has reduced the guy to a puddle of goo, sauntering away with two masks for 12/-. This was not a fair contest. Gloria was gorgeous, and it was rumored had been an exotic dancer, for which she had all the necessary equipment, in abundance. When she fluttered her lashes and wiggled her assets, I was surprised the vendor remembered to charge her anything.

There was a movie theater near the hotel, so one day I headed over that way to see what was playing. As I approached the theater, I couldn't believe what my eyes were telling me. Here was this African man wearing a loose fitting off-gray loincloth. He was carrying a spear and one of those old-fashioned sandwich type advertising boards. The boards, both front and rear, were touting the arrival of a new Tarzan movie.

The Tarzan movies of the day featured Johnny Weissmuller, an Olympic swimmer who had parlayed five gold medals from the l924 and l928 Olympics into a career playing Tarzan, Lord of the Jungle. The main cast included his wife Jane, who provided the female scenery but was often in need of rescuing, Boy, their 10-12 year old son, and a chimpanzee named, oddly enough, Cheetah. The Africans in these movies were portrayed as wide-eyed, befuddled dolts, and Tarzan had to bail their sorry black butts out of all sorts of predicaments, many self induced. If you had rated the Africans as forty-watt bulbs, the chimp would have come in at a hundred.

Hunting and Teaching in East Africa

One couldn't help but wonder what the local reaction would be. There was only one way to find out, but being the only European[5] in the audience, I was a bit apprehensive. Would there be a riot? Would indignation reach the boiling point, with me scalded in the process? Actually, ... no. The Africans viewed the show as high comedy! They laughed, they chuckled, they pointed to the screen, turning and smiling at their neighbors. My apprehension turned to curiosity. What exactly were they laughing at? Once in a while I could connect the laughter to what I saw on the screen, but mostly I had no clue as to what had caused the latest guffaw. Clearly, colored by their life experiences, they were seeing a different movie than I was. Perhaps they took it as being too ridiculous to be anything but farce. Perhaps they were just too innocent to be offended.

After this mystifying cultural adventure, I decided to spend some time on a subject I understood, namely guns. **Tanganyika Hunter** was located in Moshi. This was the premier gun shop in the country and I made more than one pilgrimage to ogle, fondle, and drool. There was an assortment of beautiful, handcrafted double-barreled rifles, from a .600 nitro down to a .418. The .600 Holland & Holland weighed eighteen pounds and was so barrel heavy it was awkward to shoulder and a strain to hold on target. However there was a very nice .500 Army & Navy double, about three pounds lighter and nicely balanced, that I took a fancy to and made a mental note of.

The rifle was a distant hope. A Car was a current necessity. Of course, a Land Rover would have been ideal, but I could not afford one. I did find a one-owner 1959 Simca Aronde with only 13,000 miles on it, all on paved roads. The car had been pampered, as was befitting that rather delicate French flower. However I was about to introduce her to a new lifestyle. The poor girl would develop many aches and pains over the next two years and 30,000 miles.

The night before our departure, we had a sundowner on the fourth floor of the hotel. Music was provided by an Indian band: drums, violin, accordion, banjo and bass fiddle. The songs were familiar American fare, but the odd assortment of instruments gave them a wholly new sound.

There was a 'stop and freeze' dance contest sponsored by TANU,[6] and the finalists were an African couple, and two from our group. Gloria, naturally, was one of the Americans, and her aforementioned assets mesmerized many a male eyeball. Her partner was Fred Drews, a White Cornell graduate and a member of the infamous porous infield. He was actually coordinated, on the dance floor. Can you imagine two Americans, half-and-half, doing the jitterbug to an Indian band at the K.N.C.U. Hotel in Moshi, Tanganyika, at the foot of Kilimanjaro, and winning a TANU youth award? Neither could the judges.

The trophy was presented by a member of a contingent from Guinea.[7] His speech was translated from French to English and Swahili, by another of their group. The Guineans wore the label 'Black' really well, plus they were noticeably taller than the locals, prosperous looking in their expensive suits, and well fed.

Moshi and Kili

We enjoyed our stay in Uchagga, but this was not our assigned place. On August 25, 1962, Lou Columbe and I left Moshi headed to our schools; Lou to Ifunda, just west of Iringa, and me to Malangali.

---

[3] In Kiswahili, the prefix Ki is used for languages, U for the land of a people, and Wa for the people: Kichagga, Uchagga, Wachagga. In Kiingereza (English), these prefixes are often left off, unless needed for clarity or effect.

[4] Moffett, Handbook of Tanganyika, 1958, p. 212

[5] In East Africa, European was the general term that covered all whites.

[6] TANU is short for the Tanganyika African National Union, soon to be the only legal political party in the country.

[7] Guinea was a French colony in West Africa, and the word guinea comes from the Berber for Land of the Blacks.

Kilimanjaro from the Sanya Plains, 35 miles to the west towards Arusha

CHAPTER 5

Malangali

Three days and 6oo miles later, I was in Malangali. I hadn't realized Tanganyika was so large: 365,000 square miles, or the size of the states of Washington, Oregon, California and New York, combined. Or, from the viewpoint of an easterner, the size of Maine, Vermont, New Hampshire, Massachusetts, Connecticut, Rhode Island, New York, Pennsylvania, Maryland, Virginia, West Virginia, North Carolina, South Carolina and Georgia.

We left Moshi just after noon heading west to Arusha, a town about the size of Moshi, with its own large mountain. We paid little heed to either however, as we were anxious to push south toward our goal for the day, Dodoma, the halfway point of our journey. Thirty miles out of Arusha we saw our first wild animals of the trip, six giraffe just fifty feet from the road. When another car came by, they took off in their slow motion fashion and soon disappeared into the bush. Shortly we came up on a male ostrich running along side the road. These animated drumsticks can hit thirty miles per hour but look like they are about to come unglued at that speed; legs flying, wings flapping awkwardly, feathers settling to earth in their wake. This one soon tired of the chase and trotted off into the open plain to join its mate. By the time we got to Dodoma, we had seen dikdik, gazelle, baboon, and one huge, ugly dead snake. We also saw our first Masai, a collection of other folk, mostly farmers, and two albino Africans, one a half-crazed girl running towards us across a sand river. She was madly rotating her head, causing her long golden hair to whirl above her shoulders like a single propeller.

We pulled into the Dodoma Hotel about 9 p.m., too late for dinner, but the lady of the house brought up some delicious cold cuts, potatoes, radishes and tomatoes. Lou and I ate in our cushy beds and amused ourselves with talk about roughing it in Africa. In the morning, before breakfast, we were served tea in bed, and our shoes vanished, shortly to reappear, polished.

We left Dodoma early the next morning, about thirty minutes after eight. Dodoma had not much to recommend it, so we did not linger. Hot, dry, dusty, depressing, that was Dodoma. We had run out of tarmac about seventy miles south

Malangali

of Arusha, and from that point it was dirt roads to ten miles north of Iringa. Some was gray and dusty, some was red and dusty, and some was rocky and dusty. The longer I drove, the faster the safe speed seemed to get and before long fifty to sixty miles an hour on those wash-board, pot-holed, undulating roads seemed perfectly reasonable.

As we sped along we spotted a long black object in the road ahead, a snake. He was too big to be anything but a python, but he was jet black, the sun glistening off his skin. He could feel us coming and tried to make cover, but we were too fast and he was too slow. Just before contact he suddenly reared his head to the level of the bonnet[8] and flared his hood: a cobra.[9] I had seen a few pictures of Indian king cobras, but they were not as large as this snake: over twelve feet long and three to four inches through. We were impressed. And excited. I slammed on the brakes and we jumped out of the car, cameras in hand, but the cobra had crawled into a thicket. We could hear but couldn't see him, and going in after him didn't seem to make a lot of sense.

Later we came into a hilly area where the road became narrow and twisted. We had to stop to let an oncoming lorry (truck) negotiate a sharp curve, but as we finally topped the hill and started rehashing our cobra experience suddenly a duplicate lay right in front of us. This time I locked up the brakes just before impact, hoping to slide over the snake and kill him in the road. We slid over him all right, but we lost visual contact. Where was he? Coiled under the car perhaps, wounded and mad as hell? Soon enough this issue was cleared up as I noticed his tail disappearing into the brush five feet from my head. With alacrity I cranked up the window and we piled out the left side of the car. We scrambled up the four-foot bank that bordered the road and could hear the cobra moving in a pile of tinder dry brush left by a road crew. Lou latched onto a large branch and began to flail the brush pile. Shortly the cobra started to stir. We heard him before we saw him, but out his head came, the embodiment of impassive death. He surveyed the scene. Lou was to his left wielding a big stick and I was ten feet or so to his right, wielding an 8mm camera. He opted for me. The jammed viewfinder on my camera made everything appear further away than it really was, so as the cobra worked itself across the brush pile towards me, he didn't appear all that close, but I noticed the acute angle between him and me was shrinking. My camera, instead of pointing out ahead of me, was now pointing down. I peered around the camera to see him only a few feet distant, still coming. I was thankful I didn't trip on anything during my hasty retreat.

We arrived in Iringa, having covered the 170 miles in four hours, with two cobra breaks thrown in. Lou's wife Reni was there, as was Vicki Dierauf, whose husband Ed was also in our group. Both women had been flown on ahead, as Vicki had a bun in the oven and Reni hadn't been feeling well. I spent the night at the White Horse Inn and had a chance to chat up some hunters in the bar that evening. The possibilities I had been harboring now sounded like probabilities.

Hunting and Teaching in East Africa

The next morning I fitted the Simca with two new tires and started the ninety-eight miles to Malangali, alone. Iringa sits on a cliff, above the Little Ruaha River, and as I descended the escarpment the view was expansive. The river banks down below were crowded with thick vegetation, while the landscape beyond was dotted with acacia trees stretching toward hills, low and rolling further to the southwest, high and closer, to the south. From the Livingstone Mountains south of Iringa to the Poroto Mountains near Mbeya, 240 miles distant, there is a continuous ridge of hills, some as high as 9700 feet above sea level. The principal drainage systems are the Great Ruaha River to the north of this ridge, and the Kilombero, to the south. Both of these rivers join the Rufiji well before it empties into the Indian Ocean, just opposite Mafia Island. The first few miles were tarmac, and then back to the dirt. At mile ninety I came to Njiapanda. Njiapanda means crossroads, and here a large green sign indicated in yellow letters that Malangali Secondary School was down the road to the right, eight miles.

The road to Malangali was narrow, much of it a one-and-a-half car road. It was rougher than the main roads, but parts of it were shaded by tall, non-native eucalyptus trees, the handy work of Europeans. I took my time, savoring the feelings of anticipation and excitement, and suffering the occasional twinge of anxiety. On the outskirts of the village another sign, white with black letters, announced the presence of Malangali Government Secondary School. Above the lettering was a green coat of arms and the school motto: Never Give In.

The single story buildings to the right were old and looked it. These were remnants of the German era: the 1880's to 1918. When the Germans lost World War One, they also lost Tanganyika. These brooding, tin-roofed buildings enclosed a small courtyard. The gray whitewash had worn away in places, leaving a pox of underlying brown clay patches. The school workshops were located here, but an air of sadness hung over the place, a lingering vapor from an earlier chapter: a chapter of terrible tragedy.

> In the early 30's a girl's school was located in these buildings. It was a brief interlude, and abruptly the school ceased to exist. The Provincial Commissioner's Annual Report for 1934 reads as follows: In October the province and the Territory were shocked by a tragic occurrence at Malangali when 37 pupils attending the girls school lost their lives as a result of arsenical poisoning by cattle dip, which was accidentally administered to them by mistake for shark oil. The affair naturally caused considerable consternation among the tribesmen in general and the inhabitants of Malangali in particular. At one time there were definite indications of hostility. As a result of personal interviews with the parents and relatives of the deceased children a calmer atmosphere later prevailed. The opportunity of expressing their feelings personally afforded them an outlet for their grief. As a measure of sympathy for the bereaved parents and relatives of the deceased children government made an ex-misericordia payment in each case amounting to the bride price ruling in the locality, and in addition paid all the funeral expenses. By the middle of December police investigations, which required the recall of an officer from overseas leave, were completed....

Malangali

Mr. Bangu presided over this complex, his sunny disposition never betraying the sad history just beneath the surface. His assistant however, looked like he wore the experience as a permanent coat.

The rest of the school buildings, built of brick with tile or corrugated metal[10] roofs, were newer and more substantial, even impressive. As I parked in front of one, the office, out stepped the headmaster, an older, florid Englishman in white shirt and shorts. He introduced himself and inquired as to whom I might be! Evidently, the message of the drums hadn't carried this far inland. Although Mr. Partner was surprised at my arrival, he was quite unruffled, being used to arrivals, departures and changes, with little or no notice.

He toured me around the school, introduced Mrs. Partner, who was head of the English department, and located the three Americans already on the staff. Eleanor DeSelms, Harold Hanson and Don Adams were part of the first wave of the Teachers for East Africa Program. Eleanor was from Colorado but graduated from Smith College, Harry was the son of a Lutheran minister in Minnesota, and Don was a Californian.

The school was fully staffed when I arrived, so I occasionally filled in for Mrs. Partner, a thin, frail, rail of a woman. I moved in with Don and Harry temporarily, as all the staff houses were occupied. Don was hard to live with. He was obsessive-compulsive about small matters, like accounts. We shared expenses, and everything had to be figured to the penny; an East African penny; one-seventh the value of an American penny. None of this rounding-off nonsense for him. He was a big man with a ready smile, but he wore his emotions on his sleeve and could blow up over some niggling matter, only to soon be wallowing in remorse, sorry for his actions. This act got old in a hurry.

Harold, whom I called H., was on the thin side, a black Lincolnesque beard covering his often animated face. Harry was emotionally secure, easy to get along with, and rational. Harry and I became good friends, hunting and traveling together over wide stretches of East Africa.

Eleanor, on the other hand, was more complicated than any of us guys. She was born in the West, but was the product of an eastern girls' school education. Though in her twenties, her hair was gathering some prematurely gray highlights and she was developing a matronly set of hips: so round, so infirm, so fully packed.[11] Her house was across from Don's and just down the road fifty yards from the house that I would soon occupy. When we boys later got into hunting, she was surely amused, in a superior, female sort of way. Men, don't they ever grow up? She was our proxy sister: critical, opinionated, independent, strong willed, and not about to take any guff from her siblings. Still, we ersatz brothers all liked her and put up with her quirks and moods.

We all got on well with the Brits: the Partners, Schofields, Thomases, and Barret. Alf Schofield was a blustery man from the midlands of England, with a big barrel chest and smallish legs. A no nonsense type of guy. He and his wife Hillary had two young boys. Cyril Barret was a spindly man in his forties or early fifties, and could he absorb the beer. I think his body was 90% beer. He didn't have beer in his blood, he had beer for blood. Yet, he never appeared at all affected, much less drunk. Ian and Ceinwen Thomas were the ones we fraternized with most, however. He was English and she was Welsh. Ian was very disciplined, while Ceinwen was a blithe spirit. They taught us how to play whist, and Ceinwen would often join us three male Yanks for tennis.

On one such occasion Don and I were standing just outside the staff room and Don asked Ceinwen to join us down at the courts. Ceinwen, in her bright, perky way said: "Fine. When you are ready, come by the house and knock me up." Well I managed to keep a straight face, but of course Don immediately lit up, his entire continence turning into one huge silly grin. When Don explained through his smirking lips what this expression meant in the good old U.S. of A., Ceinwen immediately turned a bright crimson. She recovered quickly, however, and ever after when we invited her for tennis she would reply with a mischievous smile: "OK, when you are ready come round and knock me up."

Later, when the Asian (Indian) schools were nationalized, we got two Indian teachers. Mr. Amin was ramrod straight, though slight of build. Every evening he would lead his family on a stroll, he in front, hands clasped behind his back, shoulders squared, and his wife and kids behind, single file like a row of ducks, all in order according to height. Unlike ducks however, I never heard a peep from the kids.

Mr. Phadke was wrapping up his career in Tanganyika and had sent his wife back to India, with him to follow when his contract was up. He was fiftyish, balding, a little portly, and an excellent cook, a rarity for an Indian man. He taught Don, Harold and I how to play bridge, using an Italian system that the Indians of East Africa had modified. He would make delicious Indian snacks like chevdo, bhajia, ladu or gatia, which we Yanks would descend upon like vultures. Needless to say, we looked forward to his invitations to cards.

We had only one graduate African teacher, Joseph Muwowo, but when I arrived he was making arrangements to leave on scholarship to Dublin, Ireland, so I never got to know him. However, Mr. Bangu was a fixture at the school, the only fixture. While the rest of the staff flowed in and out like the tide, he and his assistant were locals. One of the dorms was named 'Bangu House', after his father, a prominent mzee[12] in the village. Mr. Bangu had a smile for everyone and was liked and respected by students and staff alike. While he was always neat, Mr. Tumwidike was always disheveled: wild hair and tattered clothes. He did all sorts of maintenance about the school and was very loyal to Mr. Bangu. He was likable, just a little sad and wild looking.

The staff at Malangali Secondary School was thus quite diverse. The school sat on the southeast edge of the village. Malangali, at 4000 feet above sea level, had a comfortable climate, with a stated average rainfall of about thirty-five inches per year. The vegetation did not reflect this generous amount however, with acacia trees and thorn

Malangali

scrub dominating the flora. The rains were erratic, some years way below the average, then a year with eighty inches or more. The vegetation tended to reflect the low years.

During the German period, the village had been an administrative center, on the main road. But troublesome washouts caused the British to move the road to higher ground, eight miles to the south. We got the bulk of our supplies over this now usually passable road, from Iringa. The next nearest settlement was Mbeya, one hundred fifty-three miles to the west. Malangali was, altogether, a great location for living, teaching, and hunting.

---

8 In British, the hood of a car is called the bonnet; the trunk is the boot.
9 I would later learn that this python sized cobra was called a giant forest cobra. I would see two on this day, and only one more in the next four years
10 When it rained, these corrugated roofs became Mother Nature's drums, making it almost impossible to lecture.
11 Paraphrase of a cigarette advertisement of the 40's and 50's: LSMFT: Lucky Strike Means Fine Tabacco; So Round, So Firm, So Fully Packed.
12 Mzee refers to an old man, but in Swahili this is an endearing expression of respect. Percentage-wise, not many people make it to old age, so an elder is a walking treasure.

Malangali Staff - Front row: Me, Eleanor, Alf, Bangu, Ian. Back Row: Harold, Cyril, Dan, Don, Mbelwa, Tumwidike.

Ian and Ceinwen Thomas and daughter Glenda.

Meat arrives for student mess. Twice a week a cow was slaughtered in the village according to Muslim custom and the school got a portion to mix into the students' meals.

CHAPTER 6

Pre-Hunting

In Tanganyika you didn't just get a hunting license and head for the boonies. You couldn't even get a hunting license unless (Rule 1) you first purchased a gun. You could not purchase a gun unless (Rule 2) you had a license to do so. You couldn't procure said gun license unless (Rule 3) you had the serial number and description of the exact gun you were going to purchase. And, of course, none of this could be done locally, requiring multiple trips to Iringa or Mbeya.

I had been actively pursuing leads on guns since my arrival. In September I applied for a gun license in Iringa, but it was turned down as too vague: see Rule 3. So the first free day after that, October 2, Cyril Barrett and I left for Mbeya, a three-and-a-half hour drive west. About forty miles of this section of 'The Great North Road' was narrow, winding, and in poor condition, a relative term, but at least the last seventeen miles into town were tarmac.

About nine in the morning we drove up to a store that had Arms and Ammunition lettered across its façade. The Indian owner, Mr. Manji, was very cordial, but more importantly, very efficient. Once we had established what I was about, he phoned **Tanganyika Hunter** in Moshi. A half-hour later the connection was actually made and Manji arranged with Mr. Wagner for me to purchase that .500 Army and Navy double-barreled nitro express I had coveted while there. Wagner was to airfreight the rifle and fifty rounds of ammunition, twenty-five hard and twenty-five soft-nosed, immediately, at a cost of 2600/-, or $371. Manji said he would see to all the licenses and I could collect everything on the weekend, four days hence. I figured that was optimism run rampant, but he wasn't far wrong.

We were quite taken with Mbeya, a beautiful little town, higher, at 5800 feet, and greener than any town I had seen so far. Cyril and I went to the local market and I bought a basket, some potatoes, and a hand broom made of a wide, thin grass, then we headed home.

The weekend came and went, sans telegram. But on Wednesday the tenth word came via wire that the rifle had arrived, so on Saturday Harry and I hustled ourselves down to Mbeya. On arrival everything was in order, which in East Africa sometimes happens. Not only was the gun there, with case and the fifty rounds of ammo, but even the licenses were ready and waiting. As a bonus, the cost was 200/- less than anticipated. I was set to go: licensed rifle and general game and buffalo licenses.

Game licenses in Tanganyika were cheap, especially for residents. Those of us in the TEA Program were employees of the Tanganyika government. As such we were considered residents and were paid according to the local salary schedule. A.I.D. kicked in an overseas differential, which was run through the Tanganyika Department of Education and brought our pay up to American levels, or at least to Washington State levels. I was thus making exactly what I had been paid in Sunnyside, Washington: $4,700 per year. For those teachers from states like Idaho and Montana, however, this was a considerable boost in salary.

In 1962 the General Game License cost 100/-. For your $14.30 you could shoot forty antelope of various kinds,[13] from eland to dikdik. In addition to this array of antelope, two hippo, three warthog, three zebra, and an unlimited number of game birds were allowed. Dangerous and less common game, like kudu or sable, were hunted under supplementary licenses ranging from 10/- for buffalo to 600/- for elephant.[14] Yearly, three buffalo and three elephants were the bag limits for residents: three cape buffalo at anywhere up to 2000 pounds in weight, for $1.43 each!

Also, as a resident I could hunt dangerous game on my own, that is, without a professional hunter in tow. This greatly reduced cost, but greatly increased risk. The learning curve had to be steep. I would prove that stupidity was not necessarily fatal, but continued stupidity surely would have been. Luck is good. Luck is sometimes better than knowledge or skill. But luck is fleeting, and the law of averages is a 50/50 proposition. If you are hunting dangerous game, you do not want to come home alive 50% of the time.

---

[13] The antelope: Bushbuck (2), Dikdik (2), Duiker (6), Eland (1), Grant's Gazelle (2), Thomson's Gazelle (3), Hartebeest (4), Impala (2), Klipspringer (2), Oribi (1), Pigmy Antelope (2), Puku (1), Reedbuck (1), Roan Antelope (1), Steinbuck (2), Topi (2), Waterbuck (3), and Wildebeest (3). The Birds: Ducks, Geese, Francolin, Quail, Guinea Fowl, Lesser Bustards, Snipe, Sand Grouse, and Pigeons. On birds there were daily limits of from 6 to 25, but no season limits.

[14] Some other supplementary license fees: Kudu, lesser or greater, 100/-, Leopard 250/-, Lion 200/-, Oryx 100/-, Ostrich 100/-, and Sable Antelope 100/-.

Pre-Hunting

.577 case on left, and .500 on right. The Spaghetti looking stuff is the cordite powder that propells the 500+ grain bullets. Fountain pen in foreground for scale.

CHAPTER 7

The Election

Tanganyika was to hold its first presidential election on November 1, 1962. A week prior to that date Mr. Partner asked if I would be willing to help. I don't know what prompted him to volunteer me, but since I was probably the most political person on staff and somewhat vocal in my support of African self-determination, perhaps Partner thought my idealism should be leavened with a dose of reality. On October 26, a meeting was held at the middle school where eleven of us, ten Africans and one American, were given instructions and assignments. I had been told they probably wouldn't need me, but I emerged as the Presiding Officer of Polling Station #20 at Mbweni, on the road to Madibira.

The Area Secretary, a young Englishman, explained the voting procedures. The voter would have a numbered receipt that was to match a number the polling officials would have in their registration receipt books. Each voter thus identified would be given a ballot with Mtemvu or Nyerere as the choices. An X would be marked, in pencil, and the ballot would be folded and slipped into a locked ballot box. It all sounded simple and reasonable to me. But, of course, it wasn't.

Just prior to the election we learned that Julius Nyerere would be visiting our school, along with the regional and area commissioners. This caused quite a stir. The regional and area commissioners, with an entourage of twenty, had already paid Malangali a visit, but were treated rather to a roast than a reception. The students felt superior to them, asked pointed questions, and called some of their answers lies. When the Area Commissioner made some remark about a portrait of the Queen and Prince Philip hanging on a wall in the mess hall, the students reasoned that it was up to TANU to present the school with a picture of Nyerere if they wanted it displayed. One student pointed out, to loud applause, that the Queen and Prince were symbols of the Commonwealth. The students also raised questions about the new Preventive Detention Bill and were not mollified by the answers. I think some of the more political of our students felt this law might be aimed at them somewhere down the road, and well it might.

The Preventive Detention Bill allowed the government to imprison anyone, for

The Election

any reason, for up to a year. After a year, a signature from the President could tack on another year. Thus, theoretically, a person out of favor with the government, or perhaps some Regional Commissioner, could spend years in goal, without the benefit of formal charges or a trial. However the law was much worse in potential than practice. It was used, but rarely.

Julius Nyerere arrived on African time, that is, two hours late. At nine-thirty, we were all pretty excited, but by eleven-thirty the enthusiasm had waned a bit. He made a short speech and then opened the meeting to questions. The students were happy to see him, but not awed or shy in their questioning. The entire performance was done in Swahili, so I mostly just observed the interplay of emotions. Our students were polite and attentive. They rightly did not feel superior to this man. They respected Nyerere, though not always in agreement with him.

The area and regional commissioners were slavish in their fawning, a surprise to no one. They were both sycophants, people of modest talents thrust into positions of responsibility and power: eager to avoid the former and embrace the latter. There were some good and capable men at the top of TANU, but as the chain of command descended, so did virtue and aptitude.

There were two Europeans in Nyerere's party. Lady Chesham, a transplanted American from Philadelphia, was a Tanganyika citizen and a Member of Parliament. A Brit named David Ricardo was the other pale tag-along. He had a cattle ranch near Sao Hill, about halfway to Iringa from Malangali. On foot he had driven a herd of cattle over five hundred miles from Moshi to Sao Hill, with a group of Masai. I had a good chat with both of these interesting people, and even a brief visit with Nyerere himself.

Julius Nyerere was not at all impressive, physically. He was short, slight, and looked older than his forty years. The role of Empire breaker did not seem to fit this soft appearing little African man. To take on the colonial government, buttressed by the British Empire, was toil for a Hercules, not a Julius. He smiled and laughed easily and in no way appeared to be the man of granite will that he most certainly was. In short, Mwalimu[15] looked like an affable school teacher, not the founder of a rough and tumble political party or the architect of Uhuru[16] for Tanganyika.

Of course for a number of years Julius Nyerere was a teacher, an affable, popular teacher. He was born some time in 1922, one of twenty-six children from eighteen mothers.[17] His father was chief of the small Zanaki tribe in northwest Tanganyika, near Musoma. Perhaps the luxury of eighteen wives accounted for his father's longevity, as he lived for eighty-two years.

Young Julius herded the family livestock and performed the usual tasks of a boy in a traditional, subsistence family. Before long, however, this precocious youngster had talked his father into letting him attend the Catholic boarding school in Musoma, a town on the east edge of Lake Victoria. In 1937 he ventured south to continue his education at the government secondary school in Tabora. In 1943 he was baptized into the Catholic faith, and in that same year he entered Makerere University in

Hunting and Teaching in East Africa

Kampala, Uganda. At that time Makerere was the only university in East Africa and here he met other members of the African elite, including Ibrahim Sapi, grandson of the famous Hehe chief, Mkwawa.

It was at Makerere, among this privileged intelligentsia, that Nyerere's political life began to gestate. In addition to the lively discussions and debates, Nyerere saw political potential in the Tanganyika African Association, an African social study group started by colonial governor Sir Donald Cameron, in the 1920's. Talk about sowing the seeds of your own destruction! You plant beans, you expect beans. You start a social club, you expect a polite, tea-sipping, educational discussion group, but maybe you get a political party bent on your demise.

In 1945, Nyerere left Makerere and accepted a teaching post at St. Mary's Catholic Boys' School, run by the White Fathers in Tabora. Two Catholic priests, Father Walsh at St. Mary's and Father Collins in Musoma, had considerable influence on Nyerere's life and thought, and he remained a devout Catholic through all of his adult years.

Nyerere taught at St. Mary's until 1949, when he left to attend Edinburgh University and earn his Masters of Arts degree, which he completed in 1952. A year later he was teaching at St. Francis, a Catholic secondary school located at Pugu, just a few miles inland from Dar es Salaam, the capital of Tanganyika. The wolf was at the gate: not a fire breathing wolf, not a violent wolf, but an intelligent and determined wolf.

Nyerere and his fellow activists had been working within the Tanganyika African Association and used this vehicle to form a full-fledged, nationwide political organization. Saba Saba[18] Day, July 7, 1954, is the national holiday that commemorates the founding of this political organ, the Tanganyika African National Union. Shakespeare asked, What's in a name? There is plenty in this name. African meant no Whites and no Asians. National simply meant nationwide, but Union not only meant united, it served notice that all politics would be conducted under this one roof.

Nyerere argued that Tanganyika could not afford the divisiveness of a multi-party state. An independent government would need to be focused to use all of its efforts and meager resources for the national good. He felt this could still be a democratic system, but in the African mode of consensus through palaver. A multi-racial party was also not an option. Colonialism had served to humiliate the African and undermine his self-confidence. Many in TANU feared the admission of Europeans and Asians would dilute their goal of 'Africa for the Africans', or lead to White and Asian subversion, if not dominance, of their African organization.

This ban on non-Africans remained in effect until 1963, at which point independence had been achieved by TANU, and Africans were firmly in control. The exclusion of Europeans and Asians from TANU was not racist, but political in nature. That did not mean that all TANU activists were not racists, some certainly were, but the overriding mission of the party was not only to gain independence, but to re-kindle African self-respect and confidence. This could not be done with Europeans and Asians leading the way, or even visibly helping. Behind the scenes, sympathetic

The Election

Whites and Asians did aid and abet TANU, but their help was sub-rosa, and in fact of only peripheral importance. TANU was an African movement, and independence an African achievement. Nyerere's first cabinet, it should be noted, did contain one European and one Indian, not members of TANU, but members of the government, appointed by Nyerere and serving at his pleasure.

Shortly after independence had been secured, December 9, 1961, Nyerere resigned and his trusted lieutenant, Rashidi Kawawa, became Prime Minister. Nyerere turned his energies to establishing a Republic with himself as President, thus supplanting the Crown as head of state. That is what this election was all about.

The day before the election my ride to Mbweni was to pick me up at mid-day. Around two in the afternoon I motored up the road to the middle school, and although the Landrover hadn't yet arrived, it was due shortly. Evidently, shortly and mid-day were synonyms for 8 P.M. Through the dark we drove to Mbweni, which consisted of one house. The headman was not there, but his wives, frightened by the Rover or the Mzungu within, directed us to Logodo. With no more than the word of some half-scared, illiterate women who wanted rid of us, we departed for this substitute polling station. Logodo was also a one hut settlement, but the resident assured us the women were right and that the sub-chief from Malangali had been there the previous day and knew all about it, although it seemed the officials of the government were not in the loop.

They prepared my cot in a small, smoky brick shelter to the rear of the hut. The smoke kept the mosquitoes at bay, but I got little sleep and arose at five-thirty the next morning. Two hours later our polling station was set up and shortly our first voter emerged from the bush. His voter registration receipt did not match any number in our receipt books. A few more citizens arrived, but their numbers were equally non-compliant. About this time, a well-dressed African man arrived and introduced himself as the Presiding Officer of the Sandani polling station. He had no ballot box, no ballots, no registration books, and no instructions. My assistant Nathan, from the middle school in Malangali, knew the man as a headmaster from another middle school. We talked with the local representative of TANU and found out that actually there were supposed to be two polls in this one hut. Since we had no receipt books in the one instance, and the wrong ones in the other, we loaded our gear and all left for the nearest telephone at John's Corner, twenty-five miles away. After an hour's drive we reached the phone but couldn't get through to Malangali as the messenger at the post office was evidently out, and the only phone in the village was in the post office. Back into the Rover, we pressed on to Nyololo, fifteen miles further up the road. Nearing Nyololo we happened upon the Area Commissioner, the roasted one, and he informed us that the Nyololo polling agents also had the wrong books but were letting everyone with a registration receipt vote. He was going on to Iringa to see the Area Secretary, the man in charge of the election hereabouts, but suggested we follow Nyololo's lead. Under the circumstances, this seemed eminently reasonable. We continued on into Nyololo anyway, and exchanged books, as they had Sandani and

Hunting and Teaching in East Africa

Mbweni books. Eureka? Not exactly.

We arrived back at Logodo around noon and immediately set up our polling station, four hours late. In the United States we would have had a riot on our hands, but Logodo looked like a county fair on opening day. Magically, hundreds of people had percolated out of the surrounding bush and they were milling about, visiting, catching up on local happenings with old acquaintances, and just generally having a good time. Africans were not slaves to the clock, and if you were, you had better get over it.

Inside the house we had a couple of benches behind which the TANU representative, Nathan and myself sat. The TANU man could not talk to the voters, he was there to observe. Nathan was to help me with language issues, and naturally he spoke Swahili, but he knew no Kihehe. I was the Bwana Mkubwa[19] and, supposedly, fully in charge of this shambles.

The local people were wonderful: polite, patient, and positive. The women went first, but were clue-less. Only one out of three hundred fifty women marked the ballot on her own, and correctly. This slowed down the process tremendously as I had to ask each one their choice, and then mark it for them. I would ask: "Unataka Mtemvu au unataka Nyerere?" The answer was always Nyerere, or something close, or they would simply point to the black dot, Nyerere's symbol next to his name. These women had never used, maybe never seen, a pencil before, so its operation was a mystery, particularly the soft end, which didn't seem do much. So I did the marking. I figure this green, been in the country two months, white boy cast over four hundred votes for Nyerere that day.

At first we tried to match registration numbers with those in our newly found books, but this was a hit and miss proposition. A few did match, but most didn't, so after fifteen minutes we just closed the books. Anyone with a registration receipt was allowed to vote, and after all, that was the point. Mtemvu had as much chance of winning as a dikdik would wrestling a crocodile. The process was important, not the outcome. It was important that the most common of people felt they had taken part in the formation of the new government. After all, Nyerere would win, and not because the election was rigged. He would win because he deserved to win. He was the man of the people, their leader, their George Washington, their Mwalimu.

Before long we had a system that worked pretty well. Nathan would take their registration receipt, they would pass on to me, and I would help them with the ballot. A few had places to put the ballot other than the ballot box, the most popular being down the front of their dresses. I did not personally retrieve any of these, but between Nathan and myself, we were able to coax such ballots out of hiding and into the proper receptacle.

The first woman to get down on her knees and lower her head to the ground caused me considerable consternation, though nobody else seemed to even notice, much less berate her. She hadn't knelt before the TANU man or Nathan, so it was my precious pigmentation she was acknowledging. I popped out of my chair and exhorted her, with arms and voice, to stand up. "Hapana Mama, Uhuru sasa." "No Mama,

The Election

freedom now." She seemed bewildered by my reception of her homage. I looked imploringly to my left for help from Nathan or the TANU guy, but they looked perplexed, uncertain of the meaning of my fractured Swahili, and perhaps uncertain as to what this poor woman had done to set me off. I was, after all, a White man, and as such unpredictable and difficult to fathom. In short order this bowing business happened two more times. Fortunately my repeated gestures and speech convinced the TANU representative that I would not be offended if he advised the ladies to remain upright. Thereafter, if a woman seemed about to dive to the floor the man from TANU would quietly say a little something in Kihehe, and we would proceed, though the woman might flash nervous glances back and forth between the advisor and the Mzungu. Maybe we Wazungu[20] had some bad habits, like eating African babies.

About three thirty it was evident we were going to run out of ballots, so the driver was dispatched to Malangali. When he got back at six o'clock with eight hundred more ballots and some help, we had about twenty ballots left and had just started on the men.

The men were more sophisticated than the women, which is to be expected in traditional societies. The women are generally stuck at home attending to the kids, crops, cooking, washing, and other domestic chores, while the men often get out for travel and jobs. In the next two hours we voted three hundred sixty-five people. It had taken six hours to do the first four hundred. More men knew what to do with the pencil and ballot, plus we had that additional helper from Malangali, a TANU man for all I knew, who was outside issuing ballots. Every now and then he would come in with a handful to cram into the ballot box. Perhaps he was on loan from Chicago.

About eight o'clock we finished our exercise in chaos and headed for Malangali. Nathan took the ballot box to the middle school and I went home to Don's place. There was not-so-good news and bad news. The not-so-good news was that I was now a co-mother, as Don had adopted a baby monkey. The bad news was that Mrs. Partner had suffered a coronary thrombosis. The severity was uncertain, but the consensus seemed to be that she was a tough old gal and would pull through.

---

[15] Mwalimu means respected teacher.
[16] Uhuru means freedom from slavery; liberty, emancipation.
[17] An African will refer to his aunts and his father's other wives as his mothers. A European's insistence as to which mother is his real or birth mother, is mystifying.
[18] Saba means seven, thus Saba Saba is 7/7, or July Seventh.
[19] Bwana means sir, master; mkubwa means large, superior.
[20] Mzungu generally means European (or White); something wonderful, startling, surprising. Wa is the prefix for more than one of these oddities.

CHAPTER 8

First Safaris

Our first two safaris (trips) were basically exercises in exploration and education. In early October, Don, Harold and I decided to investigate the Buhoro flats, north of the school. We had tried to reach the flats once before by going north from Malangali, but past the Catholic mission at Itengule the road petered out. We pressed on for eight more miles, crossing two streams and one swampy area, before the road dissolved into a sea of stumps. This time we were going via Madibira, twenty-five miles as the bustard flies, but ninety miles by road and rut.

We left before sunrise with two Rovers and four students. Short on gas, we arrived at Matanana only to find a dry petrol station. This caused us to drive thirty miles past our turn-off to get petrol at Ifunda. Around mid-day we reached Madibira, a small settlement with a large Catholic mission, on the southeast edge of the Buhoro Flats. We visited the mission to say Jambo to the fathers and ask for directions. As is usual with Catholic missions out in the bush, this one was impressive. An extensive compound was graced with several brick buildings, including a church, a school, and a dispensary. The Catholic missions, in addition to proselytizing, try hard to ameliorate local hardship. A well-established mission will always have a dispensary, an elementary school, and often a middle school. If the mission creates or is near a population center, a secondary school will also materialize in time. The dispensary will treat a wide assortment of ailments, from malaria to worms to infections, and, the White-man's dawa (medicine) is powerful dawa.

In addition, the fathers usually experiment with different subsistence and cash crops, sometimes with tremendous and beneficial economic consequences, as with the introduction of coffee and sisal. One could say that all of these activities have but one purpose: to engender faith. And while, in the big picture, that is true, I never met a Catholic missionary who wasn't sincerely sympathetic and sensitive toward the African. To the fathers, the African was a person,[21] one of God's creations, complete with a soul in need of salvation. If the by-product of their efforts to save souls resulted in less suffering and more happiness, that was fine with this avowed agnostic, tender in the ways of Africa. By definition, we agnostics don't have the answers to life's

First Safaris

mysteries, so why cloak ones-self in the arrogance of cynicism? Cynicism is a useless exercise; an attempt to appear intellectually superior by those bereft of gumption and guts.

The fathers got us pointed in the right direction, geographically speaking, but in spite of their help, we got lost. In the bush, even divine guidance is no substitute for a local kiongozi (guide), which we found in the form of an old man willing to come along with us. An hour later we had only managed eight miles. A skilled tracker would have had trouble following this 'road' and the area was full of elephant potholes, leftovers from the rainy season but now hard edged and jarring. Shortly after noon we turned around, ten miles short of good hunting. We had to be back at the school by six so Harold could show the movies and we could placate Mr. Partner. The hundred mile return trip took five hours, four of those hours for the first fifty miles.

Toward the end of October, Don and I decided to try again, using a different route north from Malangali. The road existed in places, but that didn't mean it was better than no road at all. The worst part of the journey was driving across maize fields with washboard surfaces built to Paul Bunyan specifications. There were also streams to cross, trees to fell, logs to roll away, and hitchhikers to accommodate. About fourteen miles out we acquired a guide to show us the way. Having covered all of twenty miles in four hours, we stopped after dark and slept in some abandoned native huts: Don, four students, the guide, and myself.

After a gourmet breakfast of bread and peanut butter, we broke camp before sunrise, our guide navigating us through peoples yards and shambas (farms). Since it was the dry season and nothing was planted, our trespassing was harmless, according to the students and the kiongozi. Whatever the case, our entertainment value more than made up for any minor vandalism. The locals were quite happy to see us as many of them had never seen a car and those who had, had never seen one on their doorsteps. One elderly woman offered a "Jambo" and when I answered she lit up with a smile of astonishment. I was puzzled at her reaction, but one of the students said she probably thought the car had made the reply, and that we were just part of it.

We got to the flats shortly after sunrise and were treated to an ostentatious display of Africa's fauna: elephant, giraffe, buffalo, topi, kudu, zebra, bushbuck, and hundreds of birds, and thousands of flies. This last group seemed the most ferocious, or friendly, depending on the point of view. Don shot seven times at a small, distant buck and was rewarded with a fat lip, complements of the 30:06. I tried to close on a herd of buffalo but without success.

We then noticed some tarps and tents on the edge of the plain and went for a look-see. Three Europeans from the Brooke Bond Tea Plantation at Mufindi had established a hunting camp and they, along with a government game scout and several African safari workers, were lolling about in the sparse shade. They had had an exciting night. The game scout had been sleeping under a tarp with several other Africans when he sensed an ominous presence. He grabbed his government .404 and swung it around just in time to intercept a hyena's jaws aimed at his face. The hyena clamped down on his rifle, between his hands, and started dragging him off into the brush. Though terrified, he didn't dare let go of the gun or the hyena might have gone for him. The Europeans heard the commotion, scrambled for their guns, and scared the beast off with a few shots into the air. The scout's rifle stock was a mass of splinters and half-inch deep holes. He was all right, though still shaken, but he had received some superficial bites during the fracas, and the hope was that the hyena wasn't rabid.

Hyenas have the reputation of being slinking cowards, but they can be ferocious adversaries. They have powerful jaws and front shoulders, but were short-changed in the hindquarters. This gives their bodies a sloping look from front to back, causing a gliding, sinister looking gait at slow speed. The three Englishmen knew personally of two hyena attacks on humans sleeping in the open: one lost part of a foot, and the other lost his nose.

Two of the Mufindi whites accompanied us back out onto the stifling plains. Our targets were the buffalo, but the going was not easy. Although the flats were hot and dry, they were interlaced with narrow channels filled with up to three feet of oozing black mud and stagnant water. Wading through them was slow slogging and the additional exertion was not welcome in the searing heat. At least we saw no snails.[22]

We stalked those buff all over the plain, but they were really skittish, probably from being shot at. Finally, hot, exhausted, and out of patience, I took a long-range shot at one, probably three hundred yards. This was not a rational decision but one rooted in fatigue and rookie impatience. On the second shot, the .500 knocked me off balance as I hadn't fully recovered my shooting stance from the recoil of the first round. Consequently, and justly, I absorbed more punishment than the buffalo, the bullets meant for them falling harmlessly short.

The .500 was a brute, though a handsome one. It propelled a 500-grain bullet that developed six thousand pounds, that's three tons, of muzzle energy. No wonder those guns were so heavy. Even with the weight, however, if you had an inclination to shoot it prone, it would have an inclination to break your shoulder. It came equipped with crude iron sights, a wide vee towards the breech and a post up front. It was obviously a short-range gun due to both the ballistics, powerful but slow, and the sights. But the obvious didn't really impress itself on me until our next hunt.

Shortly after noon we decided to leave, as the animals were melting into the heat waves and it was hot, hot, hot. We hunted a little on the way home but saw only some wild pigs, which eluded us. We got back just before dark and between us Don and I drank a gallon of beer, four bottles of pop, two quarts of tea, and an unquantified amount of water. We were tired, but all in all, satisfied with our first taste of hunting in Africa.

21 Contrast this with the Afrikaner (Boer) outlook toward the African as sub-human: — just out of the trees or — just lost their tails, were common Boer expressions.
22 Bilharzia, or schistosomiasis, is a disease caused by small flatworms you get while wading in stagnant water. Over time, these parasites attack various organs and debilitate or kill the host. A certain kind of snail is part of the life cycle of these very small flukes.

CHAPTER 9

A Death in the Family

Monday, November 19, was a really glum day. Mrs. Partner's death had been announced and sadness enveloped the entire school. At noon, Don, Alf, Cyril and I screwed down the lid of her coffin and loaded it into Mr. Partner's car for the trip into Iringa. The funeral would be at five o'clock that same day.

Just the previous Saturday at baraza (assembly), Mr. Partner had explained to the students that Mrs. Partner would never teach again and would have to take it easy, but: "She has passed the crisis and I fully expect her to be getting around soon." What a quick and cruel turn of fate. Filled with optimism on Saturday, on this day he was the picture of abject misery. As we came in he was leaning over the coffin, tears in his eyes. He bent down to kiss his wife's cold lips, then found his way into the bedroom to change clothes while we sealed his wife out of this world, and perhaps into the next.

During the previous couple of weeks, we teachers had taken turns sitting through the night with the Partners, providing some small measure of comfort. Knowing someone was there, Peter would catch short breaks of fitful sleep. Gladys would drift in and out, sometimes lucid, sometimes softly incoherent. Occasionally, on awakening, she would be startled by the presence of someone in the room other than her husband, her eyes wide with terror and confusion.

Toward the end of the first week she started to improve and after the second week she seemed definitely on the mend. Our nightly vigils were then discontinued, but a few nights later she suddenly left, quietly departing in her sleep.

Mr. Partner ordered the school to carry on, so only a few staff attended the funeral. Cyril drove Partner's car with Peter and Gladys aboard; their last safari together. That hundred miles to Iringa must have seemed like never-ending torment.

The Partners had been in Tanganyika for many years and were well known in educational and governmental circles. Mr. Partner's desire to conclude his career as headmaster of the government secondary school in Tabora was well known, and soon rumors began to circulate. In a matter of weeks the appointment was made, partly a

A Death in the Family

reward for his long service to the country, but certainly also in response to his loss. Educationally, this posting was the zenith of his career, but even this new position with its added prestige could not fill the void created by the death of his life's love. He retired to England after only a brief watch at the helm in Tabora.

CHAPTER 10

Life in Malangali

Life in an African village was a definite modification on life in Tacoma. The basics were the same: food, shelter, clothing, and transportation. The differences were in the details.

I had been in Malangali but a few months when an attractive young woman arrived from Columbia University to survey my reaction to these differences. A single guy out in the African boonies, a beautiful girl fresh from New York City: romance was in the air. But, alas, she was so serious and businesslike, so self-important. Consequently my smart mouth got the better of me when she came to a question about culture shock. I responded that: Yes, I had suffered culture shock since joining the TEA Program. Her pulse quickened. Her antennae sprung to attention, all aquiver. She wanted details. With a straight face, and serious demeanor to match her own, I related that as soon as I had arrived in New York City, I knew that I had entered a different world. The deeper I developed this fiction, the cooler the immediate atmosphere became. Loose lips sink more than ships! My chances of getting to know her had abruptly become biblical: akin to that rich man trying to thread a camel through the eye of a needle.

Three months after my arrival, and a couple of weeks before the entrance of that one-woman cold front, I moved into my own place. The government rent was twenty dollars a month for a furnished, two-bedroom house with tile roof and tan stucco exterior. There was also a kitchen, living room and bath, along with more yard than necessary. The floor was concrete and red, the color coming from the wax used to keep it polished. Due to the elevation, the house also had a fireplace, though I rarely used it.

While the house was thus quite standard, the services and accoutrements were not. For instance, our electricity came from a diesel generator at the school and was only available from 6:30 to 11:30 at night. Our water came from the Little Ruaha River, which skirted the village. People, cattle, goats, pythons and who knows what all used the river. These users not only made withdrawals, they also left deposits. Drinking water had to be boiled, and for twenty minutes because of the altitude.

Life in Malangali

Then it was poured into a ceramic filter for further purification. For washing, the water was heated in a contraption behind the house called a Tanganyika Boiler, a large rusty tank with a hole in the top for water and debris to enter, and an enclosed firebox below for wood. Taking a bath in brown water amounted to exchanging an old accumulation for a brand new coat; a cold water rinse being the antidote.

Food was nothing special. Potatoes and rice from Iringa Stores and meat from Malangali cow were the staples. The local zebu cattle were, in a word, tough, and African maize is almost tasteless, producing a corn meal that is just barely yellow.

To keep meat and produce edible, a refrigerator was necessary, but with only five hours of electricity daily, this meant a special appliance: the paraffin (kerosene) fridge. Some sadistic genius invented this gizmo with the sole purpose of tormenting the owner. Mine was a small half-sized model. It existed to malfunction. Being awakened by, or coming home to, a house full of smoke was a common occurrence. The wick would mysteriously go from flame mode to smoldering mode, usually in the wee hours of the night. If you came home from safari at three in the afternoon, it would greet you with cool efficiency, but pull in at two in the morning, tired, cranky and ready for bed, then this infernal device would be in full fume. I was tempted more than once to put a bullet in the thing and trade warm beer and half-rotten meat for the frustration. Still, it wasn't on the game license so I never did put it out of my misery.

Another essential nuisance was the mosquito net. It hung from the ceiling and you tucked the bottom edge under the mattress. When bedtime came you quickly undid a section just large enough to slip through and then immediately closed this portal once inside the cocoon. Occasionally, you did not enter alone, and the extra company was not Marilyn Monroe. You learned to sleep in the center of the bed, as any body part nestled against the net was an open invitation to dine and mosquitoes like their red wine with any color of meat. At the higher elevations, like Malangali, the net was only needed six months of the year, but during those six months it was a great aid to blood retention. It was not 100% protection at first, but once you got proficient it was highly effective. In any case, if you had a phobia about bugs gnawing on you, Africa was not the place to be. In addition to the ubiquitous mosquitoes; worms, chiggers, fleas, ticks, tsetse flies, and unnamed and uncounted others all delighted in your presence and took comfort and sustenance from your carcass. Like it or not, you were part of the food chain.

Our supplies came from Iringa Stores, a general merchandise emporium with everything from ammo to zippers. The school truck would make the run to Iringa once a month to fill our orders, usually bulk items like rice, spuds, beer, and pop, and also personal items like soap, toothpaste, and paper products. We teachers would also visit the shops of Iringa, which were stocked with goods from all over the world. Tomato sauce, an absolute essential condiment for Malangali cow, came from South Africa, along with peanut butter and liqueurs. We could purchase Kellogg's Corn flakes from England; raisins from California; cookies from Pakistan; flashlights from

Hunting and Teaching in East Africa

Hong Kong; bicycles from China; hats from France; cloth from the Netherlands; beer from Kenya; radios, record players, cameras, and shirts (wash and tear) from Japan; cameras and film from Germany; axes from Czechoslovakia; cashews from India; and groundnuts (peanuts, not people) from Tanganyika.

There were two small local shops, or dukas, in Malangali, and once a month, on the third Tuesday, a native market sprouted up across the river. From the local shops we would buy sweets, meat, odds and ends, and sometimes commodities we ran out of like toothpaste, rice or potatoes. The local market was a source of African produce and products: eggs, vegetables, woven floor mats, carved ladles and stools, and the occasional keepsake like a drum, a cane, or a finger piano.

The native market was as much social as commercial. There were pombe (beer) stations just beyond the market, in the bush, and this helped to keep things festive. Cattle, sheep, goats, and chickens were sold or bartered, as well as maize and imported cloth and clothing. The transaction process was a combination of serious negotiation and social interaction. Prices were fluid, lending to lots of generally good natured posturing. If you were to walk up and pay the asking price, on anything, you would create ambivalence in the seller. On the one hand he would be pleased that someone had paid full, sucker price, but he would also feel cheated of the chance for a little friendly verbal sparring. The process is as important as the purchase, and it is, to some extent, insulting and arrogant to do the one without the other. To haggle is to get down on a human level and interact, man to man, in a bargaining contest. To just fork over the money and walk off is a cold way of doing business and tantamount to treating the vendor as someone not worthy of your time or attention.

I loved to haggle. It was fun to get going on an item, eventually getting some give and paying a reasonable price. I knew that I was paying more for the merchandise than an African or Indian would have paid, but I enjoyed both the process and the purchase, and if the former carried with it a little premium, so what.

All of our time was not spent in Malangali, however. Having a vehicle meant freedom to roam, explore, and hunt, but to get from here to there usually involved distance, bad roads, and breakdowns. The vehicle of choice was the Land Rover. These were bare-bones machines, tough and simple, but expensive. The other preferred cars, from top to bottom were Mercedes Benz, Peugeot, and Volkswagon, the 'Beetle' variety. They all had certain common traits: they could take the abuse promised by East African roads, they were dependable, and they were numerous, so parts could be had when the need arose, and the need would arise.

My Simca Aronde was a sweet little machine, unlike Attila the fridge, but she was not always able to withstand the punishment. It was like sending an eighth grader out to play linebacker in the National Football League. No matter how gutsy or determined, the kid was going to get pounded. For the Simca, the pounding came from speed. The roads were rough, but at twenty or thirty miles an hour, damage would be slight. However, at those speeds, given the distances to be covered, you would be forever getting to your destination. There were stretches where twenty to thirty was all

Life in Malangali

you could muster, but if the road were dry, wide, flat and reasonably straight, I could push the Simca up to seventy, though the usual speed was between fifty and sixty on good stretches.

Over the two years and 30,000 miles I put on my Simca, I broke every spring on the car at least once, put seven holes in the gas tank, and demolished shock absorbers and one wheel. The roads devoured tires like piranha feasting on a capybara. At the end of my very first trip, from Moshi to Malangali, when I removed my luggage the two rear shocks were staring at me like a couple of floating fried eggs. They had worked themselves and their mounts completely through the floor of the trunk.

The essential tools for continued locomotion, aside from some spanners and a screwdriver, were a hammer, some tire-irons, a tire pump, hot patches with clamp, matches, a fingernail file, and a fresh bar of Sunlight soap. Flats were a given. The trick was to feel the tyre going flat before it was ruined. On a hard surface, that was easy, but on sandy or corrugated surfaces, a tire would lose most of its pressure before you would notice and the cords inside the tire could separate. One positive aspect of my Simca's tires was that they were easy to fix. When a Landrover got a flat, that was a battle. Through involuntary practice, and plenty of it, we could fix a flat on the Simca and be back on our way in just under five minutes: jack up the car, undo the lug nuts, place the tire on the ground and beat it with a hammer to break it loose from the rim, use the tire-irons to lever one lip of the tire over the rim, remove the tube, find the puncture and clamp on a hot patch, scratch the patch to expose the powder, strike a match and watch the powder sizzle, sealing it to the tube, remove the clamp and let the patch cool, slip the tube back into the tire, use the tire-irons to reposition the tire on the rim, pump up the tire with Kismet,[23] our aptly named foot pump, put it back on the car, tighten the lugs, lower the jack, and off. My personal record for flats was seven in three days.

Besides tires, electrical and fuel problems could bring progress to a halt. The most common electrical problem was a dirty distributor and/or fouled points. The roads were dusty and eventually enough would accumulate to cause the car to sputter to a stop. We would huff and puff and blow the dust out and then use the fingernail file to spruce up the points.

Petrol problems were generally due to the lost gas[24] process. The Simca did have a quarter-inch steel plate bolted under the engine to protect the oil pan, but the gas tank had no such armor. Its little bare fanny skimmed along just above the road and it often got spanked. My first gas tank puncture I noticed while repairing the more common variety on a rear tire. Fortunately it was a slow dribble and I made it to town and had it soldered. The mechanic suggested that if I was going to bang around Tanganyika with a naked gas tank, I should at least carry a bar of Sunlight soap. A fresh bar of this yellow hand-soap was soft and malleable, perfect for plugging gas tank wounds.

Another impediment to forward motion was divine interruption. This almost always had something to do with rain. Usually it was what rain did to things like roads and bridges. Sometimes it was a swollen stream or a flash flood. On one occasion it was the rain itself, coming down so hard we couldn't see the end of the hood. Stopped in the middle of the road, we were hoping that some bus or lorry wasn't blindly headed our direction.

Seeing the road was essential. So was concentration. You had to be aware of the ever-changing road conditions or you could end up in the ditch or on your top. Most accidents involved only one vehicle and the carnage was usually self-inflicted. Speed was most often the culprit, with inattentiveness probably second.

Speed was, however, relative. Some drivers could flip a 'Bug' at twenty miles an hour and were a hazard to one and all. A skilled, experienced driver could get that same car into a controlled four-wheel drift at three times that velocity. But even the most skilled driver would sooner or later come a cropper if he pushed too hard. The best evidence of this came from the East African Safari, a 3,000 mile race held on main and secondary roads during the rainy season. Of over ninety starters each year, the highest number to complete the race during my time there was eighteen. One year only nine finished. Eric Carlson, a renowned rally driver and husband to Sterling Moss' sister, had a commanding lead on one occasion. His Swedish built Saab was front wheel driven, a definite advantage over the rest of the field, but tearing around a corner, Saab and aardvark met: dead aardvark; disabled Saab.

Which brings us to another travel challenge, moving obstacles. The only creatures that were considered targets of opportunity were snakes. Everybody liked a dead snake. But, bicyclists, cattle, goats, and even chickens, were best avoided. Away from the towns, bicyclists were not used to vehicles and would sometimes panic as one approached. Even though there was no other mechanical noise for miles, their realization of your presence was late in coming. You might be only fifty feet from one of them when suddenly his head would pop up as if out of a trance and the wheels of his bike would start to oscillate, resulting in a spill or a plunge into the ditch. Fortunately none of them ever lost control in the direction of the car. Large and small livestock were usually in herds or flocks and were easy to see and mostly easy to avoid.

Hitting any domesticated animal tended to upset the owner, even if the victim was a chicken. Chickens were a special case. The Swahili name for them is apropos: kuku. They do indeed act coocoo in front of a vehicle. If you zig, they zig: cost 4/-. If you zag, they zag: cost 4/-. After bumping off a few of these erratic performers, I happened upon a solution in an article about a race car driver. He explained that to avoid a pile-up on the track, he just kept going straight, figuring the involved cars would have spun out of the impact zone by the time he got there. Using this strategy, I never did clip another kuku. Perhaps it was I who had been the erratic performer!

Wild animals generally had the good sense to stay away from the main roads. Still, I had a couple of close calls. On one occasion my Simca got its face smacked by an elephant's tail, and on another we almost took the front legs off a giraffe. How could

Life in Malangali

such an expert, alert driver such as myself not notice these two behemoths? There are, of course, plausible, perfectly plausible, explanations. These reasonable, plausible, and persuasive explanations are fermenting. They will be revealed bado kidogo.[25]

Every so often we would come upon a black stripe across the road. On closer inspection, the black stripe was actually crossing the road: an army of black ants in an eight inch wide, closely packed column, neat as a ribbon. The choice was to drive over them, or wait, perhaps for hours. The tires would cause a bulge in the formation and temporary disarray in the ranks. But within seconds the soldiers marshaled themselves back into line and, ignoring their casualties, continued their march.

Servants, as they were known, were another part of your life. You had to have at least a cook, and maybe a second employee to keep ahead of the lawn. It was unnatural, seemingly against the laws of nature, for a bwana not to have a servant or two. If you tried to get by without one, you would constantly be pestered by petitioners, tattered references in hand.

A cook, mpishi in Swahili, was essential as there were no labor saving devices and shopping, cooking, washing, and cleaning took large chunks of time. A couple with children might also hire a dobi, a man to wash their clothes and help with other chores. A dobi might be forty years old, but his English title was, nevertheless, 'houseboy'. Similarly, the gardener would be called the 'shamba boy', shamba being Swahili for garden.

Being single and not very demanding, I got by with just a cook, in Malangali. On occasion I would take a grass whip out to tame the lawn, but often as not, some local would come by and try to take it out of my hands, explaining that such work was not suitable for a bwana. Even though these offers of help were made without expectation of payment, I hung on and continued to flail away at the grass. It was good exercise, and a display of manual labor by a European was not altogether a bad thing.

Valance was my cook. In town, he was evidently a bit of a rogue. He liked his pombe and, though married, hankered after variety, or so it was rumored. He was slight but strong and had a ready, if somewhat sly, smile. Although of average height, he had Masai like features with his thin lips and pointed nose. I paid him 200/- a month, or $28, which was at the high end of the scale. By contrast, a dobi or a gardener would receive about half that amount.

In four years I had two cooks, Valance in Malangali and Haji in Arusha. Unlike Don, I had only one minor problem with my cooks. They were used to British employers. As a consequence, they tended to show up at the crack of dawn, and hover about in the evenings, after dinner. I liked my mornings and evenings to myself. I didn't take breakfast, so there was no need for someone banging about in the kitchen. In the evenings I had papers to mark, books to read, and the BBC to absorb. If I needed tea, a beer, some cookies or popcorn, I could manage on my own.

Over his two years, Don employed a number of servants, one or two at a time. He was both unlucky and indiscriminate in his choices, but the major contribution to employee turnover was his management style. Don was a punctilious boss and if you worked for him you had better dot your i's and cross your t's. If you were told to do this in that way but you deviated, even for the better, your rump was in for a chewing. It was not a matter of race. Don liked and respected the Africans. He could be gregarious and outgoing. But he was also hard to live with and harder to work for. In other words, prolonged contact with Don was like the relationship between a teakettle and a hot stove. Sooner or later the pressure would build and an eruption would occur.

In addition to feeding and generally taking care of you, a cook provided something of a shield for your house and belongings. Not that he was there when you were on safari, but his employment in and of itself created a connection between you and the local people. He was your cook, but you were his bwana. If somebody were to burgle your house, your cook would be the first person questioned, and in a small village like Malangali, such an event would not remain a mystery for long.

Though having a servant ran contrary to American egalitarianism, I always considered my cook or gardener to be an employee, as did most Americans. These employees tended to the everyday, mundane jobs that we could not do if we were to teach effectively, and teaching effectively was our job.

---

[23] Kismet, means fate.

[24] A bad play on words: an oblique reference to the lost wax process used in West Africa to produce bronzes.

[25] Bado kidogo means in a little while, which could be a half-hour, or half a day, or some other indeterminate length of time, like several chapters from now.

CHAPTER 11

The Schools

During our orientation in Moshi, we were welcomed by Solomon Eliufoo, the Minister of Education. He spoke in general terms about the school system, but one of his statements really brought the situation into focus: "New York City spends more money on garbage collection than we do for education." Though he gave no numbers, none of us doubted his accuracy. Eight years later when I was teaching in the Federal Way School District, just south of Seattle, I did a comparison of my own. For the year l970, this one district, one of almost 300 districts in this one state, had a budget of eleven million dollars for 15,000 pupils. According to the Tanganyika Five-Year Plan for l969, this entire country budgeted twenty-three million dollars to educate 600,000: twice as much money: forty times as many students. Federal Way would spend $733 on each pupil, while Tanganyika could only muster $38. Nevertheless, while Tanganyika schools were quite austere, at the secondary level they were also quite good.

Tanganyika's system of education was a collection of missionary, Indian, and government schools before independence. But after l961 the various schools were brought under one roof as a state system, run by the Ministry of Education in Dar es Salaam, with regional education officers in each of the country's thirteen regions.

Primary schools could be found in every nook and cranny of Tanzania, ranging from open-air schools with one teacher and almost no materials, to schools with substantial buildings and sufficient staff, books, desks, and other school type paraphernalia. In the first four grades the accent was on literacy in Swahili, the lingua franca of East Africa, health, farming, home making, and crafts. After grade four, an exam was taken for entrance to grades five through seven. At this next level the courses still had a vocational bent, but academic work in English, history, government and basic science was introduced. Upon graduation from grade seven, another 'leaving' examination was taken and those with the best results were admitted to Form I of a four-year secondary school. Some of those who did not make this cut would gain entrance to a technical school, but for the vast majority, this was the end of their educational journey.

Hunting and Teaching in East Africa

The secondary schools were small, usually 280 students divided into four grades, called forms, with two classes in each form and 35 students in each class. Additionally, some few secondary schools had forms five and six, which were more vocational in nature. For instance, elementary teachers were prepared there, not at university.

At the end of each school year, in December, internal exams were given forms one through three and the students in each form were ranked from one to seventy, on the basis of these tests. The following year, the first thirty-five would make up Form A, and the rest would become Form B. For seniors, an external exam was given. During the colonial period and into the mid-60's this was the Cambridge Examination, set and marked in England. This exam took the better part of two weeks and was very difficult, thorough, and intense. Subjects that were cumulative, like English, Swahili, and mathematics, were difficult enough, but the history and science exams covered all four years of separate, usually unrelated subject matter. For instance, biology was taken in the second year and two years later, the Cambridge rolls around with a four-hour biology test: a two hour written examination, and a two hour laboratory ordeal. The same applied to chemistry, taken in the third year. In the late 60's, the Cambridge was replaced by a Tanzanian test, written and graded by the Ministry of Education, but on the same model as the British test. Those students who did well could further their education in forms five and six, or pass straight to university.

The University College in Dar es Salaam, Makerere in Kampala, and the University College in Nairobi, made up the three branches of the University of East Africa. Qualified students could go to any of these, and many also went overseas, with Great Britain being the preferred destination. The United States garnered its share, and France, Germany, Russia, China, and a smattering of other countries also got some students.

Those whose results were less than scintillating might gain admission to one of the technical or agricultural schools, or a teacher training college. There were also programs run by the various ministries to train people to fill their manpower needs, such as the game department's school for game scouts and wardens, in Moshi. Some would also join the army, though this was not the most popular of options.

Tanganyika did not even have a secondary school until 1933, and as independence approached there were only twenty-eight such institutions, educating about 8500 students in a country of twelve million people. Those 8500 were very fortunate indeed, representing as they did just 2% of the 365,000 elementary and middle school students in the country at that time. An education meant a good job, an easier and more interesting life in the city, escape from the village with its toil and static prospects, and prestige and future economic well being for not only the student, but his family as well.

Everything was taught to a syllabus, with the leaving exam looming in the shadows, a dreaded and all-important hurdle. If a teacher presented extraneous subject matter he would be asked: "But sir, is this on the syllabus?" Their futures depended

The Schools

on mastering the syllabus, and they knew its contents fore and aft. They were not receptive to someone diminishing their prospects by going off on a tangent, no matter how enlightening, interesting, or important the teacher perceived it to be. Some Americans did not like teaching to a test, but the system did serve to make both the student and teacher accountable.

During the 1960's, there was a great influx of American teachers as part of Tanzania's desire to rapidly expand its educational system. The Peace Corps and the Teachers for East Africa Project were the principal agents of this influx. By the end of the decade Tanzania was producing her own teachers at a sufficient rate to phase out the American programs.

In America not only are teachers in the public schools college graduates, they are backed up with a wealth of support, from luxurious facilities with brightly lit classrooms and well stocked libraries, to specialists in speech, reading, psychology, curriculum, finance, drug abuse, driver's education, sports, and on and on. By contrast, Tanzanian schools had poorly lit basic facilities, meager libraries, and no specialists. While American high schools are awash in electives, in Tanzania, electives were limited to what was volunteered by staff, usually on Saturdays. However, also by way of contrast, in Tanzania teaching was an honored profession. It carried great social status, was usually free of discipline problems, and accentuated basic education with stated goals that could be realized.

In American schools, the accent is on the process of learning and thinking, with considerable latitude for the individual to choose a path to the future. In this way, our schools reflect the needs of our democratic and capitalist system. In Tanzania, the accent was on what was taught, and what was thought. Educational opportunity was not universal and not a birthright, and with this opportunity came responsibility. The state provided the education and the state expected graduates to be useful, hopefully instrumental, in the process of nation building. Their schools thus reflected the needs of a poor, basically socialist one party state with no history of either democracy or nationality. So, while Tanzanian schools did not provide a free flowing, elective rich curriculum that canonized the individual, they did have direction and purpose, a direction and purpose suited to Tanzania at that juncture.

CHAPTER 12

Malangali School

It was dark inside the dorm. The students were asleep, or supposed to be, but to the right, about halfway down the aisle between the two rows of beds, a small, bright red glow flared unexpectedly. It quickly disappeared. I walked toward the middle of the long narrow room, not certain of what to do. At Malangali we were not often confronted with this sort of breach.

Our school was a typical four form, 280-student secondary school. We were a boarding school and because of our remoteness, a close, if not always close-knit, society. There were six dormitories. Bangu House was named after an important village mzee and the father of our vocational instructor, Mr. Bangu. Another dorm was called Mkwawa, after the legendary chief of the Wahehe who had tangled with the Germans in the 1890's. The Swahili poet Shaaban Roberts was also honored with a dormitory.

Besides the dorms, there was an office building for the headmaster and staff, a library, a science lab, four classroom buildings, one for each form, the mess hall, and some less imposing buildings dating from the German period. The post-German structures were all brick, with cement floors and tiled roofs, and all were more than adequate in size.

The mess hall was the most imposing of the collection. It had to accommodate the full student body for meals, assemblies and events, and the high ceiling gave it a spacious feeling, even when packed for a special event like Nyerere's visit. The following description was written by the Mess Prefect, Hassani Sanga, for the Malangali School Magazine, 1962:

The Mess Hall

In 1960 and 1961 the Dining Hall was large enough to accommodate all the boys. But as soon as the double stream was introduced in Form IV early this year, the increased number of boys could not be accommodated at one time and it was necessary to have two sittings. This inconvenience was removed when smaller tables and forms arrived and the stage was used by a few Senior boys.

The Dining Hall will appear even better when the new kitchen which is being built behind it replaces the old one which is degrading its front view. The new kitchen will be operated

Malangali School

by diesel fuel instead of wood.

Although the Young Farmers have erected several beehives within the school area, swarms of bees have ignored them and decided to share in the use of the Dining Hall. These uninvited guests have caused tremendous damage to the ceiling. Even though we felt great sympathy at first towards these poor creatures, I think now the R.S.P.C.A. members will forgive us when we apply powerful D.D.T.= in order to destroy them. Owing to the fear of attracting more swarms of bees by perfumed flowers, only a few flowers, like the morning glory, have been grown in the Mess Hall gardens.

The school had two levels of administration. The direction of the school, teaching, and over-all supervision were the responsibility of the staff. However, on a day to day basis, the students, through their duly elected student body officers, called prefects, shouldered much of the responsibility for the smooth operation of the system. The Mess Hall Prefect made sure things were in order for meals and meetings. The dorm prefects handled everything from disputes between students to coordinating activities and keeping the buildings clean and tidy. The Sports Prefect issued gear from his cache and helped schedule and organize activities and events, like the once a year Sports Day, a track and field competition attended by people, prominent and otherwise, from as far off as Mbeya and Iringa. The Head Prefect held meetings with the other prefects, kept them on their toes, made and listened to suggestions, fielded complaints, settled disagreements, and was the main liaison between the student government and the staff.

The deputy headmaster was in charge of the prefects and worked closely with them, the staff, and the headmaster, to keep things humming. Each day, on a rotating basis, one member of staff was the Duty Master. On that day he would keep tabs on the routine of the school; inspecting the mess hall and dorms, visiting sick students in the dispensary, ruling on any problems not needing headmaster involvement, and checking the dorms after lights-out at 9:30.

Being Duty Master was not much of an ordeal as the students were mature, responsible, and, though not docile, well behaved. Discipline problems were few and far between: three that I know of in my two years at Malangali, two serious and one not. I was attending to one of them that night in the dorm and as I approached the middle of the room, only the occasional snore and the sound of my footsteps echoing off the cement floor interrupted the quiet. In a low voice I asked who had been smoking. "It was I," came out of the darkness, a couple of beds ahead. I recognized the voice and told Buyuni to follow me outside.

Buyuni Jahazi was popular among students and staff, being smart, athletic and invested with an infectious smile and outgoing personality. We headed for the science lab and on the way I secured a grass whip, a long steel shaft with a two-edged blade angled out from one end. In length and shape, a grass whip could be related to a golf club, kind of like a useful cousin. I gave Buyuni a short, perfunctory lecture on school rules in general and smoking in particular, then handed him the whip and directed him to cut all the tall grass between the lab and the students' tennis court. As a motivational aside, I allowed that if that chui I'd heard down in the valley got closer, he could go back to the dorm.

Of course there had been no leopard, but the next morning as I passed the science lab, it was obvious that Buyuni had been inspired. The grass had been savaged. There were strands stuck high up in the chicken-wire fence bordering the tennis court, and even a few clumps atop the laboratory roof. I visualized him flaying away with both hands, pausing to listen, and then furiously back at it. No doubt he worked up a sweat in more ways than one.

The evening bed check was necessary on two accounts. These were serious students, and if you allowed it they would fire up their kerosene lamps and study into the wee hours. This was a short-term comfort to them, but a long-term drain on their eyesight and classroom alertness. On one occasion I had walked Bangu House from end to end, and was about to exit when a faint shaft of light registered with my peripheral vision. I retraced my steps and examined the corner bunk. There was a headless lump under the blankets, and while we did have a few lumps in the student population, they all did have heads. The covers had been carefully drawn to the floor and made light tight, no doubt by his fellow miscreants. But he just couldn't resist a peek as I was leaving, no doubt savoring the fast one he and his buddies had pulled off.

I stood there for a minute, letting suspense breed anxiety, and then I gently plucked the blanket, revealing a hurricane lamp in full flame, a pile of books, and a sheepish student grinning up at me, sure he was in big trouble. My response had to be brief as I could hardly keep a straight face. With the sternest voice I could muster I ordered him to turn off the lamp and get to bed. My voice was just loud enough to reach the alert ears of his companions in crime, who I was certain were feigning sleep, and then I left.

After finishing the rest of my round, composure restored, I returned to the Bangu dorm, entered, and strode purposefully to the corner bunk. There was, as before, a lump under the blanket, but this time it had a head attached.

The European teachers enforced the curfew, doing the rounds at irregular times after lights out. I usually waited until at least ten o'clock, but sometimes it was as late as eleven before I entered the first dorm. But no matter the time, the kids knew we prickly whites would show up, so they were mostly sound asleep by the time one of us did. It took about half an hour to walk through the six dorms, check the beds for occupants, and investigate a few favored study dens, like the tailor's shop.

The African staff, except Mr. Bangu, ignored this duty. On those nights the school was lit up like grandad on Saturday night, and on two of those nights, one of which I will save for a later chapter, this laissez faire practice had serious consequences. Not only was the bed check used to enforce lights out, it was also a way to keep track of the students' whereabouts. If they were not in the dorm, where were they? Mostly, their absences were innocent enough, but the village had attractions. These were young men in the prime of life. There were no available women at the school, and no liquor. The village, though not much, had both.

One night a junior sneaked into the village. A few of the locals welcomed him with open arms, and ulanzi. Ulanzi is a bamboo wine with a sweet taste that belies its potency. After a while he stumbled out of the hut, pie-eyed, and pointed himself in the general direction of the school. If not found out, so far so good: just a lark. But an additional temptation crossed his path: make that two. He knew that the women would recognize him as a student, but instead of being circumspect, he was emboldened by the booze. A secondary student was, or would be, a man of substance, a real prize. How could they resist his status, not to mention his well-lubricated charm? So he pestered them, propositioned them. The two women were Mrs. Bangu and her daughter.

The resulting assembly was not one to be forgotten. The staff assembled on stage, behind our new headmaster, Mr. Kabati. Kabati looked out upon a gathering of subdued and apprehensive students, their bright white school shirts contrasting with their somber mood. To the rear of the room were the elders and other dignitaries of the village, invited to witness justice being served, punishment being inflicted, and deterrence being instituted.

For several minutes Kabati harangued the students and apologized to the villagers, giving assurances that this was a one-time transgression. He reminded our charges of the long-standing restrictions on going into the village: Saturday afternoons and Sundays, only, and then to be back before dark and in time for the evening meal. Once the headmaster had whipped himself into a lather, it became the culprit's turn. He was called forward, angrily assailed verbally, and then ordered to assume the push-up position. At this juncture Ian Thomas, refusing to watch what was about to unfold, abruptly turned his chair away from the proceedings and, sitting ramrod straight, focused on the side of the stage. Kabati had on hand a pliable, still green bamboo cane and he lashed the student six times across the back of his legs. The student did not falter or cry out. He maintained his position, his body steady, but his supporting arms at times trembling.

Afterwards, things were pretty solemn, but most were satisfied with the proceedings. The village representatives were mollified and the students, though far from happy, were nevertheless relieved. They realized that it would have been much worse if Partner had still been there. A European headmaster would have had no choice but to expel the offender. In the 'good old days' a European could flog an African at will, but that was now an option open only to an African bwana.

Expulsion was the ultimate punishment; the student sent home in disgrace, a disgrace that would engulf his entire extended family like a toxic cloud. Expulsion could be unbearable and could end in suicide, a not uncommon practice in East Africa.

The students were very supportive of each other, but their sympathy on this occasion was tempered with the feeling that the abused had done something stupid, and the consequences could have indeed been more severe.

CHAPTER 13

Malangali Students

There was a puzzling hullabaloo down in the village. The race had long been decided, with Edward Mhelela coming in first, as expected, followed closely by Daudi Kalungwana. However this was not a race for individual honors but a cross-country event, seven miles round trip to the Catholic mission at Itengule and back, with fifteen members from each dorm competing as a team.

Edward and Daudi, our two best long distance runners, had crossed the finish line some thirty minutes earlier, and they and most of the other competitors were quietly milling about, sucking on orange slices, when the ruckus arose. They immediately got excited; laughing, shouting, jumping around, and then they took off en-masse toward the commotion. They shortly became part of the rolling, noisy celebration that was slowly approaching the school up the main street of Malangali. As the throng of students broke out of the trees and shrubs at the far end of the sports field, I could see a scrawny little runner, almost engulfed by his enthusiastic escort, struggling forward, dog-tired, dead last, and beaming.

Not everyone thinks running seven miles in the heat of the day is all that much fun. Most of our students had read Kipling and were not eager to enter the company of mad dogs and Englishmen...out in the noonday sun. One dorm had come up one short of a full team and much cajoling and badgering had netted nobody. Eventually Aswani volunteered, but the dorm prefects weren't doing cartwheels at the prospect of this ungainly freshman rounding out their team. Who would have thought such an unlikely performer would have provided such a transcendent moment. His courage in completing the course was an inspiration in itself, but the reaction of the other students to his efforts was just beautiful.

With students like these, a teacher could get spoiled. The majority of our young men came from three tribes in the Southern Highlands: the Hehe, Bena, and Nyakyusa, although we had students from as far off as Mwanza, on Lake Victoria. The mix was blessed with a liberal ration of intelligence and ambition, and these attributes fueled a determined work ethic. Physically they were of average height, a very few slightly over six feet, and their bodies ran to lean or stocky, but certainly not fat. At

Malangali Students

the school there was only one African awash in blubber, and that was James, the head cook. The students were mostly in their late teens or early twenties, though one had a head of salt and pepper hair and was affectionately called Mzee by his fellows. Their color ran from a few very dark, to a few very light, with most somewhere in between, and many showed diluted African features from centuries of mixing with other tribes like the Bushmen and Arabs, the Portuguese and Persians.

Their workweek consisted of forty periods of forty minutes each. They were best at subjects that required the ability to memorize or think logically: math, science, geography, government, history and Swahili. The most challenging subject was English. To almost any foreign student, English is an enigma. Its arbitrary nature frustrates. There are rules of grammar and pronunciation, but as the English expression goes: rules are made to be broken.

Swahili is a structured, consistent, logical language, much like Latin, so the fluid nature of English came as something of a shock. English boils down to usage, and it is far from being a static, inert mass. If a manner of speaking is widely accepted by educated people, that is or becomes proper English. A common construction of both African and Indian students was: I am having a book. Unless the speaker is a pregnant mama book about to give birth to a baby book, this expression is not acceptable in English. It is obviously a transposition from their languages to English, but we just don't use that phrasing, though for no good reason that I can think of.

One day I walked by a classroom and heard a British teacher lecturing about the forty-third type of adverbial clause. Fortunately for me, and my students, the British were dropping this old approach of trying to teach chaos as math, and were adopting 'usage' as the vehicle of instruction. Consequently, teaching about sentence structure and grammar gave way to more writing and speaking. Theory will only introduce a skill, practice will build and refine that skill. You do not produce a machinist by simply telling him how to operate a lathe. He must get his hands on the machine and use it. If, for instance, I wanted to augment sentence constructions, I could introduce gerundive patterns and have the students practice these until they became part of their repertoire. I could tell them what a gerund was, and I would, but that wasn't essential.

Sentence construction is one problem, pronunciation is another. 'Island' and 'salmon', for instance, each have an appendix like letter that serves no function. French adoptions like 'depot' and 'corps', look nothing like they sound. But, English abounds with its own homegrown anomalies. If 'bough' rhymes with 'bow', as in bending at the waist, then 'cough' must rhyme with 'cow'. Or, if 'rough' is pronounced 'ruff', maybe 'bough' is actually 'buff'? How about 'through' and 'though'? And, as difficult as English is, the British make it worse. The word 'schedule', for instance, is totally mangled and comes out of British mouths as 'shed'ul'. If they are going to persist in this direction, then 'school' should be equally tortured and bang our ears as 'shul'. Or, go to London and ask a Bobby how to get to Leicester Square. The British blithely erase one entire syllable, changing what should be **Ly-kes-ter** to 'Lester'.

Hunting and Teaching in East Africa

While we Americans have done what we can to correct such perversions, we are still stuck with the basic product, a bastard language with one Germanic mother, and several shadowy fathers, identifiable only through their linguistic DNA. The resulting confusion is evidenced by the fact that there are 1,120 different ways of spelling the forty phonemes in English. By way of comparison, Italian needs only thirty-three combinations of letters to spell out its twenty-five phonemes. Swahili is more like Italian, and once you learn the vowels,[26] any word can readily be pronounced correctly.

I taught one or two English classes each quarter, and while the students would have four periods a week of history, and five of science, ten of their forty weekly periods were spent harnessing English. They worked hard at it and all became proficient, though not necessarily successful on the Cambridge Examination. The best student of English at Malangali, for instance, failed this test, as I feared he would. He never welcomed a punctuation mark as a friend. His flowery, rambling, overblown sentences would run-on forever, acceptable for a Tolstoy or a Joyce, but not for the Cambridge. Part of the test had a two-hour essay section, with the choice of one long essay or two shorter ones. I had earnestly advised him to avoid the long essay like the plague. I had been very frank as to why. On test day I entered the room to observe, and sure enough, he was in high gear on the long essay.

In addition to English I also taught history, and while this subject did not present the challenges that English offered, it had its own peculiarity: cause and effect. The students would memorize the causes of the French Revolution and regurgitate them on a test, but they did not see events through European eyes, and retained a healthy skepticism toward Western reliance on economic determinism as the basis for explaining historical events. Natural Marxists they were not, but what passed for African cause and effect was suspect as well.

A case in point was the man-eating lions of the Njombe district. These lions went on a rampage from 1932 to 1947, killing hundreds[27] of people. They prowled an area about eighty miles in diameter, straddling the Great North Road and stretching from just west of Malangali to the Great Ruaha River, which crosses this road just a couple miles east of Chimala, towards Mbeya. The game ranger at the time, Dusty Arundell, had his hands full with a meager staff that got all the smaller during W.W. II. His primary task was to erect and man a pole fence to try and keep an outbreak of rinderpest from crossing the border and decimating the cattle herds of the Rhodesias and South Africa. In addition, he had the usual duties of animal control; that is keeping the elephant, and sometimes hippo, out of people's crops and villages. It was not until George Rushby took over these duties in late 1945, that a concerted effort was made to rid the Njombe district of these predators. Over the next year and a half, he and his African game scouts managed to bring the carnage to an end, with a total of twenty-two lions dead, fifteen of which Rushby considered certain man-eaters. That, at any rate, is the European view of the matter. The African explanation is entirely different.

In 1932 Matamula Mangera, headman of Iyayi, a village on the Great North Road

Malangali Students

and smack in the middle of the area the lions would terrorize, was relieved of his post. Matamula was a renowned mganga, or witch-doctor, and almost immediately after his dismissal reports of man-eaters started to reach the district commissioner at Njombe, fifty miles south of the Great North Road, and the game ranger in Mbeya, some hundred miles to the west. The locals were convinced that this was not mere coincidence, and over the next decade and a half repeatedly implored the paramount chief and the district commissioner to reinstate Matamula. The tribesmen were reluctant to discuss anything about the lions, and even Rushby's game scouts referred to them indirectly as the "dudu ya porini," the insects of the bush. To talk about the man-eaters was to invite an attack, and to hunt them was a useless provocation. The locals viewed Rushby and his game scouts with sullen irritation. Yes they had killed some lions but by definition the dead lions were not the man-eaters, as they were protected by magic and could not be harmed. All the hunters had accomplished was to irritate Matamula's lions, and thus put additional African lives at risk.

The people of Iyayi and the surrounding area got word that the district commissioner was leaving, and before a new one could arrive to complicate matters, a large deputation was assembled and went straight to the Paramount Chief at Mdandu. They begged once again that Matamula be restored to his post, as only this would end their troubles. The Chief relented. A few days before Rushby's scouts killed the last two 'man-eaters', Matamula regained his old position as sub-chief at Iyayi. There were no more killings by lions in the Njombe district.

The Europeans dismiss the African version as the superstition of a primitive people. The Africans believe the Europeans live in a different world from theirs. But do they? When Rushby visited the Lutheran Mission at Ilembula, in the heart of Njombe District, the Swedish missionary in charge dismissed the African notion of black magic as absurd. His view? The man-eaters were obviously the work of the devil.

The line between superstition and religion is a fine one indeed. Both are based on faith, and to believers are as true as the tangible world. The biggest difference between Christianity and localized religions is the hundreds of years Christianity has had to adapt, though often reluctantly, to the findings of science. When an African student looks through a microscope in the biology lab, his world is changed forever. Puncturing a scrap of cowhide with a thorn and securing it in a path for someone to pass over is no longer going to remove a curse and cure what ails him. These germs that you cannot see with the naked eye are a revelation. They are not an invention of the white man's world. They are real and the basis for western dawa. And western medicine is powerful stuff and known to work wonders, even by the simplest person out in the bush. The irony is that this abrupt introduction of western science drives people to western religion.

For a history major, one advantage of teaching English was the occasional glimpse into the thought processes of my students, concerning cause and effect. One such occasion revolved around the issue of flying machines. I had one pair of essays I set for every one of my English classes: Was colonialism good for Tanganyika? or Was colonialism bad for Tanganyika? The first time I wrote these on the board, there was some apprehension and an immediate request for additional choices. It came out that they were concerned that Mr. or Mrs. Partner would see their papers. Once assurances were given that only my American eyes would scrutinize their work, they got to it. I always arranged my essay periods back-to-back, so the students had eighty minutes to create their compositions. With this much time to consider the matter, this topic usually produced some interesting arguments and interpretations. On one occasion a student strenuously made the claim that the colonials had killed off all the African scientists and destroyed their flying machines. After going through the language corrections, I continued with a critique of their reasoning. I pointed out that since we Americans had had our own revolution to throw off British colonial rule, I did not care which side of the question they took, however, their arguments had to be logical and believable. When I offered up the 'flying machines' argument as an example of what not to include in a serious paper, immediately half a dozen hands shot into the air and in unison several of the pupils insisted that it was, as the British would say, a true fact. I was caught totally flat-footed by this response. I had not mentioned the author's name so as not to embarrass him, and here the whole class was flapping its collective gums in support of this incredible claim.

It should not have been such a surprise, on reflection. It took Westerners centuries to get beyond witchcraft and supernatural explanations for events not understood. In fact, and certainly in the United States, there are still those who believe in and even practice witchcraft, and those who will accept all sorts of hare-brained, irrational[28] reasons to explain an event or phenomenon. There is even an organization called the International Flat Earth Society, questioning what is tangible and visible and claiming that Columbus and Franklin Roosevelt were flat-earthers!

My students came directly from an illiterate, often isolated, subsistence culture into a westernized colonial and educational system that questioned and denigrated much of what they had been raised to believe by their respected and influential parents and elders. They were not stupid, and not illogical by nature. After all they did quite well at physics and math. But they were an amalgam of their life experiences, and included were some firmly held beliefs that we Europeans would classify as irrational inventions beyond the pale of the possible. We should not expect someone freshly plucked from the bush to immediately think entirely as we do. We, after all, do not have everything right either.

After this incident of the flying machines, I decided to see what the reaction would be to the name Matamula. From Malangali, it was only forty miles west to the center of the man-eaters' activity, and that activity was very recent. When I dropped the name, the students froze. It was quiet, but not just the absence of noise. It was the quiet of fearful tension, like being in the bush on a moon-less night with Matamula's lions about. I could sense the gears between their ears spinning with all kinds of thoughts. Why was this dreaded name injected into the classroom? How did this American even know about Matamula? Would trouble result? Nothing was said. I

Malangali Students

quickly regretted my cavalier treatment of a subject that so unsettled my students, and started on the next assignment.

When I first set the essay on colonialism, I would get a few tepid compositions on the positive side, and the rest would be gently critical of the colonial situation. After word got around that I really didn't care which position they took, as long as their thesis was coherent, then I got more red meat. The kids could be inventive: "Sir, he colonized my pencil," meant not only that someone had stolen his pencil, but also that theft was the essence of colonialism. The infrastructure and cash crops introduced by the colonials were there to benefit Britain, not Tanganyika, as they were necessary to exploit the country. As for the colonials themselves, they had a 'superiority complex'. Who could argue? Well, as it turned out, Stafford could.

Stafford was an unreconstructed, unabashed Anglophile. On the occasion of our classroom debate on this topic, he took the pro-colonial side, and indeed on this occasion his was the only essay on that side of the equation. As he stood in front of the class expounding on the virtues of colonialism in general and the British in particular, his classmates were animated, though not heated, in their rejoinders. There was much amused head shaking, eye rolling and finger waggling. Stafford was just being Stafford. He was so far out of step with the temper of the prevailing political climate that the others just accepted it as some sort of unexplainable, amusing aberration.

Stafford was one of our taller, darker students with a somewhat flat though engaging face, a reflection of his generally sunny attitude. But Stafford also was the lone, random recipient of a dark cloud in the form of a notice to report to the farm of a renowned wizard, as the students put it, in northern Malawi, Tanganyika's neighbor just south of Mbeya. The British teachers, especially Alf Schofield, tried to dissuade him, arguing that he was an educated man and should not be bullied by superstition. Stafford was adamant, he would go, or he would die. He went.

After three months he returned, none the worse for wear it seemed, either physically or mentally. The other students certainly did not make fun of him on this occasion. They were silently sympathetic, so as not to call any attention to themselves, and just thankful that their number had not come up.

Though Stafford missed the end of the school year, he was not a senior at the time so he did not lose his shot at the Cambridge Exam. As December rolled around, so did this all-important test of their schooling. The Cambridge was given throughout East Africa during the same two week time frame, and each individual test was set at the exact same time for all schools. Thus, if Malangali was doing the Physics test on Monday morning, starting at eight o'clock, so was every other school in East Africa. The tests arrived at the schools in individual brown packets, secured with melted wax imprinted with the Cambridge seal. The tests were invigilated by a teacher from another school, and just before each test he would report to the headmaster's office and get the appropriate packet. If the seal had been tampered with the packet was shipped back to England, and the entire class would fail that portion of the

Hunting and Teaching in East Africa

Cambridge. The teachers at the school could enter the testing room to observe, but had to remain mute and not communicate in any way. Students could not leave the room. When a test was completed, all the paperwork was placed in a return envelope, sealed with hot wax into which the school logo had been stamped, and immediately posted to England for marking. On arrival at Cambridge, the seal again was inspected, and if signs of mischief were evident, the test would be discarded. Since the Cambridge was given in many colonies and countries throughout the British Commonwealth, and since multiple choice questions had not yet been invented in the United Kingdom, the marking took time. At Malangali we did not get our results until towards the end of January, or into February. By that time, the tested students were long gone, and a new class of seniors was just beginning its final year. The tradition was for the headmaster to assemble the students in front of his office and read out the Cambridge results, name by name, as soon as they arrived on the bus carrying the post. The students were both apprehensive and eager. They wanted to know how their friends had done, and also gauge their own fate. Smiles and shouting would greet good results like a first or a second. Unfortunately, murmurs of sadness and disappointment were also appropriate at times.

Invigilating, or even observing a test is boring to the fourth power, but in 1963 a remarkable and poignant situation developed. One of the students had dysentery and it flared up during a test. He could not control his bowels, but he would not allow his predicament to affect his performance on the Cambridge Examination. Sitting in his own mess he not only completed the test, but somehow managed to block it out of his mind and concentrate on the important task at hand. All the students and staff knew of his travail and empathized with him. So when the test results were announced in front of the headmaster's office one evening in early February, the students followed the proceedings closely. Their response that evening was somewhat subdued, as name after name and result after result were recited. But finally the headmaster came to the focal point of the proceedings: how had the afflicted student done? Kabati paused, an ever so slight grin on his pudgy face. He looked out over his anxious audience and read the verdict. The students were ecstatic. The muted atmosphere of the evening dissolved into a raucous celebration. It was a replay of the joyous reception that scrawny, dead tired, dead last, runner had received.

Yes, a teacher could get spoiled, with students like these.

---

26 In Swahili, the "a" is like that in "father", the "e" is like the long "a" in "hay", the "i" is like the long "e" in "bee", the "o" should be long, and the "u" is like "ou" in the word "you". Every syllable ends with a vowel, and the accent is always on the second to the last syllable. Some adopted words don't conform to these rules.

27 Sub chief Jifiki of Wangingombe kept a list of those killed in his small area from 1941-1945. There were 230 names on the list. The Lutheran Missionary

Malangali Students

at Ilembula had a count of over two hundred for a two year period at the end of the war. These numbers, covering a fraction of the time and a smaller fraction of the area involved, represent a fraction of the lives lost.

[28] Speaking of hare-brained and irrational, here, quoted from an essay, is my all-time favorite: "Rudolph Hitler was a great man because he died of disappearance."

Malangali students. Adam Kombango wanted me to take his picture, but by the time I got my camera squared away, all these other boys horned in.

CHAPTER 14

First Elephants

My first elephant hunt was at best a qualified success: I did get two elephants with modest ivory; and nobody got killed. But it was not a model hunt. Between me and the local guides, we made enough mistakes to stock the morgue of a mid-sized city. That nobody was killed was just dumb luck.

The governments of East Africa required visiting hunters to hire a licensed professional hunter before heading into the bush. This was eminently reasonable on several counts, not the least of which were language and topography. What would happen if a guide suddenly said something about nyoka? Would the visitor know that the guide was telling him he was about to step on a snake? Perhaps the visiting hunter had done some homework and knew the Swahili for buffalo, nyati, but maybe the locals use the less common 'mbogo', as in mbogo karibu sana, the buffalo is very close. Equally unforgiving can be the landscape. Whether thorn scrub, elephant grass, or rain forest, the terrain can be very confusing, and a novice to the country would get disoriented and lost in no time.

And then there were the objects of the hunt, the animals. Those classified as dangerous were the ones most likely to kill you, of course. But a wounded oryx could skewer you like a kabob, and a hunt for something as innocuous as an impala didn't mean you were only going to encounter antelope. Is that the outline of a buffalo horn in that thick patch of bush? Could it be the one the locals wounded yesterday with their muzzle-loaders? If he comes for you, how do you like your chances with that 30:06 in your hands?

The animal that killed more people than all the others bundled together wasn't even considered dangerous game. Two of them were included on the General Game License, and on the Rufiji River they were considered vermin: shoot as many as you like. The hippo was obviously dangerous, but more to the locals out at night or people in dugouts, than to hunters.

Of the five animals classified as dangerous game, the least dangerous was the rhino. They are certainly impressive when seen up close, especially if you are afoot. Large, built like a tank, surprisingly fast and agile, they have accounted for the deaths

First Elephants

of several hunters, amateur and professional alike. But they have weaknesses. Their eyesight is poor, their sense of smell so-so, and they have little tiny brains that don't compute very well. When I was there they were protected, and you had better not shoot one, even in self-defense. When I encountered rhino, which did happen on occasion, I always gave them a wide berth. I did not want to put myself in a situation where I had to kill one of those interesting relics. No excuse would be accepted. Killing a rhino would cost you a hefty fine, your rifle and licenses, and your hunting privileges.

Two of the big five were cats: lion and leopard. I carried a license for both during my first two years but never hunted them as it was too boring and time consuming. I would have shot one had it crossed my path, but none volunteered. The professionals would set up a blind, kill anything handy for bait, drag the carcass behind a Land Rover for a few miles to either side of the blind, suspend the dead animal from a tree, and wait. And wait. According to professionals, both in print and in person, the average wait was about ten days! The result should be an easy shot, like shooting a fish in a barrel, but the light and shadows could be tricky, the cat might move, the hunter might be tired or edgy, or a poor marksman. A botched shot creates a serious problem. The cat will head for cover; it doesn't take much, and someone is likely to get hurt.

Buffalo and elephant round out the big five and are generally considered the most formidable. The Cape Buffalo is a legendary adversary, especially when wounded. He is big, strong, determined, and relative to a human, fast enough. His senses are all keen. He looks something like a Black Angus, except for the cuddly part. Somehow he comes across as sinister. Maybe it's the massive boss covering his forehead, not to mention the spread of those black horns. The lower than normal placement of the ears, usually replete with rips and notches, adds to his appearance as one tough hombre. And the eyes. He can give you that bored, bovine stare, but get him riled and those coal black eyes can pierce you to the quick, standing the hair on your neck at attention like the tail of a frightened warthog.

There were lots of stories about wounded buffalo. Mostly they emphasized two points. He was cunning. He would lay up in thick bush and attack from close range, often from the rear, having doubled back on his own tracks. He was single-minded. When he charged he would not have a change of heart just because bullets were bouncing off his boss or tearing into his flesh. A bullet will sometimes deflect a charging elephant, but not nyati. A buff had to be stopped dead, or disabled.

The weekly newsmagazine out of Nairobi carried the story of a Kenya farmer's altercation with a buffalo. Plowing a field one morning, he noticed a lone buffalo bull in amongst his cattle. He pulled his rifle out of the scabbard lashed to the tractor and shot the unwelcome intruder. The buff dropped in his tracks and the farmer continued with his work. At noon, the farmer retired to his house for lunch and a nap. Later in the afternoon, he returned to his chores, but towards evening he decided to butcher the buffalo. His African workers threw clods of dirt at the animal, but not an eyelash fluttered, not an ear twitched. Still, the workers insisted the bwana be careful. They encouraged him to put another bullet in the beast, just to make sure. After all, an animal can go down, but like a boxer it may get back up and carry the fight to you. Those Africans, they can sure be grannies sometimes!

The European was certain the buff was dead. It had been lying in the hot sun for hours, and the dirt clods had bounced off a totally inert mass of meat. With knife in hand, the farmer grabbed the horn and twisted the head to expose the throat. The buff was not dead. There was one spark of life left in him and he spent it to rip the farmer from stem to stern, gutting him in one violent, final act of retribution.

While a wounded buffalo could indeed be a holy terror, there weren't really many of them. Licensed hunters only occasionally let one get away, and the Africans with their muzzle-loaders had no real incentive to tackle buffalo. Meat was precious, but life was more so, and there were much less risky sources of meat. In short, when you hunted buffalo they were not usually pre-wounded and therefore generally not pre-disposed to aggression.

The same cannot be said for elephant. Elephant are most dangerous on initial contact. When that first shot goes off, anything can happen. Usually, the hunter is in close, in thick brush, and the number and location of all the elephants is uncertain. Add to this mix some tuskers carrying a grudge, and you have an even more volatile situation.

Elephants are cursed with a pair of very big teeth. An African could earn a year's wages poaching one average sized tusker, but muzzle-loaders are not ideal elephant guns, and the ratio of wounded to killed had to be very high. Generally, elephants realize that man is a menace, but in areas where muzzle-loaders proliferated, the elephants were seriously pissed off. Such an area was the venue for my initial hunt, though I was innocent of this knowledge going in.

I was somewhat better prepared than the visiting hunter type, as I did know some Swahili, and, as important, had made contacts. A professional hunter I had met in Iringa, for instance, had drawn me a sketch of an elephant indicating the locations of the heart, lungs and brain. The brain is on a line between the eye and the ear-hole and is about the size of a rugby ball. A big enough target at close range, but elusive at certain angles. The lungs are huge, filling much of the chest cavity, but the basketball-sized heart is low and barely back of the front legs. This was very useful knowledge, as a shot higher up his chest, as would be appropriate on most game, would result in a lung shot and perhaps many miles of tracking.

Another contact was a student at Malangali, Nicoderm Mwaduma. It was in response to Nicoderm's information, buttressing what I had already gathered from a European farmer, that we set off for Dabaga, a village about 35 miles southwest of Iringa. Harry, Don, Nicoderm and I left Malangali at three in the morning on a Sunday in November. We departed the main road about two hours later, and in another two hours managed to cover the distance to Dabaga. In low gear, the Simca barely pulled some of the grades, and the streams were crossed via rickety, home-made bridges of logs and branches. But it was beautiful, green, hilly country, thick

First Elephants

with bamboo and other rain forest vegetation, including some enormous trees.

About eight-thirty we finally parked the car, having pushed beyond Dabaga to Masasiwe (Ma sa **see** way), where Nicoderm had relatives. Masasiwe was more an area than a village. Huts were sparsely scattered about the forest and were made of bamboo, which the locals cut at an angle, leaving a short, sharp stump. As we waited for guides, a middle aged African man came by with a ghastly wound to his calf muscle. While walking in the forest, he had stumbled and run one of those bamboo stumps under the muscle, separating part of it from the bone. I put a whole tube of anti-bacterial ointment on it, but advised him to get to the hospital in Iringa. Yes, my medicine was good: dawa mzuri, but through Nicoderm I tried to explain that it was not sufficient for this kind of deep wound. Neither he nor Nicoderm seemed too concerned.

Finally some guides materialized. They estimated that elephants were a couple hours away and they were making all sorts of arrangements to take care of things, once we got some. I was taken aback. I had thought of this as an exploring safari on which we might get lucky, but these men counted success a foregone conclusion.

The first hill we descended was a lulu. The trail seemed straight as a string and straight down; and it was slick. Some of it we negotiated on our rumps, the better to get up close to those bamboo stumps that laced its edges. I couldn't help think what it would be like coming back up after a hard day's trek. The next couple of hours we spent climbing up and slithering down more of what seemed the steepest hills in creation. They were dotted here and there with huts and shambas, but mostly they were covered with towering, dense forest and thick underbrush. Along the way we stopped at a hut and were offered some greasy, very tasty, roasted peas. After our snack and some rest, we headed further into the forest, eventually arriving at another hut where we had some squash as we waited while the scouts were looking up the elephant population. Shortly they returned, and we headed off to three or four hours of utter frustration.

Within half an hour, we saw our first elephant, a group of three, some distance ahead. The guides wanted me to shoot, but at this stage I was fresh, and thinking, so I said we should get closer. Getting close was not a high priority for the locals. The guides escorted us via Australia, and by the time we got to where the tembo had been, they were a good two or three miles away, instead of the two or three hundred yards they had been in the first place. We chased elephants around for the next three hours and every time we got somewhat close, the guides figured we were too close and led us off to a place of better vision, but greater distance. I was really pooped, and disgusted. The crowning moment of their ineptitude, my own moment would arrive soon enough, occurred when we found ourselves within fifty yards of a small herd. They were having a good time breaking branches and eating, and we could hear the contented rumblings of their stomachs. But instead of going in after them, the locals led us out into an open bog, up-wind of the elephants. The breaking of branches ceased. The stomachs became silent. We were knee-deep in muck with nowhere to hide, and no way to run: a death trap should the elephants charge. I had no sooner sized up our predicament, than the elephants went crashing through the underbrush, fortunately headed away from us.

It was now a couple hours after mid-day, so we decided to give up the hunt and return to the car. We had barely started when we stumbled across a herd of seven, which the head guide said were very close. My moment had come. While they didn't look all that close to me, I nevertheless started shooting. Nothing happened. It was like my bullets were evaporating in mid-flight. Perhaps the elephants had their own maji-maji magic.[29] How far were those elephants and how much did these 570 grain[30] bullets drop? I flicked up the 300-yard leaf sight and tried again, with an even worse result: I hit one of them. They milled about and then disappeared into a two to three acre patch of dense brush. The guide and I, along with Don and his 30:06, went in after them on a narrow trail that circled into the thicket. It was hot, oppressively humid, and tension tied a knot in the pit of my stomach. After what seemed like half an hour, but must have been only ten minutes, the guide pointed through a hole in the brush. I could see two heads. They were sideways to us, staring at the real estate we had just vacated. We had walked right in front of them! Now they were close, fifteen to twenty yards. I fired at the bigger of the two. He staggered but didn't go down. I emptied the second barrel and he dropped, triggering a frenzied explosion of noise and activity. The elephants charged in our direction, bulldozing the brush and raising an unholy racket with their screaming and trumpeting. We backed into the brush under a big tree and I reloaded the .500. Just then, two elephant emerged, about forty yards off, heading obliquely away from us. I raised the gun and asked the guide if they were kubwa. "Kubwa sana," came the reply; very big. The tusks were not visible, so I took his word for it and let fly, another moment of terrible judgment. Where did I think I was, in eastern Washington snap shooting jackrabbits in the sagebrush? The two elephants disappeared up the hill to our right and vented their rage with an impressive display of power. Trees were quaking under the attack and branches as big as my thigh were ripped from their sockets and thrown to the wind. This visual was accompanied by equally impressive audio, as all manner of elephant caterwauling rent the air.

The other elephants in the herd had by now cleared out, and these two, having exacted revenge on God's green earth, crashed through the vegetation to briefly appear crossing the trail below us before disappearing, deeper into the forest.

Once the elephants vanished, the locals dropped out of the trees like ripe apples in a hailstorm. The guide was trying to tell us something about the wounded animal, but neither Don nor I could understand the local tongue, Kihehe (Key **hay** hay). Nicoderm had scampered up a large tree somewhere, so while we waited for him, we pushed our way through the underbrush to the dead elephant. He had slid down the hill about thirty yards and come to rest on his side. As elephants go, he wasn't large, and he had only fair ivory, about twenty-five pounds each tusk. But he was still a mighty and impressive animal, and as we were admiring him, Nicoderm arrived and we learned that the wounded elephant was being tracked and reports would follow.

In a matter of minutes the kill site was alive with Wahehe. The women brought

First Elephants

baked spuds, again greasy and tasty, and the men began to dismantle the tembo. First they cut the tip of the trunk off, the first three inches or so, and took it off site for burial. According to Nicoderm, this was a precaution to prevent the elephant's spirit from later sniffing out his killers and stomping them to mush. After this little ceremony, the men began cutting up the meat and extracting the tusks. As soon as chunks of elephant were severed, they disappeared into the bush on the shoulders of the sturdy women.

The elephant was killed at two-thirty, and about four o'clock, with only two and a half hours of light left, we got word and headed out. I had only three more rounds of hard nosed ammo but didn't have much time to mull this over as the elephant that had taken them ninety minutes to locate, was only ten minutes distant. The upper half of his body came into view about fifty yards ahead and slightly downhill. I was not keen to shoot without assurances from the guide that this was indeed the wounded one. He joined Nicoderm up a tree for a better view, and said it was the right tembo. I crept slowly down the trail, that knot tying up my stomach again. Since I was moving down-grade toward the elephant, the closer I got, the more he sunk into the intervening vegetation. At roughly twenty yards, all I could see was the top half of his head. He was standing perfectly still, facing me almost head-on. His eyes seemed to be closed, except for the occasional flutter of the lids. I shouldered the rifle and paused, thinking how small it seemed as the barrels leveled, and then the explosion ripped the still, quiet air. Quicker than a blink his ears flew forward from the impact and he dropped like the gods had pulled a rug from under him. When you hit an elephant in the brain, there is no dramatic posturing, no staggering about, he just goes down like six tons of brick. Also, as I was discovering, his mates go crazy. In this case there was only one other elephant with him, probably lingering as a guard, or just a friend, and he immediately let out a blood-curdling bellow and went tearing through the bush off to my right, running the gamut of elephant vocals. Don got excited and popped off a shot with his deer rifle but probably missed as he hadn't sighted it in, and later on, still not sighted in, he overshot some antelope by about three feet.

In any case, when Don shot I thought that maybe I had misjudged the elephant's direction, so I ducked off the trail and recharged the empty barrel. I turned to face the direction from which the elephant would come, as I was spot on between him and Don. I raised the gun to my shoulder, safety off, fingers on both triggers. If he suddenly loomed over me, I would ignite both barrels and hope six tons of muzzle energy would dump him on his butt, as it most assuredly would do me on mine. The elephant continued to bellow and plow through the brush, but he was in fact circling around and away from us.

Once the excitement was over, confusion set in. I went back up the trail to chew on Don, but he, the guide, and Nicoderm were all of the opinion that the elephant I had shot had immediately got back up and taken off. I was sick. I just couldn't believe that the one I'd shot had regained his feet and was now headed deeper yet into the forest.

I was pretty dejected, and resigned to pursuing the elephant into the dark, when one of the other Africans, from a higher perch, pointed to where I had shot and said

Hunting and Teaching in East Africa

he thought an elephant was down. I approached the spot, .500 at the ready, and to my relief the wounded one was there, and totally dead.

The locals were really happy. They not only love the meat, but hate and fear these raiders. While the tusks were being axed from the skull, we roasted some meat, and relaxed. It would be a long haul back to the car, with the sun fading rapidly.

Fortunately, the elephant had crumpled straight down, coming to rest on his knees. This turned a three-hour job into a one-hour job. An elephant will usually land on its side, but sometimes, from a brain or spine shot, he will end up in this kneeling position. When an elephant falls sideways, as the first one had, extracting the bottom tusk is slow going.

As we got under way, just before dark, we could hear a buffalo prowling the nearby undergrowth, but we left him alone, and he reciprocated. It was well after sunset when we passed the location of the first elephant, but in the moonlight we could see what remained: almost nothing. The entire beast was gone: meat, hide, bones, feet, everything. All that remained to mark this animal's existence was a conical mound of semi-digested matter from its innards. In a day or two, that would also disappear.

We reached the car without incident, about eight that evening. We took numerous rest breaks along the way, but that last hill was almost insurmountable. About a third of the way up, we took a breather, then started again. I took two steps, and my legs refused a third. We had to sit for several minutes before making another try. Once we got going, I knew we had better not stop or we might have to spend the night. The hill was so steep that my knees were coming into my chest. In places it was slick and we had to use the brush and bamboo stumps to pull ourselves upward. It was more like climbing a tree than a trail.

Already fully loaded, the tusks added another hundred pounds to the Simca's burden. One smelly pair was laid across the back floor, and the other draped across the laps of Harold and Nicoderm. At one stage we had to unload everything but me, the driver, and push and verbally encourage the Simca up a slippery and challenging grade. The rest of the trip went without incident, except we almost fell through one of those rickety homemade bridges. The guys got out and pushed the car back a few feet so that the left front was no longer catching air, and once all four wheels were more or less on firm footing, we crept the rest of the way across the span. When I say "we" crept across the bridge, I mean the Simca and me. The others thought it prudent to lighten the load and waited on the far bank as 'we' inched our way, lurching and bumping, accompanied by occasional snapping noises as parts of the bridge complained.

We were low on gas at this point, and did not know if we were going to have to walk some more or not. Finally we got to a farm, and Bwana Zinatoes and his wife treated us to milk and biscuits. He was the farmer Don and I had talked to earlier about hunting in the Dabaga area. They were quite surprised to see us at that hour, and even more so to see the ivory. They asked how it went and we allowed that it had been quite exciting. We were really tired, but at least for me, the adrenaline had not entirely quit flowing, so I recounted our adventure. He gave us a look. You do know,

First Elephants

he said, that the last hunting party into those woods came out in boxes. No: I shot a look at him and Nicoderm, we hadn't been privy to that bit of information.

It was another twenty minutes to Ifunda and the nearest petrol station, where we pooled our resources and bought a gallon of gas, as the man wouldn't take a check. We then motored into the trade school and knocked up Louie around midnight so we could borrow enough cash for enough gas.

On the way to Malangali, I was gently chiding Nicoderm about the timidity of his fellow Hehe. Weren't they the tribe that halted the advance of the Angoni, a branch of the Zulu, from the south, and the Masai from the north? Weren't they the warriors who, under Paramount Chief Mkwawa, almost drove the Germans into the Indian Ocean in the 1890's?

By way of defending the honor of his relatives, Nicoderm simply stated that it wasn't just Europeans that were killed on that ill-fated safari Bwana Zinatoes had mentioned. He also offered that there were still many active and skilled elephant hunters among the Wahehe, but of course now they only used their muskets for crop control and to defend themselves from the marauders. These muskets proliferated in Uhehe, dating back to their accumulation under Mkwawa and his father. Mkwawa had controlled an active ivory trade, arming hunters with muzzle-loaders captured from raids on caravans across central Tanganyika, and trading ivory and slaves to the Arabs for ever more guns.

The skirmishes between the Hehe and the elephants result in a certain amount of illicit ivory, and a large number of wounded tembo. In my two years hunting in the Southern Highlands, I dug three lead balls out of the six elephant taken; and I did not go mining for them. The other three may very well have been packing lead also.

The next few days were spent closing down the school and seeing students off to their scattered, homeward destinations. The first of December had come, and the school year was over. During this time I had no papers to mark and only mundane, autopilot type duties like supervising clean up and checking in schoolbooks and materials. I had plenty of time to contemplate the recent hunt and came to the conclusion that if I were going to continue to both hunt elephant and stay alive, I needed to build on the experience of that hunt, and learn enough to survive the next one.

I had dreamed of hunting elephant from the moment I had finished my first junior high book on Africa. I wasn't going to let the fact that I'd made a basket full of bonehead, rookie mistakes deter me. And, since I'd made a basket full of mistakes all at once, I had gained a basket full of How Not To Do It experience to analyze.

First off, I had finally tumbled to the fact that hunting elephants, and in fact all dangerous game, was a close range exercise. Never again would I take a shot of over forty yards. Over the next four years, twenty yards was probably the average distance between my quarry and me, though I am leaving out of this average the elephant shot at point blank range. There were two critical reasons to get up close: accuracy and power. The closer the target, the more likely a bulls-eye, thus greatly increasing the odds of a clean kill and reducing the chances of having to follow up a wounded animal. And with those big ponderous bullets, once out of the rifle, they lose power quickly and at any real distance, their trajectory was more like that of a mortar shell than a rifle bullet. Even up close, a hard-nosed .500 slug will not bore all the way through an elephant, side to side.

Though less obvious, an equally important realization concerned the African guides. Just because they lived in close proximity to the game didn't mean they knew how to hunt. In fact, most didn't. Hunters pay attention to the wind. Hunters do not wade into a bog, upwind of a herd of elephant. The local kiongozi[31] know their area and could often get you close to game, but the approach and the decision to shoot needed to be the hunter's responsibility. For instance, when the two elephant crossed in front of us and I asked the guide if they were big, well of course they were big. To him they represented tons of meat. But I was talking ivory, and he couldn't see that any better than I could.

The most important function of the guides was as local geographers. They could keep you from getting lost, and at this they were uncanny. You could walk all day in undifferentiated country that would just swallow your sense of direction and they would get you back to your camp, precisely. They didn't need to cut a trail or a track and follow it back: one minute you were in dense bush and the next you were in camp. I would often test my sense of direction with the guides, more to visit and connect with them than to actually learn anything. At a rest break I'd ask, "Gari huko?"[32] I would point in the direction I thought the car was. They would smile and chuckle, sometimes bringing a hand in front of their mouths to disguise their amusement. "Hapana Bwana, gari huko mbali."[33] No, they would point, the car is far off in that direction. I would just laugh, joining their good-natured fun at the expense of the hopeless bwana.

But in a sense it was not a laughing matter. I was absolutely dependent upon them. I carried no water or food and no compass, and generally didn't even tote the rifle. There was nothing to keep them from melting into the bush, leaving me to the animals and elements. I usually had someone along with me, a fellow teacher or hunter, but at times I was totally alone, a speck in the bush, miles, from anywhere. Only once did I feel really uncomfortable.

The locals couldn't help but know that my companions and I were novices, especially at first. So why would they even go out with us? We did pay them, but fifty cents American per day could hardly be enticement enough. I came to four conclusions: one, we were entertainment; two, we might provide some excitement; three, they could receive a large cache of meat; and four, should circumstances dictate, they could outrun us: the devil, or the elephant, or the lion, takes the hindmost!

The third lesson had to do with bullet placement: two brain shots, two wild reactions. Next time I would try for a heart shot, and over the years this became my favorite as the target elephant would usually run away from the source of the pain, and the direction having been set, the others would generally follow. As the panicked herd dashed off, they wouldn't notice as their mortally wounded brother lost steam

First Elephants

and faded to the rear before going down. The follow up would only be a hundred yards, give or take, and once the grounded elephant was in hand, I'd cut off the tip of the trunk, Hehe style. At first, the blood would surge from the severed end, but gradually the flow would decrease, signaling that the elephant was indeed good and dead and wasn't going to deliver any unwelcome surprises.

Once the elephant was deemed dead, the work of extraction would begin, and one small lesson learned from the first hunt was to carry a whetstone. The axes prevalent in the country at that time were from Czechoslovakia. They were made of iron, not steel, and consequently went dull in a hurry, the elephant hide being almost as blunting as the thick, dense bone. A whetstone made for an easier and shorter job.

The lessons enumerated above were ones I could and would apply, but another insight took time to evolve, and had no practical application value. From this and later hunts, I gradually came to the conclusion that the presence of native muskets equated to more aggressive elephants. In Uhehe, the guns were a product of local history. Elsewhere, an Indian or Arab duka[34] out in the middle of nowhere, was a clue. This knowledge was more esoteric than useful, however. Elephant hunting, even for professionals, is serious, dangerous business. Elephants can be plenty aggressive, with or without persecution. Hunters get killed. Even photographers in game parks get killed. I never, at any time, thought I was hunting a docile creature. For me, fear and respect were tools for survival. But so was experience.

That first hunt was a crash course. It was like my first year of teaching. I learned more that first year than during the period of preparation, or all the years thereafter. That first hunt was my baptism of fire, my on the job training. With each subsequent hunt, as with each additional year of teaching, I would bank more experience, and make fewer mistakes.

You could get killed, without making a mistake: bahati mbaya.[35] You could live through a number of mistakes: bahati mzuri.[36] But eventually, mistakes would lead you to an early grave, bahati or no.

---

[29] Maji-maji magic, a reference to a rebellion against the Germans in 1905-07 by the Angoni, who were under the erroneous impression that their wizards could turn German bullets into maji, i.e. water.

[30] Grains. Bullets and powder are measured in this unit of weight. There are 7000 grains in a pound, so twelve of these slugs would weigh just short of one pound.

[31] Kiongozi-Swahili for guide.

[32] Gari huko-gari is car, and huko means there, or over that way.

[33] Hapana means no. Mbali means far away.

[34] Duka = a small shop.

[35] Bahati mbaya = bad luck.

[36] Bahati mzuri = good luck.

CHAPTER 15

Mkwawa

The Southern Highlands of Tanzania is dominated by the Wahehe, a tribe of historically short standing. Up to almost 1860 there was no such tribe. The area known today as Uhehe was inhabited by approximately thirty small tribes, or clans, similar in speech and customs.

When the explorer Sir Richard Burton came upon them in 1860, he assessed them as follows: "Though to appearance hearty and good humored, they are determined pilferers. They are on bad terms with all their neighbors and they unite under their chief." That chief was Muyugumba, father to Mkwawa and founder of the Mujinga family, which still rules the Wahehe today.

The expansion of powerful peoples from the north and the south spurred Muyugumba to unite the thirty-odd tribes of his area into one centralized force. Muyugumba adopted the weapons and training practices of the Ngoni, a branch of the Zulu, and, inflicting their own methods on them, checked Ngoni expansion northward. It was during this early period that the tribe became known as the Hehe, from their battle cry ahela, which means the enemy runs. And, the enemy did run, as Muyugumba conquered tribe after tribe until his dominance covered some 8000 square miles.

When Muyugumba died in 1879, Mkwawa gained the throne and quickly expanded Uhehe to twice his father's legacy. Mkwawa would rule until 1894. He consolidated Wahehe structure and traditions, and the rule of his family. However his rule would be ended by the arrival of another powerful tribe pushing in from the coast: the Germans.

Mkwawa molded the politically disparate peoples into one unit through spiritual, economic, political and military means. As paramount chief he was also paramount priest. Only he could perform certain rituals, and his magic and medicines were stronger than that of those below his rank, which was everyone. Although lesser chiefs and wizards could perform certain prayers and use certain medicines, aid for the whole tribe could only come from the paramount chief as only he could summon the ancestors, and it was believed that these ancestors determined the fate of the tribe.

In the economic sphere Mkwawa controlled the four main sources of wealth. Cattle were the symbol of wealth and the paramount chief had the largest herd; some inherited, but many gathered from tribute, raids, and war. He could also conscript labor, whether to work on his many farms or to build structures like the fort he built at Kalenga, near Iringa, after the defeat of Zelewsky. Mkwawa also organized a system of regular tribute collection, and all headmen had to pay a levy of produce to him, as chief of chiefs. Finally, he had control of the ivory trade. He equipped the elephant hunters, and the resultant tusks were brought to him. At least once a year he sent the ivory to Kilosa or Bagamoyo to exchange it for guns, ammunition, cloth, beads, and ornamental brass nails. These goods he then distributed down through the political apparatus to help bind the people to their chief. The use of wealth, not just its accumulation, thus played an important role in establishing and maintaining political power, both for Mkwawa, and his family.

Politically, Mkwawa ruled the villages under his authority through the traditional, generally hereditary, village heads. The sub-chiefs had the same types of powers and some of the same prerogatives as the paramount chief, but scaled back to suit their lower status. When additional peoples were incorporated into Uhehe, their paramount chiefs were removed, surgically, but Mkwawa often kept the lesser chiefs as his sub-chiefs. If this did not work out, he sent select warrior families or relatives to rule. In this fashion, one of his sisters became a sub-chief.

Sub-chiefs had to bring their militia to general assembly when called, collect tribute in grain, and maintain order. Under them were a number of headmen who kept the peace in their areas, controlled land allotment, judged petty disputes, and carried out directives from above.

To form, consolidate, defend and expand, the Hehe used force of arms. Whether or not fighting was the principal occupation of the Hehe, as some explorers thought, they certainly did a lot of it. At the Battle of Mgodamtitu, 1874/1875, Mkwawa led the Wahehe to victory over the Wabena, and later as chief he defeated the Wangoni in 1882, the Nyamwezi in 1883, and then the Masai, who were expanding southward. In addition to these major actions, Mkwawa and his Hehe were involved in more or less continuous skirmishes against outlying areas to keep them under control, and to collect tribute and slaves. His raids even reached into central Tanganyika, where he made caravan expeditions dangerous and expensive for those traders and travelers involved.

At the apex of his power, Mkwawa controlled an area running from Usanga in the Mbeya District to the present Central Railway Line, and from there to one hundred miles south of Iringa: an area almost as large as Imperial Germany, and comprising about one-third of Tanganyika.

To maintain this level of military activity, Mkwawa instituted universal military service: every able-bodied man was liable to military duty. This not only stocked his

Hunting and Teaching in East Africa

forces with troops, but the service and obedience to the chief cut across old tribal and village lines and was a factor in integrating the tribe and solidifying the position of Mkwawa and his family.

Mkwawa continued to use the weapons his father had adopted from the Ngoni. The explorer J. Frederic Elton described the Wahehe as very Zulu-like in their war-dress, and Joseph Thompson described their weapons as follows: "In war they carry an elliptical fly-shaped shield of hide, about three and a half feet long, and eighteen inches broad in the middle. Their arms consist of a number of assegais, a stabbing spear, and a hybrid article, between a billhook and an axe...." Perhaps the latter item was what Burton called a sime, a large heavy weapon, with a double edged, squared-off blade about four inches broad and a couple of feet long. This Zulu-like weapons system was augmented by Zulu-like discipline and fortified by various medicines Mkwawa would administer to his men before battle. Thus the combination of manpower, Zulu influenced training, weapons and tactics, and strong leadership, resulted in Mkwawa becoming the most prominent chief in Tanganyika at that time, and after the defeat of Zelewsky he enjoyed a reputation of invincibility, a reputation he could bask in for but three short years.

The Germans came in the 1880's, and by 1890 had subdued the coastal and northern sections of the new colony. By 1891, they decided to come to terms with the troublesome Hehe who were raiding caravans and disrupting trade between the coast and Lake Tanganyika, and generally keeping the southern third of Tanganyika in turmoil. The Germans sent out a force of one thousand men under Lieutenant Zelewsky. As he neared Iringa, he was ambushed by two or three thousand spear wielding Hehe. German reports listed ten European officers, two hundred fifty askaris,[37] twenty-three donkeys, and ninety-six carriers, in that order, dead. Four officers and about sixty askari survived to reach Dar es Salaam. One German report claimed seven hundred Wahehe killed, but that number mirrors the number of Zelewsky's force unaccounted for. Perhaps, since they were African casualties they could be called Wahehe, thus diminishing the size of the disaster, at least in German eyes.

It wasn't until 1894 that the Germans mounted another expedition into Uhehe, this one led by their governor, Colonel von Schele. After much hand to hand combat they managed to take Mkwawa's walled capital at Kalenga, but the target of their efforts had fled. Mkwawa would be a thorn in the tender German foot for another four years, but the constant pursuit by these implacable enemies, and ill health, took their toll. In l898, a German Sergeant named Merkl found Mkwawa dead of his own hand.

Merkl had received word that Mkwawa was in the Pawaga area, northwest of Iringa. He proceeded by forced march and en route stumbled across a boy coming down a hill. The boy fled but was caught, and as Merkl explained, he turned out to be "Mkwawa's boy." The youngster stated that Mkwawa lay sick about three hours away. On the evening before, Mkwawa had shot his last companion, and in the morning the boy had run away. Sergeant Merkl immediately set off with three soldiers, one

Mhehe, and the young awol.38 After half an hour they heard a distant shot. The small group hurried toward the great chief, but only a warm, dead body awaited them.

The Wahehe seem to have taken the death of Mkwawa in the passive, melancholic, philosophical way Africans often accept death. Sergeant Merkl reported the reaction of the Hehe on the scene to seeing Mkwawa dead: "The caravan soon caught us up; the Wahehe immediately recognized Mkwawa and remained for a long time silent."

Mkwawa was the heart of his people, and when he died, the fight was taken out of the Wahehe and they accepted the new order of things. They didn't even take part in the Maji Maji Rebellion of a few years later. The Germans were no doubt pleased to have Mkwawa out of the way, for as long as he lived there was always the possibility of rebellion against their control. Whereas the Hehe gave a sad sigh of resignation, the Germans gave one of relief.

Since then the legend of Mkwawa has grown among the Hehe and the twilight stories told around campfires glorify his memory in a mosaic of truth and fiction. Tradition says that he died like an eagle during his last minutes of freedom. He is pictured as the 'Lion of Uhehe', who enriched his people, and for many years withstood the iron Germans.

The Wahehe attitude toward their old chief can perhaps best be illustrated by the story concerning his skull, which was sent off to Germany as a trophy. Partly because of a feeling of devotion for Mkwawa and partly because they believed his head was a palladium, the recovery of which would ensure prosperity for the tribe, the Wahehe were eager to have the skull returned. When the British acquired Tanganyika after the Germans lost the First World War, the Wahehe let them know that they wanted the skull back. As a result, Article 246 of Section II of the Special Provisions part of the Treaty of Versailles says: "Within six months Germany will hand over to His Britannic Majesty's Government the skull of the Sultan Mkwawa which was removed from the Protectorate of German East Africa and taken to Germany."

However, the skull proved as elusive as Mkwawa had been, and it was not until 1954, after much searching, that it was recovered and returned to the tribe. Sir Edward Twining, then Governor of Tanganyika, returned the skull to Chief Adam Sapi, grandson of Mkwawa and Paramount Chief of the Wahehe. Twining described the ceremony: "An honor guard of mostly Wahehe was present, and four hundred Wahehe ex-soldiers marched on parade. A crowd estimated at over 30,000 was present, and from the moment I arrived until the time I left there was dead silence, although the atmosphere was highly charged."

After receiving the skull, the Wahehe filed past it for the rest of the day, and after dark the old men went to speak to their revered sultan. Obviously the return meant a great deal to the Hehe and deeply moved them.

In independent Tanzania Mkwawa could not be seen as a popular or national hero. Due to the government's efforts to build a sense of national identity and their pronouncements against tribalism, he has not been deified. Nevertheless, in Uhehe he is a god-like hero, and the tribe's greatest claim to fame. It is not surprising therefore to find the best high school in the Southern Highlands named after him, and a game park about seventy miles north of Iringa called Mkwawa Game Park. His name and memory live on, not only in the tales around the village fires, but now as the name of places and monuments which proclaim to all the past glory of the Wahehe and their greatest chief.

---

[37] Askari means soldier; in English an "s" is often added to show plural.

[38] Awol is an American military expression: absent without leave.

CHAPTER 16

Got Snakes?

Yes, there was no shortage of snakes. The most commonly seen and probably the most numerous were the various styles of cobras. Second in number, at least according to my imperfect census gathering, was the lowly, sluggish puff-adder. Of boomslangs I saw two, of gaboon vipers I saw none, and of mambas, I saw one; and possibly stepped on one.

The snake of choice for myth and legend is the mamba, particularly the black mamba, which is twice the size, more widely distributed, more aggressive, and less tree bound than his mostly arboreal green cousin. Don Broadly, a herpetologist and leading expert on mambas states: "Without question, it is the most dangerous snake in Africa. It is highly strung, twitchy."

The black mamba[39] can reach fourteen feet in length and inject 100-400 milligrams of neurotoxic[40] venom; 10-15 milligrams being lethal in twenty minutes, give or take. The black is the fastest snake in the world and can attain a speed of fourteen miles per hour, which may sound pretty slow to those of us used to motorized vehicles, but let me put that in perspective for those on foot, or bicycle, out in the bush. At that rate, a motivated mamba could cover the distance of slightly over four football fields in one minute, if he had the stamina, which fortunately he doesn't. Or, to scale it down, he could do the hundred-yard dash in about fourteen and a half seconds, if he had the stamina, which unfortunately he does. On a racetrack, he would be no match for an Olympic sprinter, but in the bush, even Jesse Owens would find it difficult to outrun him. You and I would have no chance at all.

These two elements, venom and speed, form the basis for the snake's status in folklore, and in fact. European settlers told tales of black mambas chasing down riders on horseback. The Africans claim a mamba will stick its tail in its mouth and chase you as a rolling hoop. On a lighter note, the locals also claim that mambas are guilty of sneaking in at night and milking their cows. If they were my cows, I would tend to think that maybe my plump neighbor, the one with the constant moostache, might be a more likely culprit than the mamba. But anyway, as far as I know none of these stories are true, but then again, something strange is always coming out of Africa.

Hunting and Teaching in East Africa

There are, however, plenty of reliable reports to buttress this snake's icon status. The 'snake man', C.J.P. Ionides, was without doubt the most famous character in Tanganyika when I was there. He never locked his house and he was never robbed. There were snakes in there, some of them in cages. His reputation was known locally and internationally. He knew snakes, he collected and studied them, he wrote books about them, and he always had a supply on hand.

Ionides reported an incident in Northern Rhodesia, now Zambia, where a black mamba killed eleven people during one frantic melee. He, himself, captured one in Southern Province that had killed seven villagers in one spot. He gave her to the London Zoo, where she lived out her life peaceably, behind glass.

In Southern Highlands, while I was there, it was reported that a mamba killed several people who were sleeping in a thatched hut. Homes, gardens, and farms are a magnate for birds and rodents, which in turn are a magnet for cobras and mambas. It was thought that the snake had pursued a rodent into the hut, no doubt crawling over sleeping bodies in the process, and pandemonium broke out. As the people scrambled and stumbled about in the darkness, the mamba struck repeatedly, defending itself against these large, threatening figures.

My own experience with mambas was limited, fortunately. The only one I saw in the wild was crossing the road as I was driving to Iringa. This stretch was wide and straight, with a high, bare reddish bank of maybe twenty feet, to the right. The mamba was a bright green and about eight feet long, and some sixty or seventy yards ahead. Had the snake been a cobra, I would have easily run it down. This snake lifted its head slightly, in recognition of the on-rushing vehicle; and disappeared in a blink. I was flabbergasted. The mamba had been in the middle of the road. A cobra would have made perhaps a body's length before the car would have been upon it. As it was, I think it was my car that only made a body's length before that snake had zipped across what remained of the road and rocketed up the bank. I was mighty impressed. Although I was in my mid-twenties and in reasonably good condition, I now knew for certain, bila shaka,[41] that I could not out-run a mamba, not even on a clear, level track.

My other mamba experience was a maybe. In a hunt up north in 1966, I stepped on a snake and felt it scoot from under my shoe. The two African guides in front of me had not noticed it or stepped on it. Behind me was Don Morris, an American born and raised in Tanganyika of missionary parents. I turned to Don and said something to the effect that it was probably just a small grass snake. Don, mouth agape, shook his head. No, he stammered, It was big; and it was black. Oh. That left only two possibilities: either it was a black mamba, or it was a good-sized cobra, probably the latter since they are more numerous, and not so twitchy. In any case, large or small, cobra or mamba, a bite would have been fatal. We were a long way from the car, and the car was a long way from anything. In addition, even if you got bit right next to a hospital, that might be of little solace as there probably would be no antivenin, nor anyone who knew how to administer it properly.

In Southern Highlands there seemed to be plenty of cobras, mostly the small,

Got Snakes?

spitting variety. One moonlit night, tired of marking papers, I set off for a walk. As it was June, the evening air was cool, and the stars hung in the clear sky like polished gems. I savored the nights in Malangali with the sparkling stars, the fragrances of the flowering vines and trees, and the moon casting a warm, soft, shadowy light. There were no city lights and no mechanical sounds to interrupt the serenity, only the occasional chirp from a dog, or the muted note of a cow's bell. On such a night, I usually didn't carry a flashlight, though I would wish I had one before long.

I took a left out of my driveway, strolled past Don's lit up house on the right, and was approaching Eleanor's place ahead on the left. Between my house and Eleanor's was a field of knee high grass that bordered the road, and to the right was an impenetrable thicket of brush, trees, and vines that extended from Don's house down towards Harold's, a couple of city blocks away. I had almost reached the edge of Eleanor's yard when in mid-stride, I noticed a thin black presence where I was about to plant my foot. With a little extra boost from adrenaline, I leapt over the snake and then turned to eye it, once out of range. Now I regretted not having that flashlight. I started yelling for Don to bring me one. Plan A was to approach the cobra with the torch held to one side and see if I could get it to spit at the light.

Unfortunately, I was closer to Eleanor's place and shortly she was at the door. As soon as I explained the situation and my intent, Eleanor emitted an eye-rolling groan of exasperation, and disappeared, slamming the door for emphasis. Eleanor was not in the least intrigued by snakes, and was also pretty much unsympathetic toward guy things. While we guys secretly considered ourselves superior to gals in strength, athletic ability, bravery, intellect, and a host of other virtues, Eleanor had a somewhat different take. To her, there was a clear distinction between girls and women, but the distinction between men and boys was less certain. She would concede only one category of male superiority: stupidity. And here was proof on the hoof.

Even though I got short shrift from Eleanor, it wasn't short enough. During our brief dialogue, her big, brown friendly mutt had escaped the house and was wiggling his way out to me for a little affection. By the time the dog got to my side, the cobra had worked its way into the middle of the road and stopped about twenty feet distant, head raised, but not flared. It would be just a matter of seconds before the dog would notice the cobra, get all agitated and charge over there and get himself spit and bit. I quickly knelt down and clamped a half nelson on him, and tried again to raise Don.

As soon as I began shouting for Don, the dog spotted the snake and started growling and barking, straining and twisting. Finally Don responded, but with all the commotion, the snake started toward the thicket. By the time Don got to me with the torch, the snake's tail was just disappearing into the brush. I grabbed the flashlight and headed in after him, evidently intent on proving Eleanor's thesis, in spades. I didn't get very far, however, before it occurred to me that this was probably not one of my really good ideas.

While my encounter had certain comedic overtones, an event at the Catholic mission down the road at Itenguli was of a more serious nature. My favorite missionary,

Hunting and Teaching in East Africa

Father Charles, heard his dog yipping and wailing and bolted outside, only to see the dog hunkered over, frantically pawing its eyes. The priest rushed to the dog, reached out to gather it in his arms, and promptly got nailed with two streams of venom to his eyes. Somehow the good Father managed to resist the searing pain. He grabbed his robe with his hands to keep them from his eyes, and shouted for help. A couple of men rushed out of the church, threw him to the ground, and pinned his arms. Others quickly brought water, and irrigated his eyes for several minutes.

The dog died. He had scratched his eyes until they bled, and then the poison did its work. Due to his self-discipline, Father Charles not only lived, but could see vague shapes after a few days, and within three months his vision had recovered enough to read.

These spitting cobras aren't very big, but they don't just shoot a bullet or two of venom. They produce a copious stream, as I found out on a trip to Mbeya. As I drove into the village of Igawa, I saw one of these snakes in the road and ran over it. In the time it took me to stop the car and open the door, an excited African came running towards us, armed with a single shot twelve gauge. He pulled up short, raised the shotgun, and zeroed in. But on what? He held the butt of the gun free floating above his shoulder and sighted, if that's the word, down the side of the barrel. I thought: "Oh my god, he's going to kill my Simca." Fortunately, this unorthodox shooting style worked for him, and he blasted the snake into three pieces, the head segment being a foot long, and upside down. After marveling that my car had not been cratered by small lead meteors, I approached the cobra and nudged its nose with my foot. Predictably the snake let fly and the toe of my boot was soaked with venom. Just because a snake is dead, doesn't mean it is harmless.

I had generally estimated the spitting cobras in our area to be about six feet long, so I was somewhat surprised when Don's replacement as school biologist measured one I had run over just outside Malangali. Of course he waited several hours and poked it with a stick several times before he gathered it up and took it to the biology lab and its new home; a jar of formaldehyde. Stretched out straight, it was eight feet long. All coiled up they didn't look that big, but even when moving they did not look eight feet long. No doubt the curves produced a deceptive reading.

Another snake in the same elapidae family as the mambas and cobras is the boomslang, a skinny, green, arboreal snake that can reach seven feet in length. This snake can also be deadly, but it is not aggressive and is a back-fanged snake so a strike at a flat surface, like a person's leg, might not result in a puncture. But on the other hand, it is a tree snake, so any strike would be more likely aimed at the head. There are plenty of places on the human head and face that a back fanged snake could sink its teeth into, although boomslang bites were not common. In fact, in the four years I was there, I never heard of anyone being bitten by one of these handsome fellows.

Coming back to the house from school one day, I noticed the body of a slender green snake, sans head, laying in my yard. My cook had killed it and buried the head. Naturally I wanted the head to see if it was a mamba or a boomslang. Valance was very reluctant to tell me its whereabouts, whether out of concern for his bwana's

Got Snakes?

health or due to some local superstition, I didn't know. I went to fetch Don, since he and I seemed to be the only two people on campus with an interest in snakes, and we returned to badger Valance, tag-team style, until he finally volunteered the burial site. Once we had the head in our possession, we carefully pried open the mouth and the fangs were indeed hinged at the rear of the mouth, a boomslang.

On another occasion, as I was walking to class, I came across a boomslang in the middle of the road. It was trying to ingest a huge toad it had killed. This was one optimistic snake. It could barely fit the toad's head in its mouth, so there it sat, a snake with a toad's body sticking out of its snout. This would make a great photo, but just as I turned to retrieve a camera from my house, two students came onto the road and towards me. I knew the snake would not remain in one piece if I just left, so when the boys got close, I emphatically told them not to kill it until I got back with my camera. I hurried, as I knew I was on borrowed time, but by the time I returned the snake had been flailed to shreds, and the boys had left.

It is interesting that Africans react so differently to snakes than the peoples of Asia, who certainly have their share. In India, snakes, especially cobras, are revered. They are even gathered and used in festivals, and then released. Elsewhere in Asia, snake meat and blood are delicacies. In many parts of Asia, snakes are hunted for their skins, which produce some of the most highly prized of exotic leathers. It is said about these hunters: a cobra hunter always returns victorious, a subtle bit of understatement to the effect that if he isn't victorious, he does not return.

The Africans don't revere snakes, they don't hunt them or eat them, they just loath them. In South Africa alone, where some semblance of records are kept, 200,000 snake- bites are recorded each year. Sixty percent of these come from a snake most Americans have never heard of, the puff adder, a viper relative of the American rattlesnake.

The puff adder, the most dangerous and least impressive of Africa's snakes, looks much like the rattler in color and markings, but he is short; usually three feet or less in length, fat; up to nine or ten inches in girth, slow, and without rattles. He may hiss and puff up his neck, to intimidate predators, and hence his name, but mainly he relies on camouflage and stillness for protection. Because of this he is easily stumbled upon and startled into defense. And while he may be slow moving, he is quick to strike. Ninety-five milligrams of his hemotoxic[42] venom will kill an adult, and a single strike will leave a deposit of twice that. I can attest to the swiftness of his strike, as well as his phlegmatic nature and near invisibility.

On a trip to Iringa I noticed one on the side of the road, inching its way along the crease where the bare road butted into a bare bank. I stopped to get a few pictures and when I finished my passenger, Ray Cairncross, a Peace Corps volunteer stationed at the middle school in Malangali, threw a softball sized stone and hit the snake squarely in the back. The head was a blur as it arched over its back and struck: not something you would want to step on.

On a later excursion I was riding with Ian Thomas and two of our students, headed for Tukuyu, near Mbeya. At about half past six I saw a big puff adder along the edge of the road in some sparse, dry grass. I got Ian to stop, latched onto a torch, as it would soon be dark, and ran back to where the snake was. On the way I grabbed a stick, but as I approached, the snake totally ignored me and kept at his slow, methodical crawl. As I knelt to one knee I marveled at the beautiful pattern stretched out before me, slightly animated by the adder's dogged efforts. Unlike the mamba, at the glacial rate the puff adder was moving he would cover the hundred-yard dash in roughly the time it took Columbus to sail the Atlantic.

To motivate the adder I started poking it in the ribs with my small stick. Perhaps he kicked it into high gear, I couldn't tell. With this snake, high gear, low gear, or overdrive is all one and the same: compound low.

I had been at this poking and observing for several minutes when impatience seized Ian and the boys and I heard the car doors close as they headed my way. By now the daylight was fading rapidly, so I had turned on the torch. They came up close, looked, and said: "Well, where is it?" I replied that he was right there, and to shed light on my statement, I roamed the beam back and forth along his thick, three-foot body. They still couldn't see him! There was no real cover, only a few shafts of short dry grass. I looked up at them in disbelief, but with my knee a couple feet from mid-viper, I quickly realized that my not getting bit was a more important consideration than critiquing their failing eyesight. I looked back down: I couldn't see the snake either! Let's just say that my sympathetic nervous system was abruptly stimulated. Still, I knew enough about puff adders to know that he couldn't have really gone anywhere.

I stayed put, slowly moving the beam of light fore and aft, and shortly the adder materialized, like a crocodile stealthily rising to the surface without a ripple. He hadn't gone anywhere, or coiled. He was in the same attitude he had been in the whole time. I gave him a gentle thank you poke, and got to my feet. With the flashlight held further from the snake, the others could now see him. We were really impressed at how invisible this viper could be. For all the miles I walked on my hunts, several hundred over four years, I never saw a puff adder in the bush. No doubt they were there, but I didn't see any, and more importantly, I didn't step on one.

A large relative of the puff adder is the gaboon viper. Where a puff adder may be three feet long with the girth of an orange, the gaboon viper can get twice that length and as thick as a grapefruit, or in other words, as thick as a twenty foot python. This large viper comes with a head five inches in length by four in width, and inside that head he houses fangs two inches long. Like the puff adder, he is very sluggish, but he strikes with speed and agility. A bite leaves little time for good-byes; a grown person would be dead in fifteen minutes.

Like the puffer, the gaboon viper can also hiss a warning. One herpetologist says it is so loud it sounds like a tire deflating. Like the puff adder, he too relies on camouflage and stealth for protection and meals. He is a denizen of the rain forest and lies hidden among the leaves and debris of the forest floor, waiting for something edible to trip his trigger.

Got Snakes?

The gaboon viper is without doubt the most beautiful snake in the world, even with his little nose horns. His geometric designs include diamonds, rectangles, and triangles, and his coloration is almost gaudy, with browns and tans, blues and purples, and sometimes even some pink. The only one I have ever seen was not in Africa at all; it was in the Seattle zoo. I couldn't get enough of the colors and patterns. I stared at this inert beauty for fifteen or twenty minutes (he stared right back), and considered him to be the premier attraction of the entire zoo: better than bears, better than tigers, better even than elephants.

They are a rare snake. Even the zoo in Nairobi, replete with all sorts of cobras and a number of mambas, had no gaboon viper. There were reputed to be some in the forest around Mufindi, about forty miles from the school, where Brooke Bond had a beautiful tea plantation, and even a nine-hole golf course. In fact, even though par on the course was said to be "two cobras and a puff adder," there was no golfing reference to gaboon vipers. If there were some up there, they were not common by any means, and were certainly not par for the course.

During my two years up north, I had very few snake experiences, only two that I can recall. One I have already mentioned, and the other I will save for later as it occurred on the most exciting, event-filled hunt of my time in Africa.

There is one last snake encounter that I hesitate to include, as the telling of it calls my veracity into question. As far as I know, what this snake did, cannot be done. And yet, Don, Harold, two Land Rovers full of students, and myself all witnessed, and were mesmerized by this performance.

One Sunday the lot of us set out for the ruins of an old German fort, about two hours distant by foot, but only two hours and fifteen minutes by Land Rover. As we proceeded at puff adder speed, bumping and grinding our way through trackless bush, we crossed a small, dry creek-bed. When we came up the low, gently rising bank on the far side, we paused under the shade of a large acacia tree to rest, and let our vital organs settle back into place. Out of the corner of my eye I noticed some motion. I turned and saw this snake that looked like nothing I had ever seen, elevating itself toward the lower branches of a smaller tree rooted next to the acacia. The snake was a mottled brown color, thin as my thumb, and bony. He kept gaining altitude, and where arched, his body was kinky, like a person's bent finger. By now the whole troop was engrossed in the show, as more and more snake was in the air, and less and less snake was on the ground. Finally, with about eight feet of snake in the air and only a foot to eighteen inches as an anchor, he reached the safety of the branches and slowly, casually, pulled himself into the tree. Don's look of astonishment matched my own, I'm sure. I blurted: "Snakes can't do that." His response: "Yeah, I know."

To paraphrase Pliny the Elder, again, something new, and strange, is always coming out of Africa.

And the fort? It was just a middling sized pile of rocks.

[39] Black refers to the color of the inside of this snake's mouth, not the color of its body.
[40] Neurotoxic venom paralyzes nerve centers that control breathing and heart function.
[41] Bila shaka means: without doubt, no way Jose, not in a million years, when pigs fly, etc.
[42] Hemotoxic venom damages blood vessels, causing hemorrhaging.

CHAPTER 17

Dar

After buttoning up the school in early December, Harry, Don and I decided to visit Dar es Salaam. I had ivory to sell and we all wanted to see the capital and do some sightseeing and shopping.

Dar embraces a beautiful, natural harbor on the Indian Ocean, just south of Zanzibar. In the mid-1960's, 150,000 people lived in and around Dar, making it about the size of Tacoma or Spokane. Over the last thirty-five years, the population has compounded to ten times that number, and yet, just a hundred years prior, Dar es Salaam hardly existed.

In fits and spurts the Sultans of Zanzibar established Dar as a trading post, one of many along the Tanganyika coast. It remained just another torpid coastal village with no political or administrative role until the Germans came. It became their capital in 1891, though for logistical reasons they moved their center of operations to the cool luxuriant heights of Lushoto during the First World War, to keep closer tabs on the British in Kenya.

This was the first of many trips to the 'Haven of Peace'. Dar is only seven degrees south of the equator, but the trade winds do give it two seasons: hot and humid, and hot and less humid. At this time of the year, December, the trades come off the Indian Ocean bringing plenty of moisture and humidity.

Dar was an amalgam of African, Arab, Indian and European influences, in that order of concentration. Mombasa had much more of an Arab and Indian flavor, while Nairobi was distinctly European, sprinkled lightly with Indian spices. After the relative isolation of Malangali, Dar es Salaam was a pleasant change of pace.

For me, the first order of business was to sell my hundred pounds of elephant teeth. Before we left Iringa I'd had the tusks weighed and registered, an interesting process. The game department would weigh each tusk and stamp a serial number into it using a hammer and metal punches. As an example, if the elephants I had bagged were the sixteenth and seventeenth tembo registered in Iringa District in 1963, my serial numbers would be IR31/63 through IR34/63, assuming the previous fifteen came complete with two tusks each. Obviously, a licensed hunter wouldn't intentionally shoot a one-tusker, unless the tusk was huge, but elephants don't always give you a choice. Sometimes the ones with a single tusk, or no tusks at all, are the most ornery, but like it or not, two, one or none, he is yours, and you have just spent an elephant license. Once registered, the game ranger would void my license and issue me an ownership certificate, and with this I could keep, sell, or export the ivory.

I looked up J.F.M. Karim, Trophy Dealer, Commission Agent, and Manufacturer's Representative at 28 India Street, Dar es Salaam. Due to the Sino-Indian War, however, India was not importing much ivory and the dealers in Dar and Zanzibar were sitting on large stockpiles, so prices were low: 12/-, or $1.71 per pound.

Nevertheless, with my modest windfall I went shopping, confident that my bargaining skills, honed to razor sharp perfection at the market in Malangali and the stores in Iringa, would stretch my shillings enough to satisfy my desires, which ran the gamut from the mundane to the ordinary. I bought a camera with two telephoto lenses, a few books on East Africa, and a couple of curios, one a not so ordinary Makonde carving: a beautiful dark brown hardwood rendered into a regal African head.

At the time I didn't realize how lucky I'd been as regards the Makonde piece. First of all, there were no tourist ships in the harbor, so prices weren't double or triple the usual level, and secondly, the art scavengers, those sharp eyed vultures from the U.S. and Europe, had not yet swooped in to devour every single Makonde work of quality. On later visits I would see nothing to match the sculpture I had acquired before these merchants of New York and Hamburg, Chicago and Cadiz, had come to drain East Africa of its only truly indigineous art.

In addition to selling ivory, shopping, and a change of ambiance, there were bonus reasons to visiting Dar, two of which were Beck's beer, and lobster. Beck's was a very tasty lager, a nice change from the African beers out of Nairobi: Old Tusker and City Beer. The latter was pretty good, but Old Tusker tasted like it had indeed come directly from the undercarriage of an old tusker.

On one occasion I was sitting in the Splendid Hotel, escaping the heat and nursing a Beck's over lunch, when in came two German geologists I knew from Iringa and its environs. I figured I was in for a workout. They immediately spotted me and my liquid companion, sat themselves down, and ordered a round, me included. Our conversation centered around their determined but so far futile efforts to discover something, anything, in the way of mineral deposits for the government of Tanganyika. This prospecting, and even the recounting of it, was evidently thirsty work, and shortly another round was ordered. Being a lightweight, I tried to demur, but they would have none of that: three more Beck's arrived. More talk, more time, my turn. They vetoed my suggestion that two beers would suffice for this round. While they would certainly appreciate another pint, they could not accept without my inclusion: three more Beck's arrived. By now the two Germans were becoming positively Italian in their gestures and enthusiasm, but as much as they gained in animation, I lost, slowly sinking towards a vegetative state. Shortly they were dry again and started the ordering cycle all over. For me, it was escape or expire. I suddenly remembered that I had to meet my

Dar

grandmother at the airport. They fully understood: sometimes family comes before beer. I managed to get upright and mobile, and with four pints of German grog for fuel, headed for the door, my brain barely in command of my legs. A couple of hours in the mid-day heat served to boil the alcohol out of me and restore the circuitry between my brain and limbs. I had certainly had too much of a good thing.

The perfect complement to a bottle of Beck's was a tail of lobster, or two. I found a hotel on the north edge of town, close to the ocean, that would serve it simply boiled, no sauce, with a generous side of melted butter. The Oasis Hotel was not especially grand, but then it was not a workers hangout either, nor was it in a proletarian neighborhood. Naturally, the Chinese Embassy was right next door.

From the mid-50's, the Chinese tried to export their brand of socialism to Africa. But even after the African countries became independent, competition was stiff. The old colonial powers still exerted a lot of influence, and two powerful new players had entered the game, the United States and the Soviet Union. The Chinese had their best shot in Tanzania and for some time were quite influential due to a perceived philosophical affinity.

The leaders of Tanzania, with a strong pro-Chinese contingent from Zanzibar, reasoned that the African was a natural socialist. The traditional practice of living within an extended family and working for the welfare of the group as a whole seemed to fit perfectly into the socialist mold. In addition, the Chinese notions of national self-reliance, free of the yoke of Western domination, and a theoretical egalitarian work ethic of one for all and all for one, hit a sympathetic chord with Nyerere and his followers. Forget that in China, as in **Animal Farm,** some were definitely more equal than others.

On several levels Tanzania and Communist China seemed to be brothers under the skin. Both had a one party system, both had a desire to raise the living standards of their peoples, both concentrated on rural as opposed to urban development, and they both wanted to progress on their own terms, with their own efforts. Mao did not want to be Stalin's obedient serf any more than Nyerere wanted to be a toady of the British crown.

In addition, it was reasoned a nation of limited resources could not allow them to be squandered. The resources had to be marshaled for the benefit of all, a noble sentiment leading to a disastrous conclusion: state planning.

The logic of socialism makes perfect sense, given certain assumptions, and as an idealistic youth I was partially seduced by this model, though repulsed by the way it had been implemented in Russia and China. In those years it was said that a man who was not a socialist in his twenties had no heart, and a man who was still a socialist in his forties, had no brain. Just because a logical construct made perfect sense, did not mean it was perfectly true. And in the case of the socialist construct, it did not mean it would work well, or would even be less exploitative or more humane than capitalism. Certainly the communist form of socialism was neither less exploitative nor more humane, even when compared to the robber baron phase of capitalism. And, as I would learn later during my tour in Arusha, socialism could be very destructive of resources, and human vagaries could play havoc with the tidiest of theorems. The African, like the American, or given a chance, the Russian or Chinese, is a natural capitalist. People look out for themselves first and foremost, with any group loyalty weakening, as that group becomes more distant and/or abstract. Tyranny, supported through institutionalized fear, can suppress this survival instinct for a while, but eventually man's individualistic nature will emerge, as it has in both Russia and China.

On my first visit to Dar es Salaam, the Chinese presence was there for all to see in the form of an exhibition showing off the marvelous technology of Communist China. Don, Harry and I entered the large, barn like structure to view the wonders of collective achievement. It was like stepping backwards through a time warp. Roughly made tractors with iron wheels, straight out of the twenties, and crude iron lungs, were the gist of it. And to make matters worse, the Chinese hovering around the equipment were ill prepared for their assignments. They were all dressed alike in drab Mao uniforms, and wouldn't even make eye contact with us western devils. Our presence and questions made them fidgety and nervous. They understandably knew no English, but although they would look the African visitors in the eye and smile, it was obvious they didn't know a single word of Swahili either.

We marveled that the Chinese could trumpet such a pathetic display of both machinery (after all there were better tractors, not to mention road graders and bulldozers, here and there in Tanganyika) and presentation, but as we were leaving, our puzzlement magically evaporated. The Chinese ambassador, that representative of proletarian equality, glided up to the expo ensconced in the back seat of a chauffeur driven limousine, ambassadorial flags fluttering on each fender. This car was black and beautiful, and proudly exhibited around Dar as a shining example of Chinese craftsmanship. There was just one little problem. The ambassador had not bothered to remove the nameplates. These nameplates were in small letters, it was true, but they spelled out the name of the one American president that any literate African would recognize. The car was a Lincoln.

Evidently, the Chinese held the African intellect in rather low esteem.

Game scout in Iringa marking tusks from 1st Dabaga hunt.

CHAPTER 18

Central Province

After Dar, we collected Louis Columbe from Tosamaganga, outfitted ourselves in Iringa, and went on safari, eventually ending up in Central Province. Our initial objective was to visit Father Charles, as he had been posted to a Roman Catholic mission about twenty miles from Pawaga. We headed north out of Iringa in the late afternoon and reached the Pawaga sign about fifty miles later, just before sunset. Here we took a break and Harry sighted in the 9.3mm he had bought in Dar, but, as usual, Don piddled around until it became "too dark" for him to do likewise with his newly acquired bolt action .404.

Fireworks semi-concluded, we then drove another eighteen miles into this thorn treed wilderness and finally reached the nascent mission Father Charles had been sent to develop. He was glad to see us, but he looked gaunt and drained. His eyes had lost their old sparkle, and not because of his bout with the cobra. He had served the Church well, done much to improve the mission at Itenguli, and here he was, stranded in this hot, thorn-scrub purgatory. We caught him up on the news of Malangali, shared a couple of sweet, juicy pineapples, and then set off into the night for a place about fifteen miles distant where Father Charles said the Good Lord had planted some elephants.

After we arrived, we curled up in our mobile motels for the night, and the next morning a local guide was peering in at us, patiently waiting. First, however, Don had to zero in his rifle, so I guessed that we were in for a good hike, but not good hunting. We traipsed about the bush all morning, but oddly, animals of any sort were scarce, as in non-existent. Don never had sighted in his 30:06, and this time he waits until we are in elephant country, ready to hunt. I was a little perturbed.

After some discussion we decided to pull out of this place and head for an area I'd heard about in Central Province, mid-way between Iringa and Dodoma. Central Province was known for dry, red soil; baobab, acacia, and leafless flame trees: scrub brush of every sort, and the Groundnut Scheme.[43] To quote J. P. Moffett:[44]

It is said that the idea of the Groundnut Scheme originated in a suggestion made in Dar es

Hunting and Teaching in East Africa

Salaam by the Director of Agriculture to the Managing Director of the United Africa Company, one of the components of the Unilever group, to the effect that an area of 20,000 acres might be planted with groundnuts in order to relieve to some extent the shortage of margarine fats in heavily rationed England. As a result and at the instance of the Colonial Office, a party was sent from England in 1946 which included a former Director of Agriculture in Tanganyika, and it was this party which made proposals for a scheme covering not 20,000 but some three million acres, divided into units of 30,000 acres each in certain places of East and Central Africa of which the greatest were in three areas in Tanganyika. There is no doubt that the shape of this scheme owed much to the army mentality, closely following as it did the triumph of logistics in the war. It seemed that a scheme had only to be big enough for it to overcome all obstacles.

It was decided in England to proceed with the scheme under the direction not of the Colonial Office but of the Ministry of Food. In great haste, and without preliminary agricultural experimentation, parties were sent from England from the beginning of 1947 to start operations not so much in the two more agriculturally attractive Tanganyika areas but mainly in that area, the Mpwapwa District, which was the least attractive agriculturally and which offered as its only advantage its comparative proximity to the railway. The target for the first year's operations (1947) was 150,000 acres, a target which in the existing state of shortage of implements and resources of all kinds was quite unattainable. [44]

To draw the curtain on this Three Stooges production, by the end of March, 1951, thirty-five million pounds[45] had been leached into the aforementioned dry, red soil, and the project was abandoned. Sparse and erratic rainfall, severe outbreaks of the rosette and black spot diseases, and bumbling planning and hare-brained ideas like re-fitting W.W.II Sherman tanks for duty on the project as tractors, all combined to consume these worst laid plans of Crown and colony. It obviously isn't just Africans that screw up, as some would have you believe.

In fact, Moffett reports that when the government finally came to the conclusion that the Mpwapwa area was only suitable for ranching, a resident African headman wryly allowed that that was indeed what the Africans had always done in Central Province. The clues were there to see: a semi-arid landscape; people dependent on livestock, including a high ratio of goats; and only the occasional evidence of agriculture in the form of small, scraggly maize fields, often watered by hand with the women portaging the precious liquid over long distances in clay pots parked on their heads.

We reached the bridge over the Ruaha River and hung a left, only to take the wrong branch of this hint of a road, costing us about an hour's worth of petrol. We finally got on the right track, according to a local Gogo, and off we went, thirteen miles of rocks, ruts, and eroded soil showing the wear and tear of centuries. We lost the road after dark, but some Wagogo and Masai led us to a guide, who in turn led us on a two-hour trek through corn, thorn, and worn out roads, to elephant country. We were bushed. We set up camp by a dry creek bed, fixed a little chow, and again bunked in the vehicles. I was dog-tired and slept the sleep of the righteous, but when morning came, Don complained that he had heard lions all night long: a good omen.

Central Province

In spite of having lions about, a sign that there must be game in the area, the next day was not a good one, omen or no. Don started out in a foul mood, still angered from the night before when the guides had declined his invitation to fetch water, an hour's walk one way, at night, in lion infested bush. By God, if someone worked for him, he did as the bwana mkubwa said. Harold and I weren't sympathetic. Not only was his request unreasonable; not only were these people under no obligation; but there was absolutely no need; we had plenty of liquid stashed in his Rover: four gallons of water, one case of beer, and two cases of soda pop. Our support of the guides didn't improve Don's disposition any, and unfortunately his churlishness festered into a blow-up later in the day.

We set off just after sun-up and walked many easy miles as the terrain was basically flat, though hot and populated with thorn trees and scrub. This was indeed elephant country, just not at that moment in time. Their droppings were evident, but also old, lacking in form and aroma. The sun, abetted by bugs and birds, had reduced the evidence from nice plump clumps the size and general shape of half a loaf of bread, to splayed out splotches on the earth's crust. We did see a few kanga,[46] but that was all our five-hour loop turned up.

We decided to move on to the confluence of the Great Ruaha and Kisigo rivers, some nine miles and three flats further into the trackless bush. The Kisigo was mostly dry, but there were small pools of water here and there. Even though this was a good sign, the elephant debris was again vintage, though the chance of Harold getting an antelope seemed promising. But now a problem arose. Don wanted to camp on the banks of the river, and was quite adamant about it. Since we were supposed to be hunting, not camping, I suggested this might only serve to scare the game visiting the water holes. But much more emphatically, I was against it because the last two hundred yards to the river was a carpet of low lying thorn bushes and I had already had seven flats, and we were down to our last tire patch, some forty miles from the Great North Road.

Don threw one of his tantrums, which I did not want to deal with, so I grabbed the .500 and went for a walk, hoping to find an innocent elephant to blast. I got back to the car just before dark and could see the trail left by the Rover as Don aimed it at the river. I joined them for dinner, but as the tension was oppressive, I ate my fill in silence and retired to the Simca.

At sunrise one of the guides and I went off hunting buff. We had a nice walk but saw absolutely nothing, not even kanga. I got back to camp just before noon and H. brought our "rations," and then he and I headed out. Covering the forty odd miles would be a challenge, as we had to traverse the same territory that had produced all those flat tires, and even the one remaining patch was in Don's mitts. Most of the way H. sat on a front fender, panga[47] in hand, and at the slightest indication of threat by vegetation, he would fling up his hand, fly off the fender, and beat the bejeezus out of the offending weed. It took us over three hours, but we did make the main road, no flats, but short on gas.

Hunting and Teaching in East Africa

Heading north, we managed to cover only five of the necessary twenty miles to the nearest gas station. We sat for about an hour before a carload of Africans came by. I got out a coil of rubber tubing and siphoned a gallon of gas from their car. The rubber tubing acts like a straw. You insert it into the donor vehicle, suck, and get the gas to flowing. The problem is, you always get some in your mouth, or at least I always did, and gasoline tastes terrible, even worse than Old Tusker.

Our little saga wasn't over yet, however, as one more minor humiliation still lay ahead. We reached the duka on our donated petrol, gassed up, pointed the Simca south towards Iringa: and suffered a flat only ten miles into our journey. Those rural and occasional petrol oases were really just small shops with fuel, sometimes, common commodities like cloth and maize meal, and occasionally a luxury or two like warm beer and crackers. But, they didn't seem to carry such exotic inventory as tire patches.

Before long two cars stopped to help, one from Southwest Africa, and the other from Kenya. As we fixed the flat, the two Brits exchanged knowing glances, as if to say: "These Yanks, not awfully bright, eh what? Imagine motoring around Africa without a proper tyre kit."

Thus spurred, this dim bulb would amp up his cache of tire patches and in the future fairly glow with tire repair competency.

---

[43] In this context, "groundnuts" is not a pejorative reference to Californians in general, or even any particular Californian. It is merely British for peanuts.
[44] Handbook of Tanganyika, J. P. Moffett, second edition, 1958, Government Printer, Dar es Salaam, page 133.
[45] Back then, one British pound was worth about five American dollars.
[46] Kanga are wild guinea fowl and are found in much of the countryside.
[47] Panga means machete, a ubiquitous implement in Tanganyika.

CHAPTER 19

Rhodesia

After we returned from the Central Province exercise, my house was ready so I moved in and spent the next couple of weeks getting domestic and hiring a cook, namely Valance. This was good down time; time to play cards and tennis, read books, and plan further safaris.

I broached the subject of a Rhodesian trip to Harold, as H. was always game for something new and exciting. I wanted to visit Southern Rhodesia where I had distant relatives, cousins on my mother's side. Em and Charles Rowley had been in the Royal Air Force during World War Two, he a pilot and she a flight controller. After the war they left the RAF and England to seek a new life in Southern Rhodesia. I had met them in 1952 when they toured the world, including the exotic port of Tacoma. We kids considered them dazzling, and rich: they filled our heads with magical visions of Africa, and gave each of us a one pound note, the equivalent of five dollars at that time, a handsome sum. They were very fond of my favorite aunt, their cousin Sarah, and when Aunt Sarah learned of my pending sojourn to Africa, she made me promise to visit Em and Charles.

Visiting the Rhodesias at that time was not a trip lightly taken. The area was in considerable turmoil as independence was afoot, but had not yet arrived. The British had created the Federation of Rhodesia and Nyasaland in 1953, making Northern Rhodesia and Nyasaland protectorates of the British Crown, but leaving Southern Rhodesia a self-governing colony controlled by the white settlers, as it had been since 1923. With protectorate status, the Africans in Northern Rhodesia and Nyasaland knew independence was coming, but they were impatient for control and not altogether trusting of a colonial office that had left Southern Rhodesia in the clutches of the colonials. Of course, said colonials included my relatives.

The Rhodesias had been put on the map by the diamond mogul Cecil Rhodes, better known with the passage of time for the Rhodes Scholarship program of Oxford University, a legacy of his will of 1902. In the late 1800's, he used the immense wealth he had generated from several Kimberley mines, which he meshed to form the DeBeers Consolidated Mines, to push his dream of a Cape to Cairo railway. He was the vanguard of British expansion north from the Cape Colony, and the territory acquired was modestly named Northern Rhodesia and Southern Rhodesia by his British South African Company, with the Zambezi River dividing the two.

There was a tremendous influx of whites into Southern Rhodesia: miners, ranchers, farmers, and businessmen. After South Africa, Southern Rhodesia had the largest white population[48] on the continent, with Kenya following at a very distant third. Southern Rhodesia was separated from South Africa by the Limpopo River, so much of the white migration just crossed the river. But, after WWII, many an Englishman couldn't bring himself to descend from those days of high excitement to afternoons of tea and crumpets in Jolly Olde, but boring, England. Such were my cousins.

In the process of making our plans and gathering travel documents, Harold and I were cautioned about what to expect, particularly in Northern Rhodesia: surly glances, unfriendly people, maybe the occasional spear in the ribs of the Simca.

The night before we were to leave, H. and I had dinner at Eleanor's. One thing led to another, and by the time we left her house, we had acquired a third traveler. In the process of inviting Ms. DeSelms, I made her promise not to get on her moral high horse with my relatives. This was to be a convivial visit on a familial level. No missionary fervor was to be invested in the enlightenment of these political pagans. We were not to discuss politics or people, period. If hell was their intention, hell it would be.

On January 4, 1963, we left Malangali at five in the morning. We reached Mbeya before noon, after a detour via Njombe cost us a couple of hours as the Chamala Bridge was rumored to be down. In Mbeya we tried to get tax clearance papers, but while not successful at this, we did learn that the Chamala Bridge was not out, and we also received, gratis, additional negative vibes about our itinerary. Our next visit was to the District Education Officer. Begrudgingly, he did pen us a letter of permission, amid misgivings on his part about our plans, and by inference our sanity. We were puttering around town this way as I figured we should have at least one piece of official looking paper with Eleanor's name on it. As it turned out, all this fuss and feathers about travel warrants was a waste. At the border, coming and going, the only documents of any interest were our passports, and even these were only casually scrutinized.

We made it to Tunduma about mid-afternoon. After clearing customs, we were now in Northern Rhodesia, land of hostile black folk ready to shake their fists at us and impale my poor, innocent Simca. The roads, however, were the only real source of hostility we would encounter and they would indeed impale the Simca a time or two, but just the gas tank. Over the 3700 miles we would cover in the next two weeks, 1600 of it on dirt and 300 of it on strip roads,[49] the Rhodesias were brutal. We put a huge crimp in one wheel, ruined two tires, had ten flats, had the gas tank welded twice, broke two shock absorbers, and had the generator repaired in Lusaka with a Fiat bearing, Simca parts being nonexistent.

It had been raining, and south of Tunduma the roads were a composite of potholes and slippery clay. We had a number of good skids, but only one really wild one, and for relief from the strain and pounding, we would stop every so often. From

Rhodesia

Tunduma to Mpika, about 250 miles, the countryside was nothing but very green grasses and short, densely packed trees. There was only the occasional sign of life along the road, but when we stopped for breaks, people would ooze out of the woods like spirits, and soon we'd have a small gathering. Our initial effort to communicate in Swahili drew puzzled stares and a response in the King's English. Evidently Swahili stopped at the border, but these people spoke excellent English and also seemed much more prosperous than those in the Southern Highlands of Tanganyika. They had western clothes and a much higher level of general education, no doubt blessings conferred by the wealth of copper in their country.

Having put 520 miles under our belts on our first day, we pulled into Mpika about 9:30 at night. At that hour, there were no vacant rooms at the inn, so some kind strangers let Eleanor sleep in their station wagon, while Harry and I made do in the Simca. In the morning we had breakfast at the hotel, fixed two flats, and borrowed a big hammer to reshape a wheel that had slammed into the sharp, concrete edge of a bridge. Leaving Mpika, we covered about fifty miles before we had our first flat of the day, and while fixing it along the road we were surrounded by a bevy of curious, friendly kids, crowding around intent on watching this intriguing operation.

After 800 miles of dirt roads, we glided onto tarmac thirty miles north of Broken Hill. How glad was I to be on blacktop? I was ready to start my own church, and all adherents would worship The Great God Tarmac. We pushed on another ninety miles and arrived in Lusaka, the clean, modern, beautiful capital of Northern Rhodesia. Although it was about dinnertime, we first secured rooms, and then we ate, at the quite fancy Lusaka Hotel: 38/- ($5.40) per night for dinner, bed, and breakfast. After dinner we took in a movie, and then gratefully collapsed: such comfy beds.

The next morning we left for Salisbury, now Harare, via Kariba Dam. The dam was very impressive, and so high that from the top the crocodiles swimming about its base looked like harmless miniatures. We pulled into the capital in late afternoon, checked the phone book, and found no cousins. As they owned a hotel in Gatooma, twenty miles south, we visited a few hotels hoping someone in the business would know them. Having drawn nothing but blanks, we took rooms in the Queen's Hotel, a sort of once nice establishment with a 'Europeans Only' sign over the bar.

We went out for a walk about nine in what seemed to be less than the best section of town, when suddenly three police cars raced up in front of us to extract a drunken European from the wrath of a black woman who kept repeating: "He has my money." A crowd of Africans was clustered around the melee enjoying the plight of the tipsy white, but the police ended the show quickly. One white officer shoved the woman away and told the man to leave. He wove down the street, but she wasn't far behind. The police left amid much laughter, each car with one white and one black officer. The latter seemed amused by the whole affair, while the whites were noticeably embarrassed: after all, this was no way to represent the superior white race, especially in front of Africans.

Oddly, it seemed at first blush, the police totally ignored the money issue. Perhaps it was one of those professional disputes over fees charged for services rendered; she being the professional and he being the client, satisfied or not, welshing on the deal. Just speculation.

The next morning, after a couple hours detective work and much running around, we located Charles at the government store. He had shrunk quite a bit since I'd seen him eleven years ago, and instead of looking up into his face, I was looking down. He and Em took us to the Civil Service Club for lunch, and then out to her sister's place where we would stay the week, a week of shopping, visiting, and Simca fixing.

Em loved to talk, but when she edged the conversation towards politics, or those heathen Africans, we adroitly finessed the issue and redirected the conversation to a subject more in line with familial conviviality. I was especially proud of Eleanor. They weren't her relatives. She had no Aunt Sarah to upset if things got heated. Yet, she managed to keep a clothespin on her lips, and a pleasant, if slightly arched, expression on her face.

When Saturday arrived, we left for Gatooma to spend a few days at their hotel, which was run by their daughter Camile, and her husband Lee. We were ensconced in very plush rooms with a verandah out back that stretched the length of the hotel, the very same verandah where Camile had once interrupted a python's breakfast, according to one of the tales Charles had regaled us with in Tacoma, eleven years ago. Seems Camile had sat her infant daughter out on the verandah to eat her porridge. A few minutes later, Camile went back out to check on the girl, and a good sized python had wound down a pillar just in front of the girl, and had its head stretched to within a foot of the girl's face. The little tyke must have had a very obliging disposition as she had her spoon held up, offering her new playmate some oatmeal. While this picture might tempt some to smile, Camile was not amused. She dashed forward to pluck her daughter from what would have been a terrible experience, took her inside, and then, not satisfied with ruining the python's breakfast, she marched back out with Lee's service revolver and ruined the snake's entire day.

That afternoon, Lee took us on a tour of the location, as the African quarters were called. We were surprised at how good the housing was, and how tranquil the atmosphere. No surly looks here, but then again maybe they were not advisable, with the bwana present. We also toured a gold mine, a textile factory, and the local high school. The next day we were invited to Kuchena, the family resort on the Umsweswe River. We lazed about, and even went for a swim in the river, something we would never do in Tanganyika, crocs being a definite deterrent.

After a few days we bid our cousins adieu and left for Wankie Game Park, passing the industrial, somewhat ugly, town of Bulawayo on the way. The land was flatter down that way, and one farm looked just like the old homestead my father was raised on in Nebraska: a two story house with a windmill nearby, surrounded by trees, in the middle of a great grassy prairie.

Late in the afternoon we turned off the main road into Wankie and almost imme-

Rhodesia

diately were confronted with a danger-elephants sign. I chuckled to myself, remembering how my brother and I would laugh derisively at deer-crossing signs back home in Washington. There were never any deer crossing! We hadn't gone a hundred yards when we whizzed right by an elephant, not ten feet off the road. Harold had also seen one on the other side. We cautiously backed up and took some pictures, but when one old boy started to get annoyed, we excused ourselves.

That evening we saw everything but a dinosaur: elephant, zebra, warthog, kudu, giraffe, buffalo, impala, gazelle, and all sorts of birds, and the next morning, a lion. The next show would have to be really good to top this.

The next show was Victoria Falls, and it was really good. The falls were discovered by Dr. David Livingstone in 1860, though the locals seemed to know it was there and called it Mosi oa Tunya, the smoke that thunders. We paused about three miles from the falls to photograph the rising mist, and even at that distance we could hear the thunder.

When we approached the falls and hiked down a trail along the south edge, the rhetoric of Jumbo Williams didn't seem that overblown:

> The first impression was unmistakable; immense power, the raw energy unleashed when the entire Zambezi leaps wildly into a black two kilometer wide abyss. The scale is massive, the spectacle spellbinding and perpetually changing. The falls hiss and roar as if possessed, they rumble and crash like thunder. Vast clouds spew and billow out from the seething cauldron of its dark impenetrable depths. The moving water creates a magnetism that sucks you closer, so that you recoil in horror to quench a subliminal sacrificial urge.[50]

At the height of the rainy season, which it was when we were there, over 700 million cubic yards of water cascade across the mile wide basalt lip, presenting the viewer with the world's largest sheet of falling water. This wide cliff transforms the river from spread out placid to gorge constricted ferocious, as facing the falls is another sheer wall of basalt of the same height of over three hundred feet, this one covered in mist fed rain forest. I positioned myself atop this facing cliff, but the mist made such a thick fog I had to cover my camera until a helpful breeze temporarily swept the moisture aside, allowing me time to photograph.

Another excellent view was afforded from the Victoria Falls Bridge, commissioned by Cecil Rhodes in 1900. Rhodes felt: "...the railway should cross the Zambezi just below the Victoria Falls. I should like to have the spray of the falls cover the carriages." We crossed over this bridge and the Simca did get a light shower, courtesy of Mr. Rhodes.

From the Northern Rhodesia side, we took a boat excursion above the falls. The small launch was piloted by an African, but a European was in charge, and he made quite a show of apologizing to us because the other passengers were Indian, already seated in the boat, just behind him. While this open display of racism took us back a bit, there was a more pressing concern. We looked apologetically at the Indians, but apprehensively at the launch's motor, hoping it ran better than it looked and sounded. A dead engine could lead to complications. At least if we lost power and plunged

Hunting and Teaching in East Africa

to a frothy death, we'd go out with all shades represented, politically and racially.

Our marginal faith in the motor must have been sufficient, as it chugged happily upstream, carrying us to tranquil lagoons full of hippo. We also saw a small crocodile, but the main attraction was the river itself, and although wide and slow above the falls, the pull of the abyss was inexorable, and unsettling.

Once back on firm footing we lunched with some pesky monkeys at a restaurant just above and close to the falls. These bold little thieves would eat out of your hand and then for desert steal the sugar bowl right off the table. After this novel meal, I approached a group of Africans under a large shade tree just outside the restaurant. Before long, one of them had taken the shirt right off my back. Was this an example of the hostility we were supposed to encounter?

While I was silently inspecting some carvings, the carver was vocally admiring my shirt, one of those commissioned in Moshi of bright African cloth, sort of like a Hawaiian shirt, but a little less garish. Trying to appear only semi-interested, I offered to swap him the shirt for two nicely carved rhinos and a mask. He countered, substituting a carved bird for the mask. We bantered back and forth, but shortly struck a deal, and amid much animated laughter all around, I peeled off my shirt, and we made the exchange. The locals and we Yanks thoroughly enjoyed the episode, and a few tut-tuts from a couple of nearby colonial types just served to encourage our overt display.

The trip home was relatively uneventful. We reluctantly left the falls mid-afternoon, reached Lusaka, had dinner, and departed just after sundown for Broken Hill. Thirty miles out of Lusaka the generator quit, so we turned back. To save money and not unload the car, I slept in it, while H. and El took rooms at the Lusaka Hotel. At three p.m. the next day we were back in the game. From here it would be pretty much a straight shot to Malangali as we were short on cash and craving the comfort of our own beds and familiar surroundings. We ate dinner at Broken Hill and pushed on to within eighty miles of Mpika before exhaustion ground us to a halt. We awoke before dawn, got to Mpika with the sun, fed ourselves and the Simca, and left for Tunduma, arriving at one-thirty in the afternoon.

We were afraid we would get stuck for duty on our purchases, but the border guards didn't even look at our booty. They asked if we had any guns, cigarettes, skins, or spirits; we said no, they said go. We arrived in Mbeya as the sun circled out of sight, had a cold meal, and headed home.

Just out of Mbeya we had our third flat of the day, but the really irksome impediment to our finally getting home and planting our tired bones in our own beds was the weather. It had been perfect all the way from Victoria Falls, but thirty miles short of Malangali, it turned ugly. It was as if the gods of wind, rain and lightening had been husbanding their armaments for one last go at us. Three times lightning hit so close it temporarily blinded us. And, if the lightening couldn't put us in the ditch, the rain certainly put forth a good effort. At one point it was so heavy we couldn't see beyond the hood and had to completely stop, hoping any oncoming traffic would be doing

Rhodesia

likewise. Finally the gods ran out of firepower and we slithered into Malangali. I dropped off El and H., took a cold bath, and fell into bed at the stroke of midnight.

---

[48] The white population of Southern Rhodesia amounted to 2-3% of the total population.

[49] Strip roads had two eighteen-inch wide ribbons of asphalt running down the middle, axle width apart. The object was to make the roads passable year round, at little cost. But since the dirt was often worn away as much as six inches, lurching on and off these strips to avoid oncoming traffic could be treacherous, especially at sixty miles an hour.

---

[50] <u>Zambezi, River of Africa</u>, Jumbo Williams, 1988.

CHAPTER 20

Daily Life

I kept a diary while in Malangali, and wrote home weekly, so much of this story is bolstered by the diary entries and the contents of a six-inch stack of aerogramme letters faithfully saved by my mother. To give some idea of the flavor of every day life, I am going to quote several days' entries, edited just a little for clarity, starting the day after our return from Rhodesia.

Sunday, Jan. 20: Got up late, straightened up the mess, received mail, loafed, ate, and to bed early. Dinner at Eleanor's. Got my first set of slides back, they turned out ok. Partner still here, but leaves in a week.

Jan 21: Loafed and ate and made plans for going to Iringa tomorrow.

Jan 22: Left for Iringa about 6 a.m. The roads were slippery and it took us three hours. Saw Dr. Clark and have to check in tomorrow at 4 p.m. for an operation on that romantic tropical malady I've acquired: piles. The doc said he would get to the bottom of this matter. I saw the policeman, Mr. Moore, and he allowed me another 25 rounds on my .500 license and we also discussed some old guns he had confiscated from poachers. He indicated that if Judge Hildesly granted permission, I could have one (of the guns, not the poachers). Hildesly was busy, so I didn't see him. Eleanor and I went to Dieraufs' for dinner and to stay the night. Played some basketball.

Jan 23: I talked to Mr. Garas about welding my shock absorbers back in place and Eleanor and Cyril are to pick up the car and take it back tomorrow. Alf and Hillary + one (a new child) are also going back with them. I went to the hospital about four. Hillary and her baby boy were there also, so we visited while my room was being made up. Spent the rest of the day reading The History of the British Empire.

Jan 24: Continued reading about our muddling friends. The hospital meals are good, but after noon I get nothing until tomorrow noon.

Jan 25: At 8 a.m. I got into the ambulance and was driven to the operating theater, a small building in the Grade IV hospital area. About 8:15 I was put under, and about ten I woke up, though I wasn't wide awake until eleven. I stood up some, but was too dizzy to do it for long. Finished my book on the British Empire.

Daily Life

Jan 26: Vicky, Ed, Lou, and Reni came to visit for a bit. I started <u>Conversations with Stalin</u>. Feel all right, but a little stuffed at the lower end where the tube is. An Indian man came into the room next to me for a minor eye operation. He went out today also.

Jan 27: The tube was taken out early this morning. An African performed the extraction, and very well. If anyone is missing a length of garden hose, I know where it ended up. That thing must have been three-quarters of an inch thick. No wonder I felt stuffed. So today I go off my soup diet. Roger Hagler, a chap from Louisiana who is here with the Peace Corps doing road surveying, dropped in to visit. We had a nice chat and I invited him on our trip planned for June/July. He also brought some books. I finished conversing with Stalin and started a biography; <u>Rhodes.</u>

Jan 28: Had my first bowel movement. But since I get lots of liquid paraffin, it wasn't too bad. I walk much more slowly back from the water closet than I go to it, however. A fellow came into the next room for treatment of snakebite. Since he was still walking, I suggested it wasn't a cobra. I'm of considerable value here.

Cyril dropped by. He got a wire that his son had suddenly died. He is taking it pretty well, but his eyes became tearful on relating the news.

Jan 29: Cyril brought me a pen, and a letter from mom. The snakebite fellow left, vertical too. I'm feeling pretty foxy by now. Finished <u>Rhodes</u>.

Jan 30: Was dilated today. Not very painful, really. Read a book on Dag Hammersjold. An older Indian or Greek man was brought in about 3 p.m. breathing noisily. He had suffered a cerebral hemorrhage and they don't expect him to live. About 10 p.m. he died and they took him out.

Jan 31: I finished <u>The Dawn of African History</u> and about 4 p.m. left the hospital as Vicky picked me up and we went to her place. I talked to one of the nurses from South Africa today. We talked some about the racial policies there, but she said it's still the best country in Africa (she is African). I asked her why she had come to Tanganyika and she replied: adventure. She said a number of nurses had backed out at the last minute because they had heard you had to be in by five or roving lions and elephants would get you, and also that in Dar, the largest town, there were only ten cars. She and her companion nurse were both young and girlish, in the way of American teenagers. They talked and giggled endlessly about boys, but were very disparaging about the local crop, considering them unsophisticated hicks.

Feb 1: I sat around and read some, visited with Ed and Vicky, and listened to their little ones scream. Went to town and saw Hildesly, had a nice chat, and got my chit. With consent in hand, the policeman, Moore, let me have the pick of seven muzzle-loaders he was about to destroy. My choice was quite a looker; the stock decorated with brass fittings and buttons in the Arab style. The barrel was a piece of water pipe attached to a Tower action, which I would later learn was of British manufacture: mid to late 1600's. This gun was free, of course, but Moore let me know that his brand was Johnny Walker. Forty-three shillings ($6.11) seems a small price to pay for something that no doubt has an intriguing history, and might even have been caressed by the hands of Mkwawa.

Hunting and Teaching in East Africa

Feb 2: I went into town to place my order with Iringa Stores, pay Garas, and get the tires fixed on Ed's car. Garas has a Land Rover for 5500/-, which I am interested in. If I can get a clear swap, I may do it. I met Eleanor and Harry in town also. They have come to take me back. Shiviji had an auction and I bought a set of plates for twenty-five shillingi. A camera went for 5/-, and a dart game for 22/-. There is really a lot of junk here. We played bridge at night and got to bed about twelve.

Feb 3: Got up at 9 a.m. After breakfast I went to town and loaded up my Iringa Stores goods. Had sandwiches at Ed's, and then left about noon. The roads were dry, so by 2:30, we were home. I met Mr. Kabati, the new headmaster, a portly and good natured fellow, on first impression, and looked up my schedule: 28 periods (the students have 40 periods per week); 20 of them are English, four are history, and four are speech, of all things. I have a speech book at home and considered bringing it with me, but thought I would surely never need it out here. Saw the slides Harold took of our Rhodesia trip. Also had popcorn for dinner. That **was** dinner.

Feb 4: My first day of classes. I walked into them, said hello, made a few remarks, and left. Got some work done with Mr. Mtoi on the fatigues list, an assignment of chores for the students, usually allocated by dorm, with the prefects taking over from there. Had fish and veal for meat today. Quite nice.

Feb 5: Passed out books and in speech class listened to some impromptu orations: terrible. Had a rectal dilation: less terrible.

Feb 6: Assigned a few lessons and took the IA's (freshmen) to see the doc. Eleanor was over for lunch. Wrapped up my collector's item, ye olde bunduki,[51] for mailing home. Finished the fatigues list and got the Economics Society's papers in order. Got some pop, beer and soap from Manji's, a duka here in Malangali.

Feb 7: Tried to mail my ancient musket, but the local postmaster said I'd have to take it to Iringa and send it from there. Double damn. Put up the fatigues list, exchanged <u>Macbeth</u> for <u>Merchant of Venice</u>, as there will be no school certificate literature this year, thus <u>Macbeth</u> will not be in use among the fours (seniors).

Feb 8: Miss DeSelms informed me that there would be a lit group after all. Seems a change of heart has taken place. I felt sort of odd collecting the books I'd passed out the day before!

Feb 9: Corrected compositions, most of which aren't too bad. Had baraza,[52] as is usual on Saturday mornings, and Kabati talked about punctuality. I had an announcement broadcast by Alf about an Economics Society meeting immediately after baraza. Twenty minutes after the assembly was over, the meeting started. I could see that the headmaster's talk had really taken hold. For our students, twenty minutes late is as punctual as it gets, at least for electives. To classes and mandatory gatherings, however, there are few stragglers. There are no school clocks, but a smattering of watches among the students suffices.

Feb 10: Corrected exercise books (English compositions and précis paragraphs), after getting up at 9:30. Listened to records on Eleanor's portable set, and Harold came in with the mail and my film; eight rolls of slides and one 8mm cine film. We

Daily Life

viewed them in the evening at my place, and later had popcorn, beer, and Pepsi. Most of them turned out all right, but some were way underexposed, and some were just missing, especially the Salisbury pictures. Mystery. To bed about 10:30.

Feb 11: Don put a note in my box with a list of items and how much I owed him. He also deigned to consider any itemized bills I might have, surely an interesting suggestion, as he had lost the kitty in which my records were kept. According to his tally, I owed him 719/75, or $102.82142. I paid him 532/- ($76). I guessed I had 150/- credit in the missing kitty, plus I refused to pay for the water I'd thoughtlessly consumed, at Don's expense, on our last hunt: "That's my water," quoth Donnie. I attached a little note explaining my maji maji rebellion, and sent it to him via Valance. Childish? Yeah, but also recreational: think of all the exercise he'll get ranting and storming about over my response. Speaking of my faithful servant Valance, seems he got it into his head to dry out some wet wood on top of the stove. Of course the stove was going full blast and soon the wood started smoking, a prelude to it catching fire. And my cook? After preparing this recipe to roast my house, he had gone into the village, shopping for meat. Presumably we would roast that over an open fire, or smoldering embers. I hope I live through his care.

<u>Comment:</u> Recently Nyerere had five articles published in the Tanganyika Standard explaining why, although opposition parties were now outlawed, Tanganyika was still a democracy. This clever, slick one might say, argument ran along these lines: there is no real opposition to TANU; opposition parties only sow disruption and rivalry; since the people almost entirely back TANU (Nyerere's party), there is no need for opposition parties, and besides, the factions within TANU will serve the same purpose, but in a responsible manner. A one party system is certainly preferable to the situation in Kenya, and many other African countries, where rival parties represent rival tribes, sometimes exacerbated by religious differences, as in Nigeria and Sudan. A one party system can more easily set a consistent direction for development, with fewer dislocating disruptions based on tribal, ethnic, religious, or narrow political considerations. And, TANU is a benevolent dictatorship, far sighted usually, and sound at the top. But, to call the outlawing of opposition parties democracy, is strange logic to western ears, though not to our students. While the schoolboys might be critical of the area and regional commissioners, Nyerere and TANU central are held in high esteem. After all, Nyerere is the George Washington, The Liberator, The Savior. He and TANU brought Uhuru. They can be criticized, but below the surface is a deep respect. In any case, Tanganyika is just an infant, as an independent country. How long did it take the United States to organize, free the slaves, allow women to vote? Tanganyika has had no Whiskey Rebellion, no Civil war. Our founding fathers had grave misgivings about the growth of political parties, and recently the Supreme Court outlawed the Communist Party in the U.S., justifying their position by placing the state's interests above those of individuals! Democracy is truly an elusive creature.

At present, the one party system in Tanganyika is probably more representative of the vast majority of people here, than our two party system is for us at home. But, comes a bad egg into control of TANU, goodbye fairness and tranquillity, hello Latin America.

Feb 12: An incident of some note happened today. In speech class, one of the lads started to describe the performance of a stripper, in Dar. Well, this dialogue was halted mid-stream and a lecture given about this being a schoolroom, not a bar room. After class, this same student comes up to remind me to inform the headmaster that he is a Seventh Day Adventist, and as such, can do no chores on Saturday. I was pretty sure the Adventists did not include stripper watching in their curriculum, but as I relayed the message concerning their outlook about chores on Saturday, I also mentioned the contents of the speech. Kabati just smiled, a grin of quiet amusement, and commented that the boys don't have a Western sense about these things. The school truck brought some kuni (wood) today, big stuff. Valance was shaking his head. I can only hope he puts it in the stove, not on top of it.

Feb 13: Wrapped up nine boxes of slides and six reels of film to send home; $30 by air, $2 by surface. I decided to save twenty-eight bucks. Went over to Harold's to eat some cake he and Eleanor had made. Not only was the cake good, but Kabati was there and gave us some info on hunting in the Tabora area, as well as permission to go hunting on an upcoming five day vacation. Quite a nice chat.

Feb 14: Got tapped for 5/- today by Stafford, for worm medicine. He said this medicine was at Manji's, so I guess it is some Indian or African herb. Stafford is the young man who left school last year just before tests because of threatened witchcraft.

Feb 15: Mailed the butt end of my beautiful .500 to Moshi for repairs. I sure hate to part with any of that gun, however it needs some work done as the stock is loose around the breech and it might break loose and catch me in the teeth. That in itself would be bad enough, but it would be a whole lot worse if it self-destructed while I was harassing an elephant or buffalo.

Feb 16: After barazza a student asked to borrow my rifle, of all things. I was somewhat taken aback. Seems he only wanted it for the play that night, a skit given during a two-hour concert. Such innocence of the laws of this country, not to mention common sense. Later in the day two of the young men came to Eleanor's and borrowed three dresses for the skits. Had dinner at Eleanor's and made plans for the trip to Mufindi tomorrow.

Feb 17: Left about 9:30 and the roads were in good shape as it hadn't rained for a day. We got to the Grahams' at about eleven, after some shopping in Mufindi. Unfortunately, they had sold the fridge I coveted, but I did buy a lamp, some paraffin, and will get a cat out of the deal. They showed us around the tea plantation and took us up to the escarpment to view the scenery and take a hike that left us pooped. We left after dark with some flower cuttings, but hadn't gone three miles when some Africans frantically stopped us, shouting Swahili through the open car window. We couldn't make out what they wanted, but it appeared a fight of some dimensions was going on so we left for the police station. We managed about a hundred yards before

Daily Life

we saw a man stretched out on the edge of the road. We sped on to the police station and after about fifteen minutes, nobody seemed too concerned, the top cop was located. He dressed, as in "I've got my pistol," rounded up a couple of like minded folks, and we led them back to the scene of the embroilment, but only the scene was there, no broilers, so to speak. The police went on to the work camp, and we lit out for home, only to shortly be stopped by someone with a rifle. He acted like a policeman, but wore no uniform. Still, he was pleasant, and after a short wait, he allowed us to go; and we did.

Feb 18: Nothing much.

Feb 19: Went to the local dispensary to get dilated and the medical assistant showed me a young man who had been stabbed by his brother in a drunken brawl up at Njiapanda; a neat one inch puncture of his abdomen. His father was with him, and they both looked up imploringly at me, perhaps taking me for a doctor. He was to be sent to Iringa to open him up and see if anything inside was damaged. Also, at dinnertime, a student came by saying he was suffering from gonorrhea. I gave him a chiti to see the medical assistant.

Feb 20: Checked on my long-suffering student and he has no signs of gonorrhea, according to the medic. Guess he just wants a bit of notoriety. Saw slides at Harold's.

As I would learn a couple of weeks later, the stabbing victim would die of his wound only three days after I had seen him at the infirmary. They had not taken him to Iringa immediately. Gangrene had set in. If only I had been more insightful, or involved. I could have taken him to Iringa that day, right then, but nobody asked, and the thought didn't even cross my mind. I can still see the faces of the father and son, the fear and hope in their eyes. But oblivious to the severity of the wound and the slight training of the medical assistant, I walked on by. A request unmade, a word unspoken, an omission of expressed concern. A life surrendered so needlessly

---

[51] Bunduki means gun.
[52] Baraza is Swahili for an assembly, or a meeting.

CHAPTER 21

Scouting

In late February, during a pause between the short and long rains,[53] Harold, Roger Hagler and myself decided to do some scouting for future hunts, and possibly get H. a zebra or an antelope as an aside.

We had heard of a place called Scotty's Camp, seventy miles northwest of Iringa. An Australian and his wife ran this tourist/hunting camp right on the edge of the Great Ruaha River, complete with roundovals: round, whitewashed huts with thatched roofs. Soft beds, mosquito nets, home cooked meals, and cold beer were part of the package. It sounded like a suburb of paradise.

Nicoderm had agreed to come along as interpreter, so once we got to Iringa and loaded up Roger, the Simca was squatting a little low. Not that it was weighed down with armament. Half of my .500 was still in Moshi, and Roger had, of all things, a .22. The only real rifle, then, was Harold's 9.3.

The dirt road quickly deteriorated into a dirt track with the two ribbons of soil partially overgrown on both sides and down the middle by grass. After about fifty miles of slow going, we came to a wide, shallow, we hoped, stream. The Simca edged forward, like a swimmer reluctant to enter a cold, high mountain lake, and we bounced and jarred our way across, the underside of the car taking several solid hits. We breathed a collective sigh, drove a couple hundred yards, and were promptly introduced to the twin of the stream we'd just battled. We decided that it too was navigable, so forty yards later, with several additional bruises and scrapes, the Simca pulled onto the far bank.

A habit that I'd already acquired from driving in East Africa was to monitor the gas gauge regularly. We hadn't got fifty yards from that last watery bed of rocks when I glanced at the gauge: the needle should have been comfortably nestled against the 'Full' mark, but instead had sunk to the left, indicating that three-quarters of our gas was gone. "Soap!" I shouted. Harold immediately plunged one hand into the glove box, flipped the car door open, and half disappeared under the rear of the car. In short order he had stemmed the flow, but now we faced the unpleasant prospect of having to re-cross the two streams and limp back into Iringa, rocks and damp grass

Scouting

caressing the gas tank and the water soluble soap the whole way.

We crossed the first stream, got out, looked: no leak. The second, probably where we had been reamed, was a bit deeper and populated by an army of sharp edged rocks and boulders. Again we inspected: still no leak. Speed-wise, for the next several miles our progress simulated that of an aardvark on an oil slick, but as our confidence in Harold's patch grew, the inspections dwindled. In fact, by the time we got back to Iringa our faith in the curative powers of Sunlight Soap was such that the following day we would embark on a 500 mile trip without bothering to get the half-inch wound sutured by one of the local daktari ya gari.[54]

Since we couldn't get to Scotty's Camp, 'Plan B' more or less formed itself. The area around Mikumi, where there was a small game park, was rumored to be loaded with all sorts of game. We arrived in the late afternoon, located a Peace Corps chap's house and made arrangements to sleep there, though he was gone and nobody knew us from Adam. We then went to talk with the head game scout, about fourteen miles off, and ten miles into the reserve. In the park we saw elephants all over the place, some zebra, gnu, and giraffe, a warthog with nice tusks, and a harem of over one hundred female impala, all jealously patrolled by what must have been one industrious and indefatigable buck.

We arose before dawn, eager to hunt. We had spent the night on the Iringa side of the reserve, so had to traverse the park to reach the bountiful area recommended by the game scout. We cruised by a lion, always a good omen, whipped around a bend, and there it was: a huge problem.

My high beams were on the fritz, and at fifty I was overdriving what vision my anemic lows could provide. Coming off the curve, pedal to the metal pretty much, we suddenly realized that most of the road was already occupied. The low beams first revealed the feet, of course, but at short notice; too short.

Now a car is a poor match against an elephant. As a weapon, it is certainly of sufficient caliber, however it is nevertheless no substitute for a rifle. Firstly, it is impossible to execute a brain or heart shot with an automobile. Secondly, even if you could somehow pull off a miraculous shot, the intrepid big game hunters are themselves encased in the projectile. The signs all pointed to a counter-productive event.

The elephant was broadside to us, feeding on the shrubbery above the bank to the left. There was no time to stop, and our rapid approach was putting the big boy in swivet mode. In nervous, mincing steps, he started to back up, closing the gap between his rump and the bank to the right. I briefly thought of going under him, between his legs, but that brilliant idea was tabled immediately and I swerved around his hind legs, climbing part of the bank to get through.

For a short while it was dead quiet inside the car. Finally, when one by one we began to breathe again, a few nervous titters escaped with the exhaled tension. Harold slowly put his hand to the windshield, and in a voice tinged with awe reported that the tail had hit the edge of the glass.

Following our near-death experience with the road hog, the hunting was a bit anticlimactic. After almost sticking in the mud, we parked and hunted for a few hours. We saw a few zebra, several nuisance giraffe, and some female impala, maybe awol from the harem. The zebra were skittish and wouldn't cooperate, the giraffe meddled in affairs that didn't concern them, and the impala, being female, had no horns. Still, as scouting expeditions go, this one had been interesting, and all such safaris are useful, even if negative as to immediate results. We saw some new country, learned a thing or two (like: **GET THE HIGH BEAMS FIXED**), and one wild goose chase executed, means one down and one less to go: hopefully.

---

[53] The short rains were from November to mid-January (+/-), and the long rains from March to June (+/-).

[54] As it sounds, a doctor of cars, as in a mechanic.

CHAPTER 22

Rujewa

Who's a monkey's uncle? What does streep mean? Who would chase a hunting lion with a camera, on foot? How do missionaries have a deleterious effect on African scenery? Do Minnesotans harbor unnatural cravings for animal hides? These questions, and no doubt others of equal consequence, will be addressed in this chapter.

Early in 1963 we made the first of several trips to Rujewa, a village seventy miles west of Malangali, and thus readily accessible for weekend safaris. Rujewa rests in the southwest sector of the Buhoro Flats, a plain extending from east of Madibira to near Mbeya. The Great Ruaha River ambles through this area, though Rujewa is some thirty miles south of the river.

My .500 had just been returned from the gunsmith in Moshi. He had run a bolt through the stock to hold it firmly to the breech flange, and I was so elated to have it back I immediately collected Harold and we took our rifles down to the Little Ruaha River past Itengule to shoot a few rounds, and also to make sure they were zeroed in. The big double was right on, but the recoil was substantial, and, as always, more noticeable when shooting at a target. In fact it bloodied my trigger finger. When I pulled the back trigger the front one came back and took a piece out of me. Adding to the recoil was the fact that I had placed the Simca's rear seat on the hood, and was leaning into the kick. Harry said it was lifting me "this far" off the seat, spreading his hands a foot apart to indicate the gap.

We left after school on Friday, arrived about an hour before sunset, lined up a guide for the next day, and settled down in the Simca for the night. When on safari we generally had two choices when it got dark: sleep in the vehicle, or sack out on the ground. The car was no doubt safer, though uncomfortable and far from mosquito proof. The ground was more comfy, but carried some risk as the possibility always existed that unwanted visitors might drop by. Some visitors might just bug you, like mozzies, ticks, and scorpions. Others, like lion, leopard and hyena, might actually eat you, or parts of you. Then, there were the snugglers; long, slender, cold blooded creatures looking for a little warmth on a cool night. In other words, a sleeping bag would be a welcome and cozy haven for things that go slither in the night.

Hunting and Teaching in East Africa

The next morning we headed out with our guide and a few tag alongs. We hadn't gone far when a young man came running towards us and excitedly reported that animals with streeps were just ahead. Harold and I drew a blank. The man grew quite agitated that we didn't comprehend his English: "animals with streeps!, animals with streeps!" Finally, in exasperation, he reverted to Swahili: the animals with streeps were punda milia,[55] literally, donkeys with stripes.

Zebra were definitely on Harold's menu, so we began a stalk. As we crept up on them we noticed that they were ignoring us and concentrating on something to our left. The brush was semi-thick, so a shot would be difficult, but they solved the problem for us, suddenly taking off at full speed as a tawny blur sped after them. Harold and I, in unison so as to allow neither of us a claim to superior status on the ladder of stupidity, gave the guides our guns and raced after the lion, as it in turn pursued the zebra. We closed to within fifty yards of where she had pulled up, under some brush but in plain view. We immediately shot her several times with our 35mm arsenal while she was alertly eyeing us, tail twitching, no doubt counting calories.

Now Rujewa was in the heart of the man-eating lion territory of a few years back, and a hungry lion can cover fifty yards in about the time it would take the main course to mentally say; oh,oh, realizing that cameras weren't much of a defense, and the guides had the guns. Fortunately the guides had more sense than the bwanas and they rushed up behind us and emphatically thrust the guns back into our hands. The look on their faces was a combination of admonition: as in you idiots!; and confusion: as in do you dummies know what you are doing? I am certain that our actions, and the mental prowess of bwanas, were fodder for many a fireside chat in the ensuing years.

Later in the day Harold got a topi, an ugly member of the ugly hartebeest family. After his shot, it had taken off, only to go down after a brief flight. Our guides, all Muslims, ran hard toward the animal, said a brief prayer over it, and slit its throat while the animal still had a little wiggle in it. If the animal had been stone dead before Allah was praised or thanked, it could not have been eaten.

Harold had the guides skin the topi, and he himself finished the process, carefully removing any bits of meat left clinging to the pelt, before salting it down. Over time, I noticed that H. had a strong hankering for hides, and was very diligent and purposeful in their cleaning and care. Unlike our Muslim brethren, he didn't mutter any incantations that I could perceive, but he did go about his work with the earnest dedication of a monk. After some reflection I decided that this behavior was basically normal for a Lutheran from Minnesota. After all, the hides were a gift from God not to be squandered, and you never knew when a good, thick cloak might come in handy, blizzards being a constant threat in the frigid north; though we hadn't had one recently in Tanganyika.

Geography and religion had combined to foster this craving, but I concluded on two counts, that he didn't have some sort of hide fetish. Firstly, he never suggested, or even obliquely hinted, that we should skin an elephant. Secondly, though I visited his cave almost daily, I never caught him hunkered down in front of the fire, layered in hides, quietly chanting to absorb the karma and chi of the slain beasts.

Our other hunts to this area were not productive of game, but were nevertheless entertaining and educational. Giraffe abounded in this area and were inimical to our hunting efforts. Giraffe have a great vantage point, and as they kept a wary eye on us, all the other animals would use these tall sentinels as their lookouts. If twiga[56] got nervous, the others became concerned and alert. If twiga broke into a canter, nyama wote[57] would do likewise: safari amekwisha.[58]

However, there was more than game on these flats. There were people as well, and people can also be interesting. On one occasion Harold and I, and a couple of students from Malangali, came across one of those pockets of Masai that dot these plains. Our students were genuinely scared of these tallish herdsmen, and with good reason when one considers their reputation. Even then Masai raids were not unheard of, and the **Tanganyika Standard** reported some of those cattle reclaiming projects. The Masai has a sort of chosen people attitude. He is condescending to all others, including the superior acting whites. His ways, and all cattle, are a gift from Ngai[59] and he cherishes them. He flouts the law, swirls his mud-caked hair about, laughs, derides, and generally acts the lord of the land. He is not to be trifled with!

Our students called out in quavering voices from the safety of the Rover: "Jambo, rafiki,"[60] with a heavy accent on the rafiki part. An old woman came up to the car, followed closely by a nubile young babe, bare to the waist. Occasionally you could come across one of these beautiful creations of nature that the missionaries had failed to shroud. Whereas the old gal was about a thirty-six long, the babe was both perky and peaky, a gorgeous example of natural African scenery. The Masai are sometimes sensitive about having their pictures taken, so with my camera on my hip and Harold's directions, I captured her image for posterity, or so I thought. Dark skin tends to absorb light, and I ended up with an underexposed photo of this overexposed young beauty. On the bright side, her perfectly formed and brilliant white teeth stood out prominently, even if nothing else did.

We had another installment with the young distaff side of the race. Harold and I were driving towards a small village through high grass when we suddenly came upon two young women walking towards us. They were completely taken by surprise; and terrified. They bolted for the safety of the village and the men-folk. H. and I looked at each other and couldn't help but wonder what sort of reception awaited us. We proceeded cautiously, and on entering the clearing of this little hamlet we saw the two girls pointing at us with agitated and fearful enthusiasm. The men, seeing the ferocious beast that the women had encountered, broke into howls of laughter, much to our relief. When the beast disgorged two pale imitations of people, the girls were even more amazed, but as the men didn't seem scared, the young women slowly sidled up close to us, their curiosity overcoming their fear. One of the girls pointed to my bare forearm, said something in the local tongue, and giggled.

Pretty soon we were the focus of a small crowd, and the braver of the two teenagers was now up close, within arms reach. She pointed again, said something again, and giggled again. I asked for a translation, as she did indeed seem fascinated by my forearms. One of the men informed me in Swahili that because of the hair on my arms, the girl thought I must be some kind of monkey, or a close relative of one. The irony did not escape me.

I held up my arm and motioned her to feel it. Her hand came forward, a little hesitantly, and she gently stroked my arm like I was an exotic, though perhaps still unpredictable, pet. But since I hadn't bit her yet, she became more comfortable with the situation, and her friend soon joined her in forearm exploration. They caressed the fine red hair, occasionally sifting it between their thumbs and forefingers, all the while murmuring softly at the marvel of it. Such innocent curiosity, both refreshing and amusing.

---

[55] Punda (donkey) milia (stripes) = zebra.

[56] Twiga are giraffe.

[57] Nyama wote in this context would mean "all of the animals."

[58] Safari amekwisha would indicate that the hunt was over, finished.

[59] Ngai is the Masai god, and for the Masai, and only the Masai, he created cattle. Thus, by definition, all cows belong to the Masai, and a cattle raid is not theft, it is merely recovery.

[60] Jambo (hello) rafiki (friend).

CHAPTER 23

Hasan

During the April school break we decided to try for Ifakara, in the Kilombero Valley. This area was reputed to be great elephant country, and was situated just west of the Selous Game Sanctuary. The largest game reserve in Africa, larger than Switzerland at 21,235 square miles, the Selous was chock-full of game that hadn't been hunted in several decades. Recently, however, it had been opened to foreign hunters, at a price. Capitalism at work in a socialist country: only the wealthy need apply!

The road to Ifakara swings south from Mikumi, but when we consulted the game scout in Mikumi we learned that the long rains were inundating the Kilombero area, so we gave up on Ifakara and continued on into Morogoro. We contacted the game warden there, and he suggested a couple of areas to consider.

After dinner at one of those hotels that once was, we headed for Ngerengere, about forty miles out of Morogoro along the road to Dar, and thirteen miles south of that road. The game warden doubted we could get very far, as wet weather prevailed here also, but we did manage to make it, only to find that the nearest elephant were a ways off yet.

H. and I spent the night in the car; slept would not be an accurate verb to use, with Nicoderm sleeping in the nearby headman's house. Before retiring we made arrangements to leave shortly after sun-up on a certain road to the south which was thought to be passable.

In the morning we departed Ngerengere with a town councilor as our guide. We encountered some terrible roads but finally, after many stops to talk with the locals, set our course, and allow the engine to dry off and start again, we reached a small village about twenty miles further into the heavily forested hills. The roads here offered many steep grades, as well as their own smaller undulations, the low spots full of water deep enough to invade the distributor, temporarily disabling the car. All we could do was lift the hood, remove the distributor cap, and sit back and admire the scenery while things dried out.

After securing the services of a couple of locals, Harold and I headed out while

Hunting and Teaching in East Africa

Nicoderm stayed in the village, as it was raining and he had no rain gear. H. and I had waterproof ponchos, the old fashioned kind that didn't breathe, so while they kept the rain on the outside, they manufactured their own moisture on the inside. Suffice it to say, carrying our own personal saunas through this hot and muggy terrain, we were marinated in our own juices.

The trail we followed wound up, down, and around, and was enveloped by tall grasses, most of it way over our heads, and much of it sharp. While the grasses were busy slicing the white meat, the guides were often busy cutting a path. Running into elephant in this stuff could be a health issue, but our luck held and our existence was not compromised by any sudden encounters.

However, in the course of events one of our guides was certainly compromised, executing a vertical leap that defied the laws of physics. Though only five-and-a-half feet tall, he could have dunked a basketball with that leap, and in fact, had there been a hoop present, he no doubt would have used it as a place to park his quivering cheeks. Generally speaking, while walking in the bush you do not come across a lot of Africans popping off the ground just for the fun of it, like impala. Usually there has to be motivation, and there is no motivation on earth like bare foot on snake. At apogee, his knees were at my eye level!

Since we had seen no fresh elephant sign, and since the guides were a little spooked by the snake incident, we decided to return to the village. We had walked for miles and seen nothing, but shortly after our U-turn, we cut fresh spoor. An elephant had crossed just behind us, leaving a pile of steaming dung and a splash of still frothy urine. He was very close, five to ten minutes at most, and he had huge feet: his footprint being large enough to sit in. Elephant hunters like big feet.[61]

The guides said it was Hasan. Only the really enormous old bulls, with tusks to match their bulk, are given names. There is a certain amount of reverence involved, not to mention some measure of awe, and these old boys all seem to be Muslim, since they all have Arab names.

If our guides had been cautious before, and they were in this dense, green jungle, they now became glacial. Any little tree represented an opportunity to stop, as it was carefully scaled for a better view. Here I was, so excited to be this close to a legend packing ivory in the hundred plus pound range, and the guides were progressing like dung beetles, slow and skittery.

After about an hour of this frustrating and methodical approach to the elephant of my dreams, the guide in front signaled me to come forward: Tembo karibu.[62] He forgot to add: ndogo sana.[63] I parted the grass, and my spirits were immediately grounded. The elephant was not close, and it was not big, and it was not Hasan.

Somehow the old tusker had given us the slip and we had trailed and come to within a hundred yards of a ten pounder.[64]

The tusks were about a foot long, and as I watched dejectedly, his smallish gray rump disappeared into a grassy swamp.

Our guides were just guides, not trackers, but even had they been expert hunters, tracking in such a wet grassy area is almost impossible. The elephants leave only a hint of their passing, with parted and bent over grasses, but a legible footprint, like we saw initially, is rare, and there were lots of wispy partings in the grass, any one of which could have been made by Hasan. We turned back for camp and after arriving, downing several glasses of water, eating a few bananas, and paying off the guides (5/- each, or about 70 cents U.S.), we left.

 The trip home was more or less typical, given our location, and the persistence of the rains. On the way out of these hills we got stuck twice and the engine flooded once. For about six miles it ran very badly, each hiccup a threat to our deliverance. However the Simca didn't keel over on us and we made Ngerengere an hour or so after dark. We had a cold beer at an Indian shop and discussed the area with the owner, and then left for Morogoro to spend the night with some Americans from Harold's group at Mzumbe Secondary School. We ate, talked, and got to bed about two a.m.

 Later in the morning we left blurry and early for another place the warden had mentioned, about twenty miles west of Morogoro on the road to Dodoma. On the way a car came barreling towards us and we discovered we were going against the grain of the East African Safari Rally, the three thousand-mile rainy season race I mentioned earlier. Since we got no hot leads on elephants thereabouts, we stopped to observe and photograph the cars in the race, and then decided to go home via Dodoma. En route we encountered several more Safari cars, though eventually only seven of eighty-four would finish the race, and one of them, a Simca no less, spit a rock through my right wing window presenting me with a lap full of glass.

 We made Dodoma in the early afternoon, had lunch, and headed for our favorite BP station,[65] twenty miles north of the Ruaha River. We gassed, had a coke, got a lead on some elephants, and took off for the Ruaha. Just north of the river we drove west into the bush to investigate our lead, but the locals said that although the elephants had been there a week ago, the water had dried up and they had all shuffled off into the surrounding hills. This wasn't going to work, so we decided to return to Iringa and give up on this safari.

 When we came to the river, there was a manned gate across the bridge. They were stopping trucks from taking food into or out of the Southern Highlands, to what purpose I did not know, probably something to do with some crop disease. By now it was getting late, we were tired, and of course, we had a flat. As we were mending it, we heard a very vocal leopard prowling nearby, meaning within fifty yards, so Nicoderm concentrated one flashlight on the surrounding bush, while we proceeded apace. That fixed, I drove another fifteen miles, but couldn't keep my eyes open any longer, so Harold took over. H. wasn't familiar with my car, so when he fiddled with the light switch, instead of getting high beam, he got no beam, so we punished a large boulder, much as you would punish a boxer's fist with your nose. This bunged up the clutch and broke a tire, so we slept (?), three in the car, at that spot, thirty miles from Iringa.

[61] Even the woman I married has big feet, though no notable tusks.
[62] Tembo karibu means the elephant is close.
[63] Ndogo sana means it is very small.
[64] Ten pounder - elephants are judged by the size of their ivory: a ten pounder would carry about twenty pounds of ivory, ten per tusk; indeed: "ndogo sana!" Hasan would have had over two hundred pounds of ivory stuck into his upper jaw.
[65] BP is short for British Petroleum.

CHAPTER 24

Sports Day

The rains finally quit by mid-May, just in time for the organization, practice and work to begin for the biggest athletic event of the year: Sports Day. This was a track and field competition between the houses (dorms), and the largest social occasion of the year for the village of Malangali. Over 200 people would come, some from as far away as Iringa and Mbeya. Politicians, village elders, parents, European settlers, Indian shopkeepers, and local spectators would line the field to take in the races and field events.

I had volunteered, in an army sort of way, to host the V.I.P. afternoon tea, so I had to spruce up my yard and then run into Iringa for extra supplies, mostly biscuits (British for cookies), and saucers and cups; ninety of each, which I managed to borrow from Manji of Iringa Stores. The roads were now dry, so the trip into Iringa took only a couple of hours, but the rocks that had previously been dormant, imbedded in the mud, were now liberated and free to bounce playfully about, through windshields and the like.

While my windshield was being replaced and biscuits and cups and saucers were being readied, a number of us went to hear the American ambassador open the Iringa Agricultural School. After the speech, Derek Bryceson, the Minister of Agriculture, thanked the ambassador for America's generosity in funding the new school, but it was a bit odd that there were no prominent TANU representatives present, not even the Regional Commissioner. Perhaps the gift, though accepted, smacked of neo-colonialism and was an affront to the government policy of self-reliance. Perhaps it was geopolitical: the school was a present from the United States, not China.

When the big day came my cook became a busy man, something he was not used to. Being a cook for me was generally a leisurely occupation, but not on this day as he had to wash all those cups and saucers, both before and after the tea, get the biscuits ready for serving, clean up the mess afterwards, and then prepare dinner for me and my guests: the Dieraufs from Iringa, Mr. Phadke, and Eleanor.

The sports went very well as my house, named after the Swahili poet Shaaban Robert, came in first, and our Francis Louis (Louie) won 'victor ludorum'; that is he got more points through the course of the day than anyone else.

Francis was a very likable and popular young man and the other students called him Mzungu because of his light complexion. Ian and I were judging the high jump, and the boys surrounding the pit would encourage him with shouts of "Go Mzungu," all the while grinning and shooting sly glances at Ian and myself. Francis, using the scissors jump common at the time, did not disappoint. Whereas a few of the other competitors used the western roll, Francis cleared 5'6 by just bounding up and over, first one leg, then the other, with his rear clearing the bar while his body remained upright the whole time. In addition to the high jump, he won the 440, the shot put and the discus.

We had relays, sprints, the 440 and the mile, the long jump, shot put, discus, javelin, pole vault and high hurdles. The hurdles were a real challenge for our untrained and shortish runners, but the pole vault was more so, and not for the meek. Using metal poles and lacking training, our pole-vaulters didn't exactly soar, but that was probably a good thing, as a sunken pit with a bed of gravel to cushion their fall was all that welcomed them on touching down. Pilika, bloody but unbowed, won this event at 9'8.

The regular track and field events were augmented by a tug-of-war between the school staff and a team of students and locals, and by a spear-throwing contest. The staff won the tug-of-war as we had some big boys on our side, especially Alf and Don, and Don took second in the spear chucking.

There were no female entrants in these two special events. Eleanor was the only woman on staff at the time but was not athletic to any degree and probably would have found a way to hurt herself if armed with a spear. And the local gals were constrained by tradition, though the local tug-of-war team could have certainly used the postmaster's wife and her Joe Louis sized biceps.[66]

However, there was one all-girl race, and it proved to be both exciting and novel, probably the highlight of the day. While there were no girls at the secondary school, there were a number at the middle school just up the road. Five of them were featured in a special 100-yard dash, and none of our boys could have defeated the winner, in this particular race.

Each girl was given an open beer bottle, filled to the top with water. The bottle was then perched on the girl's head, and the idea was to run the hundred yards without touching the bottle or spilling a drop. The young lady who won covered the distance in 18 seconds flat, didn't steady the bottle once with her hands, and delivered it brim full.

It had been a busy but enjoyable day. The tea had gone off without a hitch, thanks to many helping hands, and especially Valance. After dinner I drove him home as he had not had a break all day, and I had given him more food than he could haul on his bicycle. The Dieraufs and Phadke stayed and we played bridge until one in the morning, taking advantage of the extra time the school generator was run to accommodate the many visitors staying over.

Sports Day

Unfortunately, Sports Day came around but once a year.

66 She was a remarkable and very tough woman. On one occasion she was working in the fields, nine months pregnant. The time came, so with the help of the women working along side her, the baby was delivered, cleaned up, strapped to her back, and she finished the day in the field, hoeing and nursing, hoeing and nursing.

Middle School girl winning 100 yard dash in 18 seconds with open beer bottle on her head.

CHAPTER 25

Third Elephant

School let out mid-June, about a week after Sports Day, and recess meant time to hunt and travel. First would come the hunt. And Harold had bought a Land Rover. My Simca might survive our torturous relationship yet.

We decided to try the Buhoro Flats again, and we tried the short cut behind Itenguli again, and we failed again. So we retraced our tracks and went via James' Corner, 23 miles from Malangali towards Iringa, and by nightfall had cut the Madibira-Rujewa road about forty miles into the scrub. We spent the night at this intersection, though the short wheel based Land Rover was a bit cramped as Eli, Harold's cook, was also with us.

In the morning some people came by who were hoofing it to Rujewa, about forty miles to the west, and since they had left Madibira just an hour earlier, this put us only about three or four miles from there. We went in to get information and hopefully a top-up of our petrol. As we entered Madibira, we came across a game scout, and it turned out to be the one whose gun had been chewed on by that hyena near Igawa, when Don and I had been there the previous year. He said there were elephant all over the area and he offered to get us a guide: an irresistible combination.

We then proceeded to the mission where we hoped to pry some petrol from the padres. A ruddy-faced Irishman welcomed us, his accent pronounced and a little difficult to fathom. After a brief visit he took our request into the next room to discuss with another priest, one fully his equal in Irish obfuscation. After a few minutes of free flowing baloney and blarney, the two 'Irish' fathers emerged from their gabfest. We got more than our petrol: Harold and I stared at the second priest, and then, mouths still unhinged, at each other. This was the darkest Irishman either of us had ever seen outside a University of Notre Dame uniform. He was black as soot. H. and I could not muster that inscrutable look. Our expressions were an open book, and one the black priest found highly amusing. Once our speaking apparatus came back on-line, we had a nice visit over tea, the corners of the fathers' mouths slightly turned up the whole time.

One couldn't help but wonder about the black priest's background. To speak per-

Third Elephant

fect Irish, identical to his linguistic twin, he had to have gone to Ireland at a very young age. Most Africans have a soft, lilting, almost musical accent, when speaking English. I would think the Irish version would produce even a more noticeable variance, unless immersion occurred from an early age. The man was also West African black, anthracite black. He could have been an orphan raised by Irish fathers, initially in his homeland, perhaps, but surely for years in Ireland. One of those intriguing mysteries best left to the imagination.

Once outside, whom should we meet but Roger Hagler, the Peace Corps chap from Louisiana. He had been hunting in Dabaga, then crossed the Great North Road and arrived in Madibira from the east. He was about to turn around, but seeing us and hearing of our irresistible combination of elephants and a guide, he decided to tag along.

The guide was a grumpy old headman, evidently not too pleased about being volunteered by the game scout. We started across an open flat stretch, but it became so rough due to potholes left by hundreds of elephant feet that we had to stop and proceed on foot. Numbers of elephant had crisscrossed this area during the rainy season, sinking ten to twelve inches into the soft soil, but with no cover, this soil had already dried out with the potholes set to axle threatening hardness.

A sea of elephant grass lay a mile or so in front of us. We soon entered, but I didn't like the stuff as visibility was usually close to nil. Roger and I climbed onto a tipped over tree, a common sight in elephant country, and from there we could see two or three elephants a couple hundred yards to our right. The tree swayed under our combined weight, so I jumped off while Roger kept an eye on them. They were moving slowly, and with their movement came a flash of ivory. Roger estimated the tusks to be in the forty to fifty pound range, so we decided to circle down wind and close on them.

We followed the wide paths elephants had tamped through the grass. It was hot, buggy, and humid, and there was water here and there, not deep, but populated with snails, a warning that bilharzia might be present. This would not be the last time I would wade with the snails, though when I could I avoided doing so. The threat from bilharzia would be at the end of a long road and hunters of elephant and buffalo don't always travel a long road, and, in any case, for a person into this kind of hunting, risk avoidance wasn't a high priority.

We could not see the elephants, but as we got close, we could hear their stomachs gurgling, a sign they were enjoying dinner, relaxed, and unaware of our presence. Amid a swirl of heat and tension, we inched forward until we could see the tops of their bodies, about twenty yards ahead. I stopped, and Roger went another ten yards or so to the right to better view the second one. I raised the .500 and brought it down on a line from the back of the elephant's front shoulder. At about the level I thought his heart would be I pulled the trigger and the bullet sped through the grass to its totally obscured objective. The bull let out a grunt and started to move off, but gauging where his shoulder would be, I quickly emptied the second barrel into him and

Hunting and Teaching in East Africa

down he went, the bullet plowing into that area and piercing the spine.

Out of the corner of my eye I saw Roger's go down, on the second shot also. His was alternating between high-pitched screams and low volume groans, while mine was silent in his determination to get back up. He was raising up on his forelegs, and since at that moment I didn't know that the connection between his brain and hind legs had been severed, I thought he would succeed. I sent two more rounds into what I could see of his body but he still continued to struggle. I reloaded again, waited, and when he raised up, I shot for the head, which he swung about wildly, trunk in the air, tusks swishing from side to side. Then he collapsed.[67]

We cautiously approached and found him on all four knees, like in prayer, and still twitching. Roger put one into his brain from about two feet away and he just shuddered, his prayers unanswered, his life spent. Roger's tembo was still making guttural noises, so we parted the grass and finished him off also, happy at the outcome, disappointed at the ivory.

The headman went back for Harold who had a distant front row seat in a small tree, while I cut off the tails and the tips of the trunks. Even from his somewhat elevated position, Harold hadn't seen much, however, and that was the problem: visibility. How many? Where? How close? How large are the tusks? You finally see one twenty yards ahead, but is there one you don't see five yards to the left, or behind you? Where do you aim? Aiming is guesswork. Guessing at the target is not a healthy practice with dangerous game, and not a good practice with any animal. I would eventually conclude that hunting in this dense, tall grass was not only really hairy, but also really stupid, though it would take one more such hunt for this wisdom to fully penetrate my sometimes-opaque brain box.

When the mzee came back with Harold it was late afternoon, so we decided to return to base while our guide went to organize a party to cut out the tusks the following morning. We camped on the bank of the river opposite the mission, washed up, and after a good and welcome dinner prepared by Eli, we settled down for the night, H. and Eli in the Rover, Roger and I under the stars.

In the morning we took our time breaking camp and then drove over to the headman's house, our rendezvous to collect the ivory. No big surprise, it wasn't there. By now we had all logged enough time in Africa to know that 'morning' was an approximation. We took out the cards, played some hearts, worked our way through a couple boxes of cookies and some local tomatoes, and mid-afternoon the twenty pound tusks arrived, one per porter, and the headman came in laden with meat.

We dropped Roger off at the mission and headed for Igawa, twenty miles to the west via a good road with no water to hinder our way. We soon found out what hakuna maji[68] really means in bush Swahili: it means there are no oceans, no rivers to rival the Congo, and no swamps the size of Lake Chad. Nevertheless, we got good and stuck in some stuff that looked like water, and even felt like it, so the night was spent bogged to the hubs, with us providing nourishment for a myriad of mosquitoes.

Third Elephant

The next morning Harold and Eli dug the Rover out, while I dug a tusk out, one that had been splintered near the base by a lead ball some while back. An elephant tusk is embedded in bone to about eye level. The ivory is paper-thin where it ends, and capped by a bone cover over the nerve. The nerve itself is a cone shaped gelatin like substance, white with pink tinges from the fine blood vessels that feed into it. At about the spot where the tusk leaves the jaw, the nerve has tapered down to a point, and the tusk becomes solid all the way through.

Normally, to remove the nerve you simply crack and remove the bone cover, run a finger around the edge of the nerve to break the filmy membrane that anchors the nerve to the end of the tusk, and tip the tusk and let the nerve slide out and plop onto the ground. This nerve was not normal, however. The wound had caused the nerve to fester, and it was a putrid, liver colored gravy. The lead ball had gone through the tough lip-hide that surrounds the ivory as it enters the head, and had penetrated only to the inner edge of the tusk. Since the bullet entered from below, I would guess the hunter was directly under the elephant when he fired what was surely the last shot of his life. Over time, the ivory grew around the lead, coating it with a thin layer armed with a half dozen sharp little horns. As I worked to clean out the nerve cavity, these little spikes imparted some nasty cuts, especially to my trigger finger. No doubt there was some irony here, and perhaps a little poetic payback.

While I was up to my elbow in this thick, but not delectable gravy, H. and Eli were up to theirs in mud, jacking up the Rover and stuffing branches under the tires. Once the Rover was unglued, we continued towards Igawa, but five miles further on, we sloshed to a stop facing an expanse of water as far as the eye could see. Maybe Lake Chad had expanded more than usual, but Lake Chad or no, our journey to Igawa was over.

Still, there was a silver lining. Our fan belt had just broken, the Rover was running hot, and here, right in front of us, was an inexhaustible supply of coolant to feed our developing boiler. Eli and I filled every container we had for the return trip home, while Harold tried in vain to fix the belt. Since H. could not salvage the original, he jerrybuilt a new one out of rope and copper wire.

There was elephant sign, footprints and droppings, all around us, so instead of heading home immediately, we decided to camp here and give it a go. With no guides, Harold and I went off to hunt on our own. We walked a few miles north, toward the heart of the plains, but saw nothing but vegetation; short grasses and short scrub. After a while we turned back as it was getting dark. We had a hard time following the nicks I had cut in shrubs and small trees along the way, but eventually we made camp, and Eli had a big meal waiting. That night we all slept in the Rover to a constant symphony of frogs croaking, and mozzies humming.

The next morning Harold was sound asleep, so I headed off alone, following a small creek. I walked for an hour or so, seeing lots of elephant spoor, and some buffalo tracks, but the only game on the hoof was a dik-dik. When the land turned to marsh, I had no creek to follow, so I turned back, rather than risk getting lost. Not getting lost was a high priority.

Hunting and Teaching in East Africa

When I arrived back at camp, two game scouts from Igawa were there. They said the game hadn't moved down from Rujewa yet, which fit with our observations, so we said our good-byes, collected our gear and off we went for home. The rope fan belt gave us enough juice to keep running, and three and a half hours and several gallons of water later, we steamed into Malangali.

---

[67] The head shots did not collapse the elephant. One or more of the body shots invaded a vital organ, and these type shots require a little time to take effect.
[68] Hakuna (no) maji (water) would imply that the road was perhaps: dry?

Elephant shot near Madibera on the Bahoro Flats

Same tembo - made bracelets (good luck charms) from the tail hairs.

CHAPTER 26

3500 Miles to Malangali

The day after the Madibira hunt was but a brief respite between hunting and travel. We rested up, did a few chores, and I finally got the rest of the goop out of that pungent tusk.

Saturday we left for Tabora via Mbeya. Nobody goes to Tabora via Mbeya, at least not in a sedan. We weren't privy to this morsel of intelligence up front, but by the time the day was over, we were well informed.

After fixing a flat in Mbeya, we headed north and for the first seventy miles, though dirt, the road was in good condition. It was on this stretch, where we could make good time, that a pair of stationary giraffe legs suddenly whizzed by my open window. I looked in the rear view mirror to see a large giraffe, still frozen in place. Neither Harold nor I had seen him as he was standing in the mottled shade of several tall trees that bordered the road and his own pattern fit that mosaic perfectly. Our tracks indicated that we missed his couple of feet by a couple of feet. Our heart rates, and no doubt his, were severely elevated for a while, once we realized how close we had come to taking a major hit.

The road from mile 173 out of Tabora to mile 40 was terrible. This road was evidently used mostly by dual wheeled lorries, and in places the ruts were deep, with the middle elevated. These opportunities to get high centered were fortunately intermittent, allowing us enough distance to build up some speed before taking them on with our skid plate, the car lurching from side to side, the rear tires occasionally touching down, aiding our momentum. We only had to dig out twice, but on one mad rush we hit a rock hidden in the grassy center and banged up the clutch and brake pedals so that they would not return on their own.

Just after dark we pulled into Sikonge, forty miles south of Tabora and the font of good roads ahead. We stopped at the nearest duka for a break and drinks, and the Indian owner asked where we'd come from, knowing full well we had entered town from the South but not really believing it. When we replied Mbeya, he looked at us, then at the Simca, and said: "In that?" You could tell from his expression what he was thinking. "It's time to lock up the womenfolk and the kids, we've got crazy people here!"

510 miles and eighteen hours from Malangali, we arrived at Pat Patterson's house in Tabora. In other words, we had averaged 28 miles per hour. He was, like us, gone on safari, but his houseboy wasn't, so we bunked out there. This was common practice among us Americans, and since there were TEA people in almost all the secondary schools, we had an informal network of hostels at our disposal throughout East Africa.

The next morning we explored Tabora, a hole of a place, worse than Dodoma. Unlike Dodoma, however, there were artisans about, creating drums and carvings, and to the east, twenty miles up the rail line, there was reputed to be a colony of these craftsmen creating and marketing their wares.

After getting stuck three times in thirteen miles, we gave up on the treasures just seven miles ahead. In the process we finished ruining the jack which had twisted on us for the second and last time, the car having rolled on us in the slippery goo, and we noticed a new hole in the gas tank. Ah well, back to Tabora, a beer at Pat's, a cold-water bath, dinner at the hotel, and to bed.

The next morning we loaded up, had a flat fixed and the gas tank soldered, tied the right rear brake line to the frame with rope as the bracket had been ripped off, and bought a jack, along with some carvings and drums. Just before noon we put the Simca in gear and headed for Mwanza on the southern shore of Lake Victoria.

The land around Tabora had been a surprise for we had expected it would be all thorn scrub and bush, flat, almost desert, like Dodoma. But it was mildly hilly and the landscape, though some bush, was dotted with tall, stately trees graced with actual leaves, instead of thorns. It was also marshy in places, something totally foreign to the Dodoma area. Around Mwanza we expected opulence, a fat kitty slurping nourishment from an endless saucer of milk. Here again, we were in for a surprise.

Mwanza sits in a swath of low lying, slightly undulating land. Vegetation is sparse, but large granite outcroppings abound. These rocks attract pythons, plentiful in this area, as they come to sun themselves and snooze. They look docile and lethargic in their slumber, but they aren't, a bad combination for the curious.

Snakes are predictable. If you press them, they will respond. It is people who are unpredictable. Sometimes we act with intelligence, sometimes we don't. Ignorance is rarely bliss.

A British teacher, camera in hand, approached one such python behind her house on the outskirts of town. To make a good picture better, she got closer, too close. The snake struck, and then began to coil around her body. She went hysterical. Her cook heard the frantic screaming and came running, panga at the ready. It must have been pandemonium with her screaming and thrashing about while the cook tried to kill the snake without hurting his memsaab.[69] Finally he was able to cut the python off the young woman, but the damage had been done. She was so traumatized they had to send her back to England, her mind askew from the horror of the experience.

We explored the rock formations, saw no pythons, but did get a nice view of the lake from atop one monolith: water to the horizon, and then some.

The next day we left for Kisii (Kee **See** ee) and on the way stopped by an Indian restaurant with a view of the lake from its open-air seating. Our meal, chicken curry, was soon served, then the whole family scampered inside, their dark brown heads popping up in the window frames, faces grinning in anticipation: could the wazungu handle it?

Harold had a good view of the lake, but I had more a view of the spectators. I noticed their rapt attention but assumed they didn't get many European customers and were admiring our regal presence. Well, that wasn't it! Harold and I sunk our teeth into the chicken, and it bit right back. Our mouths and tongues were on fire. One bite and the contest was over, the nobles vanquished, the wazungu gulping water and scrambling for the car. It is so nice to bring pleasure to others, to put smiles on their faces.

All curries are spicy, but not necessarily hot. Curry powder just imparts flavor, it's the peppers and other spices that add the heat. And not all Indians like flaming hot curry, but I have a theory: the darker the Indian, the hotter he likes his food. As a consequence of this predilection for hot food, the Indian is gradually cooked from the inside out, and the closer he is to well done, the darker his once Aryan skin becomes. And the babies, why are they also dark, right out of the womb? Natural selection. The genes of the adults have adapted to the constant marinade of peppered sauce, so when passed on, the babies come out pre-cooked and ready to survive the molten flow of mother's milk, and the solid fire that follows. Although this insight is of considerable value, it is being provided gratis to anthropologists and all others who study the human condition. In keeping with the theme of providing pleasure to others, no thanks will be necessary.

In Kisii we had dinner at the hotel, refreshingly English, meaning pallid with no hint of hot, and then we went shopping. I purchased a number of fine soapstone carvings, small figurines of animals, my favorites being the frogs. I bought a rabbit, two dogs, a crocodile, a couple small bowls, and half dozen of those beautifully done frogs.

The Kisii also produce four-legged wooden stools with patterns on the top formed by pounding small beads of various colors into the wood. Most African stools are plain, practical, and three-legged. A four-legged stool is much more difficult to make, as all the legs have to be the same length, or it will wobble. A stool with only three legs won't wobble, so the legs do not exactly have to match up. Forty years later, my Kisii stool looks as good as the day I bought it, and it doesn't wobble. It is very colorful, with the triangles, trapezoids, and circles in red, green, blue, olive and orange topped on one edge by a red, four-inch locust, outlined in white.

From Kisii we drove to Kampala, the beautiful capital of Uganda. Kampala is a few miles from the shore of the lake, almost directly north of Mwanza. It is nestled into a number of low hills with luxuriant foliage. It was clean, with wide, well-kept roads and numerous modern buildings.

Hunting and Teaching in East Africa

TEA consisted of three groups: those with teaching credentials and experience, those with teaching credentials but no experience teaching, and those with a degree, but no teacher training. Harold fell into this latter group, and to satisfy the countries of East Africa, he, and the others in this group, had to spend a year at Makerere College in Kampala to get certified. Harold talked fondly of his time there, and part of the reason for our trip was to revisit Kampala, the college, and friends stationed there or nearby.

The African headquarters for TEA was also in Kampala, and these folks were constantly monitoring and evaluating the program without making a nuisance of themselves or compromising our impact or effectiveness. One of these administrative types, Raymond Gold, recounted the reaction of the Faculty of Education at Makerere to the influx of Americans:

> The presence of TEA students seemed to motivate African students to work a bit harder, appeared to improve class discussions, and seemed to stimulate extracurricular activity. Without intending to become a negative influence, the TEA students mildly corrupted African classmates in at least two respects: one, they took such an intriguingly casual attitude toward punctuality for class that some Africans followed suit; and two, their habit of going away for the weekend was eagerly emulated by some Africans who thought they knew a good vice when they saw one...however, the staff felt that the Americans' virtues as students far outweighed their vices...most of the time, anyway.[70]

We stayed with friends of Harold's, and they led us about the town and also introduced us to the City Bar, a dingy, dark green single story structure with a corrugated red tin roof and a large Pepsi sign over the entrance. This was not one of the clean, well-kept, modern buildings of Kampala, but it did have seating outside, under some large, multi-colored umbrellas, and from here we could watch the world go by, or at least odd bits of it. We often did breakfast and lunch there, and although there was no floor show, entertainment was occasionally provided by an unpaid performer, serious of intent, but comic of effect. This character would come by, a long stick in one hand and a wad of papers in the other, and this is what followed:

> Russians are excellent! Russians are excellent! Russians are excellent! British are pigs and thieves. Uganda is independent and I will be president in six months. My enemies are Egypt, Sudan, Somalia, Britain, and America. Communists are good for they are Christians, but Europeans do not follow Christ, nor do Moslems follow Islam.[71]

This was the gist of it. There was more, but it was so incoherent that I couldn't connect the dots and make any sense of it. At the time, this was just a good laugh. But in retrospect, with the advent of Idi Amin and Uganda's many other troubles, it seems this little bit of madness was just the first drop from a powerful storm that would grip Uganda for years. Those nightmares that followed certainly had their surreal aspects, but there was nothing comic about them.

The night before we left for Nairobi, we had dinner at Makerere College, amid a number of educators and politicians. I had an interesting talk with the Attorney General of Tanganyika and what stuck with me was his observation on the simplicity of the American constitution. He was amazed that such a large, complicated, and prosperous country could be governed by such a short, simple document. By contrast, Tanganyika's constitution, though short on character development and plot, was a Tolstoy novel.

Nairobi was next, and a good place to shop, plus there was a Chinese restaurant, and one could even get a cone of soft ice cream. However for us the main attraction was the game park on the edge of the city. The Nairobi Game Park is small, maybe only a hundred square miles, but it had a wonderful assortment of game and in large numbers. Being close to the city, it was fenced, and since fences and elephants were incompatible, there were no elephants, but we found plenty to keep our cameras rolling. I took slides of Thompson's and Grant's Gazelle, zebra, ostrich, Defassa Waterbuck, impala, hippo, crocodile, hartebeest, gnu, giraffe, secretary birds, one beautiful cheetah, and a pride of eleven lions chewing on a gnu they had just killed. There were no maned lions in the group, but one was so huge I couldn't believe it was female, but then, from all angles, there was no evidence to the contrary.

Another car drove up, edging between us and the lions and coming to a stop only ten feet from the pride. Two young Indian men occupied the front seats, with their girl friends in the back. One of the boys made quite a show of working his body through the open window and wildly waving his arms about while yelling at the lions. The large female grew annoyed. She lifted her head and let out a blood-curdling roar, exposing a mouth full of bloody teeth. The young man flew back into the car, audibly crashing the back of his head into the frame of the car door. He sat woozily in the front seat, his body slowly wobbling from side to side. We smiled. I'm sure the young ladies were also properly impressed.

Next up was Arusha where we stayed a few days at Joel Watney's place and took in the Saba Saba Day festivities on Sunday, July 7. This celebration of the founding of TANU was a national holiday and was marked throughout the country with speeches, displays, and singing and dancing. We missed the political enlightenment, but saw the displays (a few new, bright blue tractors), and the dancing. With the Masai and Waarusha (Wa a **roo** sha) in attendance, it was a lively and colorful show. The Masai women were highly ornamented with rings of brightly colored beads around their necks, wrists, and ankles, while some of the Arush men looked very fine in their white fringed Black Colobus Monkey headdresses and shoulder garments. However, the peacocks of the event, as always, were the Masai men. These lanky, elegant, fierce but almost feminine looking men had a fresh coat of ochre on their bodies, and hairdos to kill for. Most were braided, with a single pigtail trailing half way down the back, a touch of orange for highlights. But a few had gone for the helmet look. Their hair was caked with cow dung, colored the bright orange of ochre, and the pigtail was brought up over the top, crowning the entire effort with a ridge. This body magic, when combined with their finely decorated shields and seven-foot long spears, made them the belles of the ball, bar none. And, when they went into their rhythmic, jumping dance, not an eyeball strayed elsewhere.

Hunting and Teaching in East Africa

From Arusha we crossed over to Moshi to visit Jack Humbles, my roommate at Columbia, and to look up Ignatious Sarakoki, a Malangali graduate. We ate lunch with Jack and in the evening went up the slope of Kilimanjaro to find Ignatious. His house was a fifteen-minute hike from the car through a forest of banana trees. We found him, but down with malaria. He begged off on the movie we had in mind, but we had a good visit, and his father treated us to some pombe. This time, at least, I did not pay the price for being polite: dysentery.

The next morning we left for Morogoro, and it was a miserable trip. Corrugated roads and a broken shock really slowed us down and shook us up. On the way we got a few pictures of Kilimanjaro, the clouds having cleared, and we arrived in Morogoro about nine that evening, staying with some Americans at Mzumbe Secondary School.

Our destination was now Dar es Salaam, where we would stay with Tony Luzzaro, a TEA teacher who was going to marry a Goan girl in a month. We spent the evening with Tony and a group of Goan women, including Mary from Lorando's Store, in Iringa. Two of the young women, Mary included, were planning to go to Canada to make a new life there.

Since I was teaching a class in Tanganyika government, and since there were no texts from which to teach, one of my goals while in Dar was to get a copy of the afore mentioned novel: The Constitution of Tanganyika. The clerk at the Government Printer's Office seemed confused by my request, though it well could have been suspicion about an mzungu wanting a copy of the country's constitution, especially since certain aspects of it, notably the one party state and the preventive detention sections, were controversial, and to westerners, unsettling and potentially menacing.

At first he said it was out of print! Then he insisted that it hadn't even been printed, which I knew not to be true, as I had already seen a copy. Finally, after much argument and many affirmations that I was indeed a teacher from Malangali and a sympathetic friend of Tanganyika and TANU and Uhuru na Umoja,[72] I got my copy. This became the core of my classes on government both at Malangali and later during my two years in Arusha. In fact, by 1967 I may well have been the last mzungu in the country teaching Tanzanian government, with the full knowledge of the party and the Regional Commissioner in Arusha.

In town one afternoon we bumped into a Malangali graduate and invited him to share an ice cream at the Cozy Cafe. Another African, lean and confused looking, asked if he could join us, and thinking him a friend of Daudi, we said yes. Harold was talking with our ex-student when this forlorn type loudly blurted out that the student shouldn't be talking to us. We were a bit confused as he made little sense, so the conversation continued until he interrupted again, saying whites were bad and would all be driven out of Africa. We took offense and told him to leave, whereupon he vigorously proclaimed that we couldn't speak to a Tanganyika citizen like that. Well we did, and he finally got up and left, muttering something about the Peace 'Corpse' in particular and Americans in general. As we left the restaurant we noticed that he had cornered another American and was earnestly giving him the benefit of his version of things: The World According to the Utterly Clueless.

After a few more days in Dar, we headed for home, stopping overnight in Morogoro and Iringa. We had made a meandering circumvention of East Africa, and at mile 3500, we were back where we had started, home, Malangali.

---

69 Memsaab is a respectful term for a woman of importance, or any white woman.
70 Gold, Raymond, from a manuscript entitled: <u>A Teaching Safari: A Study of America's Friendly Teachers in East Africa</u> (1963-1965), page 93.
71 From my diary, July 1963.
72 Uhuru na Umoja was a government slogan meaning Freedom and Unity.

CHAPTER 27

Scotty's Camp

While Harold and I were touring East Africa, Don had been doing something useful, namely hunting. He had gone to Scotty's Camp and got a hippo, as well as the most impressive trophy in all of Africa: a large, in the record book, greater kudu. Don was about six three or four, and from the ground, the spiraling, annulated horns reached to his shoulders. I was as green as fresh grass after the early rains.

Naturally H. and I immediately started planning our next trip. Scotty's Camp was the destination we had tried to reach on that earlier trip on which we crossed two streams and gouged a gas gushing hole in the tank of the Simca. This time, however, we had a Land Rover, and it was the dry season.

We arrived Friday evening, had dinner with Scotty and his wife, and discussed the area and its contents. We spent the night in luxury in a rondovel with soft beds, mosquito nets, and hippo music from the Great Ruaha River, thirty yards from our hut.

In the morning we located Kibaraka, a guide Scotty had recommended, and before long we came across a large herd of impala. We pursued them for about a mile and Harold got a small male. H. went for the Rover while Kibaraka skinned it out, beautifully. He used my knife very little, as he pulled and punched most of it off. By 10:30 it was skinned and cut up, and we went down to the river to wash the skin and salt it, keeping an eye out for crocs all the while.

In the butchering process we were amazed to see that the gazelle had no ball and socket joints at the front shoulders. The leg bones simply merge into muscle and sinew. No doubt this contributes to the fluidity of their graceful and stupendous leaps, but to us it came as a total surprise.

We drove along the river and saw some elephant across from us where one couldn't shoot: game reserve and all that. We then decided to go after kudu, and walked a couple miles away from the river, but Kibaraka had confused our intent and he was hunting buffalo. We saw none of either, but after getting our wires uncrossed, we headed for kudu country.

We were pushing our way towards where the kudu were known to hang out,

Scotty's Camp

when Harold suddenly jumped on the brakes and said he had heard what sounded like an elephant's grunt. I piled out, .500 ready, and sure enough, about fifty yards back and thirty yards into the brush was a herd. Kibaraka tested the air, took one look and said: "twende," let's get out of here! They were all small and the wind was carrying our scent right to them.

The day was running out, but all the way back to Kibaraka's hut we came across elephant, dozens of them in small bunches heading for the river. The bush near the Ruaha was generally pretty thick, so around each curve we would get out to check.

In addition to cautiously checking at every bend in this winding track, we often stopped to wait while they cleared off, admiring and photographing them in the process. On one occasion I saw a small group with a toddler. I cut diagonally through the bush to head them off, not certain how the little one would handle the river. As they broke cover the baby latched onto the tail of the female in front, and the female behind gripped the tail of the precious little bundle between them. Off they went, the river presenting no obstacle to their reaching the opposite bank.

We set up camp near Kibaraka's village and about a hundred yards from where they told us not to sleep as it was too dangerous; that is, too near the river and therefore a likely place for elephants to wander through during the night. Still, I didn't get much sleep. Harold's cough had returned, and a hyena visited the Rover to investigate the impala meat. Finally I left the truck and slept outside on the ground, though I spent most of the remainder of the night picking burrs out of my hide. Once I did drop off I was shortly awakened by something in the brush near my head. I grabbed the .500, whose right barrel was loaded, and the thing ran away, probably a hyena.

I wasn't the only one who got little sleep that night. As I lay awake I listened to the party the villagers were having. Menu: impala and pombe. It broke up about 4:30, so while Kibaraka and his mates had a lot more fun than I did, the old guide didn't get much rest either.

The previous evening, after we had set up camp but before sunset, three locals came by and reported a large elephant close to the village. We walked very rapidly as we had only about thirty minutes of daylight left. We hurried right past a herd of about twenty, but Kibaraka didn't even pause to give them a look. We got to the place where the big one had been, but all that remained was his signature, in the form of footprints. This quick jaunt served to whet our appetites for the following day, and being so keyed up probably contributed to my sleepless night.

The next morning we rousted our guide out of bed and started off along the road looking for spoor. We saw plenty, but yesterday's, and older. We circled into the bush and cut some fresh, fair sized tracks, which we followed up. Shortly we came upon a herd of four, in very thick brush. Kibaraka thought the big one of the previous night might be among them, so we approached to within thirty yards, three times, from different directions, sifting sand the whole time to monitor the air currents. After about fifteen minutes of this nerve wracking stalking, the guide was convinced the big boy wasn't there.

Hunting and Teaching in East Africa

Harold was sagging, as a lingering cold had sapped his energy, so Kibaraka and I continued hunting while H. rested in camp. At one point we ended up in a cornfield minus the corn, and a young bull emerged from the surrounding thicket and confronted us. We backed off and he lost interest, which was considerate of him as it saved me some ammo and a license, and him an early departure from this earth.

Harold wanted to head home and forego the afternoon kudu hunt, so we packed up and drove back to Scotty's where we had a cold beer, some coffee, and a chat. Scotty figured locals had been peppering the elephants with their muzzleloaders, as he had been chased twice in the last two weeks while escorting tourists through the game park.

We left for Iringa, dropping Kibaraka off at a village eighteen miles from Scotty's and washing up a bit in a cool stream that crossed the road at that place. It had been a great trip. Harold had got an impala, and we had seen all manner of game: kudu, impala, eland, monkeys, a giraffe, foxes, a variety of birds, hippo, and of course, elephants, lots of them, the real royalty of African animals. We would be back.

View of Scotty's Camp 70 miles NW of Iringa and situated on the Great Ruaha River

Kiongozi Kibaraka leaving his hut for the morning hunt.

CHAPTER 28

Back

A few weeks after our initial trip to Scotty's camp, we went back for more. It was mid-term break, and we needed one. The caning incident previously mentioned had just transpired, and one of our African teachers had been hauled into local court for entertaining one of the villager's wives. While the former incident was very stressful, the latter one was mostly just amusing, though still unsettling for the school.

I walked with David to the court as he didn't want to travel through the locals unescorted. At the trial he claimed that his houseboy was the guilty party, but the court wasn't buying and fined him 150/-. It was common knowledge that David was a serial womanizer, so his reputation for carousing doomed any plea of innocence on his part. And, as an affirmation of the court's verdict, the very next week he was caught with another woman, by the woman who had cost him the 150/-: hell hath no fury…, and the scorned one proceeded to bash in the windows of his government house.

These distractions called for a safari, so we headed for Scotty's as soon as we could escape. We got there on a Friday evening after a hot and dusty drive, rented a hut for three nights, and set out for kudu while there was still light. We saw a good male, but H. got a little excited and by the time he was through fumbling with his rifle the ever-alert kudu had sensed our presence and bolted into the bush.

We slept well, but the pleasant serenade of the hippos was missing as some African with a musket had killed one right in camp when Scotty was gone, and the rest had moved upstream.

Saturday was a hot, tsetse fly bitten day, frustrating, but capped with luck. We had spent most of the day chasing about for kudu and waterbuck, but all we saw were females, which in both species are horn-less. Down river from Scotty's we had come across three wealthy Texans and their two South African professionals, and they were shooting everything in sight. They had an open five-by-eight foot trailer stacked with hides of all descriptions, even a hyena's. They had shot a nice, well maned lion, and a fifty-pound tusker as well. They sported Weatherbys of various calibers, from a .257 to a .460, and the younger hunter had a diamond ring the size of a small star. We had a beer with them and then left.

Kibaraka wanted to try for elephant in a spot he was optimistic about, so we drove to a hut eleven miles from the camp. Here we acquired a pint-sized gun-bearer, age fifteen, according to Kibaraka. I suspect he was the son of our guide getting some on the job training, but in any case, he was eleven or twelve years old, slight of build, and only marginally taller than the .500. He was eager to go with us, and just as eager to carry the rifle.

We walked from there through some extremely dense, sort of rubbery, almost leafless scrub which cut visibility to five or so feet, at times. After about an hour we knew we were close, as we kept coming across fresh sign, steaming dung and foaming urine, but we could hear nothing. The youngster was carrying the rifle, unloaded, when suddenly Kibaraka leapt back towards us. While reaching for the .500 I took a look into the cover, and there he was, a single elephant, ears extended and slightly flapping, intent on locating us. I loaded and we backed off. We positioned Harold, Eli and the wee gun-bearer off a ways, then Kibaraka and I went back in for a closer look. We approached from a different direction, paying close attention to the fickle mid-day breezes. We got in close, about ten yards, had a good look at the disappointingly short tusks, and eased our way back out.

At dusk, after the aborted but exciting elephant hunt, and yet another unsuccessful stalk of some kudu, we jumped into the Rover and zoomed past Scotty's and up another road above the camp. We hadn't gone more than a mile when we saw two buffalo. Since we were after kudu for Harold, I was driving. I frantically reached for the .500, wrestled a couple of bullets from my ammo belt on the dash, and tumbled out. I worked myself into position for a good view of the quarry and sat down just as the larger one started to move off. I fired. He caught his breath, and I fired again. He ran about thirty yards, stumbled, took a few more steps, and a cloud of dust arose into the evening air as he collapsed, a big brute. His companion stopped, eyed us, and then trotted off.

I reloaded and Kibaraka and I approached, carefully. The guide bounced a rock off the boss and pronounced the buff dead, but I noticed he didn't touch it. I put a foot on nyati's rear flank and gave a shove; all was calm. The horns were good sized and had a nice, deeply curved shape. By now it was dark and supper was waiting, so we left him there and went back to camp with the good news.

We relished our meal, immensely pleased with our good fortune, and then returned to cut off the head and some steaks. The head was so heavy it took two of us to carry it to the Rover and mount it atop the tyre on the bonnet. Scotty came along with us to get a portion of the meat, and Ceinwen joined in, as she and Ian had come down for the weekend. Scotty was always in need of fresh meat, as he had hungry tourists and hunters to feed, and Ceinwen was quite intrigued by the whole business. The following evening we would have buffalo steak, and either it was extraordinarily good, or my taste buds had been deflowered by too much Malangali cow.

The next morning Ed Dierauf and George Livingstone, a Scot, went out with us

Back

and we spent most of the day up-river, among the tsetse fly. We saw some more female kudu, but that was all. We doused our feet in the Ruaha, lolled in the shade for a while, and after Ed went skinny-dipping, returned to camp.

That morning we had seen some buffalo. They were going into some thick stuff, heading away from the river. We gave chase, but they lost us. It seemed they came off the river early and returned around sunset, so we made plans for Monday.

Monday morning Harold, Eli, and I went up the same road, and after about four miles we encountered a couple of buffalo on the river side of the road. I piled out and Harold ran the Rover past them. They ran parallel to the car for a ways and I was running along the road trying to keep up. Finally they stopped, their concentration on the Rover disappearing in a tan cloud of dust. I got into a comfortable sitting position and waited. They were positioned behind a small mound and I could only see their shoulders and horns, but I knew they would cross in front of me. They walked up to the edge of the dusty track, stopped, peered after the Rover, took a step, and heard an explosion of noise from the left. One of them fell instantly. The other charged back into the bush.

I reloaded the right barrel and approached. The buffalo was digging furiously with his hind legs, dirt flying, murder in his eyes. The hair on the back of my neck stood on end, a cold chill shook my body. His intent was singular, but my bullet had broken both front shoulders,[73] so even the great determination of this formidable beast could not propel him forward. At about twenty feet, I let him have one between the front legs, hoping to hit the heart. He didn't even flinch; he just kept churning. I came to within five feet of him, stared into those angry black eyes, raised the rifle and put one shot into his neck, and then another between his eyes. My adrenaline was pumping hard, as was my heart. I approached with trepidation, grabbed a horn and pulled. He was dead.

I was wondering where Harold had got to when I noticed the Rover on a hill about a quarter mile away, Harold on top of it. The second buffalo had gone after the Rover! Harold had stopped, got out of the vehicle, and this buff had burst out of the bush. H. grabbed his rifle but in the excitement got it jammed, and had to scramble to safety on the roof. He was now treed, but not for long.

It was early in the morning and our voices carried clearly over the distance. I shouted at him to find out what was going on, as I could only see the top of the car, and in a few short words he explained his predicament. But he quickly added that the buff now had a new target.

On hearing my voice the second buffalo sized up the situation and headed for the real culprit. I could hear him crashing through the brush, the racket getting more and more pronounced as he got closer and closer. I looked for the biggest tree I could find and positioned myself six to eight feet behind it, the idea being to force the buffalo to veer to one side or the other, thus exposing a shoulder. A charging buffalo is both a challenge and a nightmare. They can absorb a lot of punishment, especially when riled, and they will not be detoured by a few poorly placed shots. The experts say you have to go for the brain, a small enough target when a buffalo is stationary, but a very difficult shot to make with the beast in full flight. In addition, the buffalo charges with his head thrown back, so the route to his brain is through his mouth or nose, while the natural tendency is to place the shot between his eyes. Such a shot will skip like a flat rock off water.

He cleared the brush about fifty yards in front of me. I had chosen a tree on the far side of the road, about twenty yards behind his partner. He galloped to within a few feet of the dead one, spun to his right, and then plunged into the scrub in front of me. He hadn't even seen me. Evidently the four inch, branchless trunk of the tree had broken up my silhouette just enough to conceal me, saving his life, or mine.

Harold and Eli arrived shortly, we cut off some meat for the home fires and dropped by Scotty's to have a beer and give him the buff's location. The horns were strapped to the tire on the hood, so all the way to Malangali our adventure was riding in front of us.

And to complete the picture, a few miles from Scotty's a small batch of elephant crossed the road, momentarily framed by the horns of the buffalo.

---

73 Unlike an elephant, a buffalo can get going with only three working legs, but even nyati can't move with just two.

Harold's cook Eli trying to lift the head of the 2nd buff I got near Scotty's Camp.

Me and same buff. Note size of trees and refer to story for significance

CHAPTER 29

Bro Arrives

One of the great joys of my stay in East Africa was the visit of my brother. Dave and I had been corresponding for months, he had saved his shillingi, and here he was: somewhere.

He arrived on November 8, 1963, and I drove down to Dar to pick him up. Problem was, initially he couldn't be found. I had suggested two hotels, and he was at neither. I checked with the customs people at the airport, and yes, a redheaded American with two guns had arrived, his stated destination Iringa. O.K., he was in the city. After a few hours of checking the other hotels, I found him at the Metropole. The hotels I had recommended were full when he arrived and though he left notes, those notes seemed to have evaporated in the coastal heat.

Dave had got the lion's share of my father's mechanical aptitude. The Simca sensed this, took it as a challenge, and as soon as we got far enough into nowhere, she quit. I assured my bro that I could get her going again, trying to show off my fledgling mechanical skills, but the car was resolute and refused to so much as sputter. I had some tools, to my brother's surprise, and the battle was joined. Off came the carburetor, innards were cleaned, words were spoken, and the Simca, delighted at some professional attention for a change, purred like a cub.

His first few weeks in Malangali Dave really earned his keep. Not only did he spend considerable time on the Simca, he also went to work on the decaying mechanical state of my other possessions, fixing my shaver, record player, movie camera, and fridge. Next, he tackled Harold's Rover and its tendency to boil over at bush speed. H. was so appreciative he let us borrow it for the weekend, a generosity we would repay with an eight inch tear in the left front fender.

Dave and I headed for Pawaga, about thirty-five miles north of Iringa. About half way, we inched up to a raging stream swollen by a flash flood. We could wait or proceed, but neither of us was habitually long on patience. The water was thigh high and had carried a couple of broken trees along with it, depositing them directly in our path. I wrestled with the trees, mid-stream, while Dave tried to maneuver the Rover between them. One pointed stub of a branch tore a clean gash in the fender,[74] just behind the tire. H. would not be happy.

When we got to our destination, we were assured that elephant were everywhere, we would have to beat them off with a stick. So the next morning we went for a walk, a long, circular walk through hot thorn scrub and sparse, week-old elephant droppings. This day was especially trying for Dave. He was not fully acclimatized yet, he had a few things to learn about walking in the bush, and it didn't help that I was somewhat casual about small details, like carrying water.

The morning was cool, so Dave started out with a coat and no hat. In addition, he was carrying the .375, not as a matter of safety, but as an expression of egalitarian principle. In half an hour there was no need for the coat, but a hat would have been nice. Within a couple of hours, water would have been nice too, and that rifle was getting heavy. Four hours into the inferno the guides were carrying the .375 and the coat, and Dave was parched, cramping from dehydration, and generally miserable. By this time, as there were no elephant for miles, we were headed back to the car, and liquid, but Dave had to stop every ten minutes to rest and give me dirty looks. I began to contemplate parking him in the shade with one guide, while the other one and I went for the Rover and some water, but just as I was about to suggest this course of action, the most beautiful of all vehicles hove into view, an oasis in the wilderness. At that moment, that plain Jane, dull gray Land Rover looked more alluring than a red Ferrari with Gina Lollobrigida at the wheel.

We didn't accomplish much on this hunt, other than Dave's initiation into the pleasures of hunting in Africa, but we did come across something of interest. Out there, somewhere, we found a cement pillar about six inches square and two feet high, and on it were engraved the letters "MMBA," and some numbers, probably longitude and latitude. This was most curious. At a later date I asked an old-timer in Iringa about this find, and he indicated that it was indeed a survey marker. I further inquired about the letters. He gave me a sly grin: "MMBA," he practically shouted, "Miles and Miles of Bloody Africa!" Dave could agree with that.

When we got back to Malangali, we found that Don had got himself into something of a bind with the game department. A few months earlier he had bagged two elephant near Scotty's Camp, unfortunately right on the riverbank; right across from the game reserve. The law said nothing was to be shot within 500 yards of surface water, excepting hippo of course, but as no action had been taken for a couple of months, we thought they might let it slide. Wrong again. It just took them a while to figure out the what, when, and who of the situation.

One afternoon before school was out for the end of year break two government Land Rovers pulled into Don's driveway, confiscated his modest cache of ivory and all of his licenses, and fined him 200/- ($30). The timing tagged a sad postscript to Don's two years. School was out November 30, and Don was leaving shortly thereafter. I felt sorry for him, in spite of our sometimes contentious relationship. He had finally dialed up his courage, gone out and done it, and then he screwed it up.

In early December Harold, Dave and I went to Scotty's Camp. We arrived late in

Bro Arrives

the day, after failing to get any hard-nosed ammo for the .375 from Iringa Stores. We found that all the people down river, including Kibaraka, had been moved to Tungamalenga, about eighteen miles back towards Iringa. This, and new regulations, were a direct result of the Texans and their Boer professionals. Not only did they shoot everything in sight, the Game Warden thought they had shot their lion and elephant in the reserve, though he couldn't find evidence to that effect. In addition, the game had been shot and scared out of the legal area, and to protect the reserve and encourage the game to return around Scotty's Camp for the tourist trade, the boundary for hunting was set a mile from the river. However, Africa did gain some small measure of revenge on those rapacious and indiscriminate butchers: one of the elderly Texans had suffered a heart attack. He died along the Ruaha, south of Scotty's Camp. Hook'em horns.

We stayed the night at Scotty's. At least the hippos were back, cavorting by day in the deep, wide pool that bordered the camp, snorting their bass and baritone notes at night. Crocodiles were also present. They were secretive during the day, but at night you could take a flashlight down to the river and illuminate their bright, red-pink eyes, causing them to sparkle in the darkness.

The next morning we picked up a guide, Kiumbe, and proceeded to Kitagaza, in a flat, tree and shrub dotted plain about forty miles up river from camp. There was no fresh elephant sign here, but elephants were reputed to be plentiful, another ten miles distant. We set up camp near the river, rested for a few hours, then headed out.

The locals knew we were after elephant, but they took us on a meat hunt. We came across buffalo tracks, followed them for half an hour, and then came up on two. Dave stalked them and shot. Off they went, but one of them was losing a lot of blood, and in flight it had stumbled a few times, so we knew it wasn't going far. We trailed the blood spoor for about half a mile through open, park-like woodland. We spotted his silhouette in the only cover he could find, a small thicket of brush no bigger than a bedroom. We closed to within thirty yards and evaluated. The buff was lying down. Dave thought maybe he was dead. I thought maybe he wasn't. My axiom with dangerous game was: "Kill'em twice." Dave put one into the prone beast and the thicket exploded, the buff charging to our left, directly in front of us. We both broadsided him and down he went, 1500 pounds of meat, one horn broken half off.

On the way back to Scotty's I spotted two warthogs, excellent eating. We tried to get close, they spooked, but Dave made a terrific shot on a running hog at 150 yards. Unlike the buffalo, this beast carried a nice trophy: two good-sized tusks.

We returned to Scotty's, as it had started to rain and we didn't want to get stranded. The pork made for a nice dinner, going well with a cold beer. The next morning it was still raining, so we loitered around Scotty's until noon. I took a stroll along the river, so peaceful and relaxing in its brown, slow flow through this deep wide stretch. I was standing close to the water, looking idly up river, when I sensed something measuring me, a tingle of concern climbing my spine. I glanced to my right and a croc was intently watching me from about ten feet out, only his nostrils and eyes showing.

Hunting and Teaching in East Africa

Snakes I don't mind. Scorpions I don't mind. Spiders, bees, mosquitoes, tsetse flies and ticks are all acceptable. Crocs give me the willies. I backed off, keeping my eyes on him. He stared right back, but with his meal now out of reach, he submerged without a ripple. No tracks, no telltale wake, nothing to indicate one might be lurking in clouded water, except, sometimes, those nostrils and frog-like eyes.

Having had enough of peaceful, relaxing contemplation, it was time to go hunting. The serious rain had dwindled to intermittent drizzle. We headed for a plain at the base of some hills, about eight miles up river. We were after zebra or kudu, but cut some fresh elephant tracks and we decided to investigate. We had no Africans with us, so we followed them up ourselves. After about an hour we heard the familiar sound of branches being cracked, and shortly we could see an arched, gray back, about eighty yards ahead of us. The bush here was patchy thick, with fine, newly grown bright green leaves. We got a bit closer and I got a glimpse of the ivory and thought it stuck out of his head four or five feet. I was pretty excited. As we sat there watching him another one broke into the clearing below us, caught our scent, and raced off through the brush. We snuck up on the first one, mounted an anthill and peered over it down into a small ravine. There he was, right below us and about thirty yards out, a perfect shot. But, his tusks were nowhere near five feet long. They would go maybe 30 pounds at best, and I had already shot some ivory in that bracket and was not about to settle for more of the same.

We passed on that one, but continued to explore along the edge of the ravine. Shortly, we decided to cross over to the other side and look up the one that had scented us. As there seemed to be elephants about we listened carefully before slipsliding down one side and scrambling up the other. We had just crested the steep, muddy bank when we saw a small bull heading right at us, about fifty yards off. He was looking towards where we had been, his trunk up, catching our scent. He broke into an amble, trunk still raised, head still directed to his right. We were in some bushes, our backs to the ravine, and though he had not seen us as yet, he was getting very close. At about ten yards I stepped out of the brush and tried for a brain shot. The force of the bullet temporarily stopped his momentum, his head knocked back into his shoulders, his front legs splayed apart. But he did not go down. He gathered himself and I put the second round into his shoulder, dropping him about five yards from our position. Then the excitement began.

He started bellowing and trying to get back up. I was frantically trying to pry a couple of rounds from my web belt, which was damp and had constricted somewhat, and Harold and Dave were bombarding the poor elephant with everything they had, which wasn't much. They had put several soft-nosed bullets into the thrashing animal, only infuriating him further, before I finally freed two shells from the python grip of my belt and finished him off.

We were disgusted. He was a miserable excuse of an elephant, probably a teenager, with ivory half the size of the one I had just passed over. It was now around four in the afternoon, so we cursed our fortunes a bit and called it a day.

Bro Arrives

We got back to the Rover, drove it a couple miles to a place where the rain couldn't stick us, and set up camp. It continued to rain so we all spent the night in the Rover, cramped and getting very little sleep. Daybreak was a relief. We hiked up to where the elephant was and past it, looking for zebra or kudu again, but getting skunked we returned to the tembo for its tusks. Even though the elephant had landed upright, on its knees, it still took us four hours to extract the ivory with our dull ax and blunt knives. However it was educational as we learned that the top third of an elephant's head was nothing but honeycombed air pockets, presumably to lighten a head weighted down by two large oversized teeth, present company excepted, unfortunately.

It was hot, as usual, we were out of water, as was not uncommon, and we were beat, so we headed for Scotty's to indulge ourselves and spend the night. An outdoor shower and a beer, both cold, and a hot meal, and all was right with the world.

The next day Harold and Dave went down river looking for antelope while I stayed in camp and cut the bone from the ivory, a two hour task with our state of the art, sharp as a basketball, Czechoslovakian ax. The boys came back empty handed, just after I had finished, and we loaded up our treasures and left for Malangali.

We rested up for a day, before our next safari and Dave made good use of his time by writing a letter to the folks on a typewriter he had won from Don over the pinochle table. (Don was lighter of goods and coin, before he escaped our little card parties:).

What follows is quoted from Dave's letter home, dated December 15, 1963:

> We got back from hunting Fri. night, quite a trip. I shot a buffalo on the first day out. It turned out to have a busted horn but gave us a bit of excitement anyway. The 375 with softnose is quite adequate for Buff. We ate part of the Buff and it was very good. Coming back from where we got the Buff to Scotty's Camp I dropped a Warthog that is fair size. Dan, Harold and I went out Wed. with no guides and found a fresh elephant trail. We tracked it for an hour and when we came up on it we also jumped a second one. We crept to within 30 yards of the first one and found it too small. We backed off and went downwind about 300 yards to cross a muddy little ravine and get a look at the other one. When we came up the other side of the ravine we ran head on into the other one and he advanced to within 10 yards then caught our scent and started our way. Dan shot one shot in the head to stop and turn him and the second in the shoulder to bring him down. The beast was trying to get up and Dan could not get the shells out of his belt so Harold and I opened up; altogether we put 12 or 13 shells in him. The 375 with softnose is worthless on elephants as it barely punctured his hide. We spent the night in the Rover and cut the ivory out the next morning, it took us four hours to do it. We turned the ivory in to the revenue office as a government trophy so Dan would not have to put it on his license. We are going out tomorrow to see if we can find some bigger Buff, Elephants and maybe some Hippo. The hunting here is quite a bit more exciting than at home, but except for the actual shooting, is not much fun. Lack of drinking water, mosquitoes and tsetse flies make it rather rough, I average about one bite per square inch all over.[75]

Our next hunt was to Lake Rukwa, at Luika on the southeast corner of the lake and about sixty miles northwest of Mbeya. Lake Rukwa is like Lake Chad, rather shallow, with wild fluctuations in size. In the 1950's, Time Magazine had pictures of the lake, or what remained of it, and it had shrunk to one narrow, fifty mile long mud hole with thousands of hippo barely clinging to life, and thousands more dead. When we arrived the hippo and the lake had not only recovered, but both were becoming nuisances. The lake now stretched to over ninety miles from tip to tip and was up to fifteen miles wide in places, overflowing its normal high water boundaries and flooding crops and villages. With the expansion of the lake, the hippo were now nosing into settled areas, eating the crops and killing people.

When we arrived, the Game Scouts welcomed us with open arms, letting us stay in their camp. The next day they led us down to the lake, encouraging us to have a go at the hippo. For some distance into the lake, the tops of otherwise submerged trees were visible. The local Africans had been backed up onto a hill, and at night the hippo would come out of the water, open their huge jaws and march up and down the rows of corn, vacuuming the contents into their ample stomachs. The locals were helpless, and even afraid to leave their huts after dark.

Dave took a prone position and zeroed in on one about seventy yards from shore. The hippo is a big critter, but in the water only the top of his head shows: his nose, eyes and those goofy, little, constantly flicking ears. There were a few inches of skin showing, between his left ear and eye. Dave aimed at the water line and fired. Without any fanfare, the hippo sank. The scouts thought he had missed, but I had watched the shot closely, and there had been no bullet splash on the water, either in front or behind the target. And when you hit the brain, there is no fanfare.

I seated myself in a Mapagoro Tree[76] and waited while Harold and Dave went looking for another hippo. After a while I heard another shot. Harold had got one also, but Dave's hadn't popped up yet. Another thirty minutes in the tree, and Dave's hippo bobbed to the surface, the gastrointestinal gasses finally inflating the animal, like helium does a balloon.

Two villagers waded into the lake and towed the hippo in until it touched bottom. Then a team of several rolled it over a few times into knee-deep water and started cutting it up. Hippo meat is a lot like pork, I'm told, but as the butchering proceeded, a complaint arose: "Hamna mafuta, hamna mafuta!"[77] Evidently my brother had done the impossible and shot a skinny hippo.

Still, all in all, everybody was happy. Harold's hippo was sufficiently fat for local tastes, and there was plenty of meat, fatty or not. The Game Scouts and the villagers were pleased that a couple of the Visigoths had been shot and the rest scared away for a while. And we were happy to have helped out and in the process garnered some hippo ivory, as both animals had large sets of teeth.

The next day we searched for elephant, but evidently it was too early for them in this area. The Game Scouts suggested we come back in a month or so, when the elephants would be as plentiful as ticks on a zebra. We said we would, and we did, and they were right.

---

[74] Land Rovers have lightweight aluminum, i.e., puny fenders.

Bro Arrives

75 The ruse about turning in the ivory as a government trophy did not work, however, and I did end up with two eighteen pound tusks on my license. If you are out there and you get charged, it's not the government's fault if you put yourself in front of a small one instead of a Hasan. You hunt them, you shoot them, you keep them. End of story, government version, the only version that counts.

76 Mapagoro trees have fist sized pods, and when these drop to the ground and ferment, animals, from monkeys to elephants, can get quite drunk on them. The question is: do inebriated elephants see pink people?

77 Hamna mafuta: the villagers were complaining that there was no fat, no fat.

Too small to shoot, if given a choice.

Dave extracting a nerve from a tusk. Note the honeycombed air pockets in the top part of the skull, and holes at the end of the tusks that housed the nerves.

CHAPTER 30

Travels with Dave

A few days after our hippo hunt, Dave and I set out to visit some game parks and Nairobi, and generally to give Dave a chance to see more of this amazing part of Africa.

The first day we made Kondoa, 150 miles south of Arusha, and spent the night at a government rest house: round, clean, white-washed, with a thatch roof. These accommodations were few and far between, but were kept up in out of the way places at government expense for traveling civil servants and other important government employees, namely us. If occupied, tough luck, you slept in your car or maybe wrangled some space on the floor. But on this day it was available, so we looked up the man in charge, a local caretaker, pronounced our worthiness, and got the key.

The next day we left for Moshi, but we had only covered a few of the 200 miles to our destination when the road presented a cavity six feet across and four feet deep. We came to a dust raising, rock spewing stop and surveyed the ditch, a perfect impediment. We were well equipped, as usual, so Dave broke out the panga. We partially filled the gap with boulders, tapered the edges with the machete, and within the hour were back in the saddle. About two miles further on, we stopped at a Public Works Department building to inform them that the road was out. There were four gents playing a game of mbao,[78] fully aware of the situation, and fully involved in their game.

We spent Christmas eve at Jack Humbles' place in Moshi. Our Christmas present on Christmas Day was a trip through Tsavo National Park, just across the border in Kenya. We saw lots of the usual game, plus an impressive male waterbuck sitting in tall grass, and two oryx.

It started to rain as we left for Nairobi, making the clay of the main road very slick. In a hilly stretch we came up behind a Mercedes going ever so slow. As we came to a sharp, banked curve, the driver slowed even further and gravity took over, pulling him down to the edge and sticking him there. Dave and I got out to help and found an Indian man and his family, totally addled by the conditions. We pushed them into motion and advised they keep their speed up enough to negotiate the curves. At the

Travels with Dave

next banked curve, he did an encore, much to our dismay. We got out again, in the mud and rain, and repeated our performance and advice, but this time, once we got them moving, we zipped around them and continued on our way. We were not about to push them all the way to Nairobi.

In the big city we shopped, had a soft ice-cream cone and some Chinese food, and spent most of one day at the Nairobi Snake Museum and in the Nairobi Game Park. There were lots of snakes to view, and the least impressive, behind glass, were the mambas. The cobras and puff adders were impressive. The mambas were small, and from the safety on the other side of a glass partition looked like slender, innocuous grass snakes, though they did have those coffin-shaped heads. The hundred square mile game park on the edge of the city was mostly open, undulating country. Though small, it nevertheless had an abundance of game, sans elephant and rhino. The park was fenced due to its proximity to the city, and elephant and rhino are not user friendly when it comes to fences.

From Nairobi we headed south for Tanganyika, through another famous park. Amboseli is on the other side of Kilimanjaro from Tsavo, and is less brushy, and therefore not as interesting. In Tsavo you are more the hunter, the game not always out in plain sight. That waterbuck we saw in Tsavo was spotted with a hunter's peripheral vision. We were following yet another slow Mercedes and were eager to get to Mzima Springs to see the hippo and croc, while these people were gawking for game. They totally missed the buck, but I caught a glimpse of it out of the corner of my eye while attempting to nudge them along, as one dung beetle does another. We stopped and photographed this beautiful animal, relaxed and chewing its cud about thirty yards from the road in knee-high grass.

One thing that Amboseli does offer, however, is rhino. We saw the daughter of Gerti,[79] now fully grown, but without ears. She was born earless, but since she stayed in the park and was protected, this was no great handicap, or so one would think. Mature rhino have nothing to fear but lions after their young and man, and their chief defense, besides their bulk and aggressive demeanor, is their well-developed sense of hearing. I would see this particular rhino several times when I was later stationed in nearby Arusha. But on one visit I didn't see her and inquired of the game scouts. They said she had been killed by Masai: speared several times, eventually succumbing to her wounds. The Masai are certainly brave, and not shy about proving it, but this was sad news.

After Amboseli we spent the night in my future home, Arusha. By this time I had been through here four or five times, and I liked this small town, nicely laid out and with enough altitude to guarantee a pleasant climate. We replaced our muffler the next day, had a couple of holes in the gas tank soldered, and away we went, south for Iringa and Malangali.

In mid-January, Alf Schofield and I went to a conference for history teachers in Tabora, and Dave came along for the ride. We drove to Dodoma and took the train from there to Tabora. The roads were decent for January, but Alf didn't help the rear springs any. Dave purchased a first class[80] ticket, 100/- ($14), for the 450 mile round trip so he could ride with us important government employees, but 'first class' was something of a misnomer, there being only three very crowded first class cars on the train. In fact, they were so crowded we had to stand all the way on the return leg of the trip.

A noteworthy aspect of the conference was the number of White Fathers present representing the Catholic Schools. These men were always intelligent and caring, and good conversationalists. But the most interesting aspect of the trip was a visit to the leprosarium on the outskirts of Tabora. Ellen Dodge, a teacher in my TEA group, drove us out there, and that in itself was an adventure. She drove like an abstraction, a Pollock to be precise. I could not help gritting my teeth and planting my feet firmly on the floor. It was small comfort knowing that we were at least headed in the direction of a hospital.

When we arrived, miraculously in one piece and not in need of intensive care, we found the hospital to be run by an American mission. Before being admitted, we were remonstrated to treat these patients as people, not lepers. Staring was strongly discouraged.

Leprosy is a wasting disease caused by the germ Mycobacterium Leprae. This microorganism was discovered in 1873 by the Norwegian, Dr. Armauer Hansen, and hence is sometimes called Hansen's Disease. Dr. Hansen showed that leprosy was not hereditary, not caused by a curse, and not punishment for sin, commonly held beliefs in various parts of the world.

Leprosy causes skin lesions, the thickening of peripheral nerve endings leading to loss of sensitivity and loss of extremities like fingers, toes, ears and nose, and upper respiratory problems. The untreated disease is contagious, though the exact method of transmission is not clearly understood. Physical contact, respiration, insects and mucus are considered likely possibilities. A study in 1977 reported that in tropical conditions M.leprae in nasal secretions could survive for up to nine days, thus opening up the prospect of getting the disease from contaminated clothing, food, utensils, etc.

The patients we visited were somewhat shy, but nevertheless receptive to our presence. We shook hands with fingerless people, passed pleasantries, and tried not to stare or look horrified. The hardest sight to treat nonchalantly was a face with no nose. Leprosy once affected every continent and where is still exists,[81] it still results in mutilation, rejection, and exclusion from society. However the people here did not sit around idly bemoaning their fate. They were surprisingly upbeat, and had become skillful artisans. We bought several items from them, including a bow with arrows, a drum, and a spear.

The return train got us to Dodoma at eight in the evening, and we left directly for Iringa with Alf footing the gas bill. Dave and I had used all of our money for souvenirs and gifts, and since Alf had not previously offered to share expenses, we relied on his wallet to get us home. We stole into Dieraufs' about one o'clock in the morning.

Travels with Dave

The next day we purchased some essential commodities and headed back to Malangali and the start of a new school year.

---

[78] Mbao is played on a board with two rows of pits filled with seeds or stones. The object is to "eat" your opponent's seeds, like capturing chess pieces, and a good player will plan several moves in advance, again like chess. In places without a board, holes the size of a cupped hand are dug into the ground and pebbles, kernels of corn, seeds, etc. serve as the pieces. Like little kids playing soccer with a ball of tied up rags, mbao can be played on the cheap.

[79] Gerti was famous for her five-foot long horn and appeared in many magazines and even a couple of movies. Female rhino have longer, more slender horns than the males, but Gertie's was exceptional, and probably more of a nuisance than useful, much like the two-foot long fingernails grown by some Chinese men of high class before Mao arrived with his 7.62 caliber clippers. Of course there is a connection here, as rhino horn and Chinese fingernails are made of the same basic substance, keratin. Further, this connection takes an odd turn when you consider the Asian belief that rhino horn is a powerful aphrodisiac. You would think they could just chew their own keratin when horny and leave the naturally horny rhino alone and alive.

[80] Yes, evidently there were still first class people in socialist Tanganyika.

[81] As detailed by American Leprosy Missions, 91 countries reported leprosy in 1999/2000. In order, the ten countries with the most cases of leprosy were: India (73% of the total), Brazil, Myanmar (Burma), Indonesia, Nepal, Madagascar, Ethiopia, Mozambique, The Democratic Republic of the Congo, and Tanzania

Dave repairing road with all the tools at our disposal.

Eland in Nairobi Game Park.

Huge tembo in Amboseli Game Park. Tusks over 100 lbs. each.

Cheetah in Amboseli.

CHAPTER 31

Zanzibar

In mid-January, rumors were careening wildly around Malangali like bats in flight. Troops had mutinied in Dar, a bloody uprising had taken place on Zanzibar, and locally, all the Protestant missionaries in the Southern Highlands had fled to Mbeya, ready to bolt to Zambia at the first sign of political instability. These were the rumors. Due to the confusion in Dar, we in the hinterlands didn't get much hard news until towards the end of the month.

The first rumor to be confirmed, at least by word of mouth, was that indeed there had been an inordinately large gathering of Protestant missionaries in Mbeya, and yes, they did seem to have their vehicles packed to the brim, and yes, they were getting documentation that would allow them to enter Zambia. Oh ye of little faith!

While this local act seemed like some comic confusion straight out of Shakespeare, the news filtering in from Dar es Salaam was anything but amusing. At first we received reports that the mutiny in Dar had been just about wages and promotions, but had no racial overtones or revolutionary intent. This sounded like relatively good news, but rang hollow. Since the officers were British and white, and the Tanganyikan army was in formation and training mode, promotions were likely to be slow in coming, at least for the foreseeable future. And further, what do armies do? They protect and support, or overthrow, governments.

A few days later there was some clarification and it seems the situation was more serious than originally reported. Some twenty people were killed, the British officers were shipped off to Nairobi, and the government quickly acceded to the troops' demands. This of course put the government in a very vulnerable position, accenting its basic lack of muscle and inviting all sorts of future trouble. In Africa a sick or wounded animal doesn't last long.

Then news, mostly on the BBC, started trickling in about a bloody revolution in Zanzibar. It seems the mainland mutiny had come on the heels of the African overthrow of the Arab dominated government on the island, and had possibly been the result of an airborne virus wafting across the Zanzibar Channel, infecting the troops in Dar.

Hunting and Teaching in East Africa

In any case, Nyerere was not about to roll over and let his government suffer the same fate as the newly independent government of Zanzibar. As soon as he agreed to the demands of the army, he called on the old colonial power to come and bail him out. The British sent troops to Dar, the army was disarmed, and once disarmed, disbanded. Court-martials followed immediately, and the police fanned out across the country to round up trouble-makers. In Malangali, local union leaders were rounded up and whisked off to the poki. One of our clerks was netted, as was the headmaster of the middle school up the road. Evidently the unions were mixed up in the army rebellion, or the leaders had been too visibly vocal and hostile to Nyerere's recent statement that all citizens of Tanganyika would be treated equally, and qualifications, not race, would be the criterion for selection to government jobs, and promotions.

Tanganyika settled down quickly, and in fact our students were quite embarrassed by the whole thing. Not only did the affair make their country look like one of those South American Banana Republics, but the cavalry riding to the rescue was British. Zanzibar, however, was a different matter.

Zanzibar had been known to the Egyptians, Phoenicians, Greeks and Romans long before the time of Christ. By the 8th Century, the Arabs controlled the trade routes along the East African Coast and this preeminence was strengthened in the 12th Century by the Shirazi, an Arab trading empire based on the nearby island of Kilwa Kisiwani. As the Arabs settled among the Bantu-speaking residents of the islands, a new culture developed, resulting from the spread of Islam and the gradual formulation of the trade language Swahili.

Vasco da Gama, and the Portuguese who followed him, interrupted Arab hegemony for a couple of hundred years, but in 1729, the Sultan of Oman reasserted Arab dominance, a dominance sanctioned by the British from the time of Sultan Sayyid Said, in the mid-1800s, until independence in December of 1963. This minority control of the island's political and economic life met with little resistance until 1948, when the mainland independence movement inspired Zanzibari dock workers and trade unionists to protest British colonialism and Arab dominance. As ethnic divisions deepened, the Arabs, Asians, and Africans began to create their own civic and political organizations.

The British tried to meld these competing interests into a functioning parliamentary government under Sultan Jamshid. Elections were held from 1957, with the African parties winning, but the Arab parties prevailing. The last such election was held in 1963, with the African party garnering over 54% of the vote, but the minority parties gaining a plurality in the Legislative Council. The British accepted these dubious results, declared Zanzibar independent on December 10, 1963, gathered up their troops, and left.

A month later a Ugandan named John Okello ignited African resentment and overthrew the Sultan's government. Hundreds of Indians and Arabs were killed, how many, no one knows for sure. An Italian photographer flew over the island shortly after the revolution and took some disturbing pictures of large mass graves full of bodies. Estimates range from 2000 to 20,000 dead. Navin and Azmina Hasham, two Asian pre-teens who would later become my nieces, had to scramble across the roofs of shops to escape detection, and perhaps death. Another future relative, Nizar Bawa, was a government employee at the time and he estimates the dead at 4000 to 5000. Okello himself put the toll at 13,000.

Most of the carnage came in the days following the flight of the sultan. Settling old scores and the fear of reprisals fueled a killing spree led by the charismatic but unstable Okello. He demonstrated his eccentricity with his attachment to symbolic numbers. For example on January 13, 1964, he broadcast the following messages: "The government is now run by us....should you be stubborn and disobey orders I will take measures 88 times stronger than at present." and, "If anyone fails to comply... and locks himself in a house, as others have done...I have no alternative but to use heavy weapons. We, the army have the strength of 99,099,000."

His threats and his ability to act on them panicked citizens, especially minority groups of all types. On January 14, 1964 he broadcast these chilling words.

> "Here is the Field Marshall of Zanzibar and Pemba....I am thinking of going to Mtendeni (village) to destroy it if the people there do not obey orders. After 40 minutes I am coming to finish you off, especially the Comorians". And "To all Arab youths living in Malindi; I will pass through Malindi armed with weapons of which I alone know. I want to see everyone stripped to his underpants and laying down. I want to hear them singing...father of Africans. God bless him in his task and that of the Field Marshall." [82]

Okello had no political standing on the island,[83] however, and soon Sheikh Abeid Armani Karume, head of the Afro-Shirazi party, formed a coalition with the radical Umma Party and installed himself as the new head of government. Fearing resurgent opposition and perhaps outright foreign intervention, Karume cast about for a protective umbrella. He immediately initiated negotiations with Nyerere and a marriage of convenience was arranged. On April 26, 1964, the United Republic of Tanzania and Zanzibar[84] was formed. Karume got a measure of security and legitimacy, Nyerere got a handle on this volatile island and hoped he could tame the passions and politics of Karume and his communist followers without fouling his own nest.

Under this new arrangement Zanzibar retained a great deal of economic and internal independence. The Zanzibaris elected their own president, who controlled Zanzibar internal affairs and served in the national government as one of two vice-presidents under the Tanzanian president. In addition, Tanzania gave the much smaller Zanzibar overrepresentation in the National Assembly (50 of 169 seats) and control over its own judicial system. Despite these concessions, however, some Zanzibaris, even Karume himself, viewed the union as a mainland plot to take over the island.

Although Karume had initiated and agreed to the union, he did much to prevent real economic and political unity between the countries and consequently guided Zanzibar on a course separate from the mainland. Dismissing Nyerere's socialist program as ineffectual, Karume attempted to institute hard-line communism in Zanzibar.

He nationalized private property and deported Asian non-citizens, who he said were plotting to take over the economy. He also sought to boost export revenues by building new state-run clove plantations with funding from Cuba, China, Bulgaria, East Germany and the U.S.S.R. But persistent economic stagnation combined with unpopular social laws, such as a mandate for interracial marriages between Africans and Arabs, cost Karume public support. In 1972 he was killed by an unknown assassin.

For those of us in Malangali all of this was distant, and life went on as usual. School had started and Dave was due to go home soon. He and I were focusing on a return trip to Lake Rukwa.

---

[82] http://home.globalfrontiers.com/zanzibar/zanzibar_revolution.htm

[83] Okello would return to his homeland and disappear from history in the morass of Idi Amin's Uganda.

[84] In October of 1964, the name changed to The Repbulic of Tanzania. Tanzania sounds like some effete flower. 'Tanganyika,' there was a name with muscle and verve.

CHAPTER 32

Dave's Elephant

As the events along the coast unfolded, Dave and I departed Malangali for one last safari together. Hunting with my brother was always a pleasure, but especially so here in Africa. With elephant and buffalo, things could get exciting and unpredictable. In a tight situation, the last thing you wanted was a nervous companion behind you with a loaded gun. Though Harold had a cool head, he had no previous hunting experience or familiarity with guns. When it came time to close on dangerous game, I would proceed ahead alone, dependent on my own resources, but on the other hand comforted in the knowledge that if life came to a sudden halt, at least it would not be because my backup got excited and blew my head off.[85] With Dave, I had no such concerns.

We had not been able to get him an elephant yet and the game scouts at Lake Rukwa had assured us there would be plenty of them in the area come February. On the way to Luika, the game scouts' headquarters near the lake, the generator on Harold's Rover gave out, again, but we made it, and elephants were indeed about. The next morning we drove further up the road along the southeast corner of the lake and soon cut tracks crossing the road into the fresh, brilliantly green grass born of the rains.

After an easy hour and a half walk through knee-high grass populated with clumps of trees and thorny brush, we came onto our first group of elephant. The next hour was spent following and evaluating a couple of them, one with longer but thinner tusks than the other. Dave and I made the approach, but in trying to decide which had the heavier ivory, they got our wind and charged off, but in different directions. We followed what we considered the larger one, and within the hour Harold spotted its back through a screen of trees.

Leaving Harold and the guides behind, Dave and I once again stalked forward. At about thirty yards, the elephant suddenly started to move rapidly crossing our line of march. Dave shot and it whirled toward us. We both fired head-on and it changed course for some thick bush off to our left. Dave's initial shot had raised a pouf of dust on impact, indicating a perfectly placed heart shot, so I figured it would not go far.

Hunting and Teaching in East Africa

About a hundred yards off, and before it could reach the patch of thick stuff, the big bull turned sideways to us and minced about in place. Dave was eager to pursue, but before I could finish my cautionary tale about avoiding an unnecessary flattening, the elephant collapsed. Dave wanted to fire the .500 so he finished it off with my rifle at point blank range just as it raised up in an effort to regain its feet.

We gathered up Harold and the guides and returned to the Rover. Dave stayed with the vehicle, to try and fix the generator, while Harold and I went back with the guides, taking just the .375 as it was much lighter than the .500. The job of extracting the ivory began, but as a storm was threatening Harold headed back for the Rover with the .375, to keep it dry, an example of socialist planning in its purest form: take something that isn't a problem, and turn it into one.

By late afternoon, the guides and I returned with the ivory. Harold was not a happy camper. He had gotten soaked, as the storm had reached the Rover before he did. As for me, I didn't help matters any by happily recounting how I had escaped with only a light sprinkle by dodging under a tree right near the elephant. By now the storm had long since passed and Harold was getting steam cleaned in the heat. Soon he would be as good as new, though not without complaint. I tried to explain that since we were in a socialist country, we had just practiced a small measure of socialist planning, and it had turned out just as it should have. Sometimes H. didn't seem to have the sense of humor you would expect from a minister's son.

The next morning we went after buffalo as Dave wanted a nice horn and not one broken off half way up one branch, like the one he had shot earlier. Elephants were all around us, gurgling their stomachs and occasionally letting out a trumpet blast, but we had no license for another one. Buffalo, for which we did have a license, were not to be found.

There were plenty of kanga, however. These noisy birds are always calling attention to themselves with their loud, abrasive cackling. Dave had brought a twelve-gauge pump with him, so we decided guinea hen would be a welcome change of diet. We approached a large flock, and when they flew, Dave went into action. On the first shot one crumpled and as the guides made a move to fetch it the gun went off again; and again. They were amazed: one barrel, three shots. The shotguns prevalent in Africa were single or double barreled, and the number of barrels determining the number of shots. They were quite impressed with this marvelous gun, and also with the fact that three birds had bit the dust. Dinner would be good.

We made it back to Malangali on our generator, as Dave had somehow managed to coax some current out of it. It had been a pleasant and successful last hunt, and Dave was pleased at the result. The ivory weighed in just shy of fifty pounds per tusk, so it was the biggest on my licenses in those first two years.

The following weekend I drove Dave to Iringa so he could catch the bus to Dar es Salaam. School had started, so that was as far as I could take him. We played tennis and bridge with the Dieraufs, weighed the ivory, got ownership certificates for Dave's hippo and warthog tusks, and said our good-byes.

Dave's Elephant

It had been great having Bro over for three months, but the following Monday was rough. For the first time since arriving at this small, remote village, I felt homesick, deep-in-the-pit-of-the-stomach homesick.

---

[85] Read Hemingway's The Short Happy Life of Francis Macomber.

Dave's hippo finally filled with gas and bobbed to the surface. Two of the local men waded out and towed it to shallow water for butchering. Lake Rukwa - Dec. 1963.

Game scout, Harold and Dave with upper and lower jaws of hippo taken at Lake Rukwa.

Dave and I with his tembo: tusks were 50 lbs. each. Lake Rukwa area.

Removing elephant teeth is not delicate work.

Dave's Elephant

The tusks are embeded in bone to behind the eyeball

Dave and guides back at the Roiver with Dave's tusks.

CHAPTER 33

Back to School

Monday did come, the sun made its usual appearance, school was in session, and thankfully there was work to do. We had four new staff members, including a replacement for Kabati, a relief to all. Lawa, Ndunguru, and Muhitira were the three new African teachers, the last two straight out of teacher training, and Lawa with only a high school diploma. Lawa was in transition from school to teaching to university, he hoped, but Muhitira had no such visions and instead was stuck in the only too real and ugly position of teaching English to Form III. Since his linguistic proficiency was no better than many of the students, it would be interesting.

Our new headmaster was an elderly man named Mabele. Unlike Kabati, he was a quiet fellow, not given to speech making, showmanship, or butt kissing. Kabati it seemed had three priorities: pucker for the politicians; research and catalog every beer joint between Malangali and Mufindi and Iringa; and spread as much joy as possible to the female population of Southern Tanganyika. In contrast, Mabele actually taught classes, and when not teaching he plied himself to the tasks of running the school, a concept seemingly lost on Kabati.

Mabele did have one vice in common with his predecessor, however. He did like his pombe. But at least he kept it local, only going the eight miles to Njiapanda for his fluids. Though his drinking did not interfere with his performance as headmaster, there was one small problem. The road **to** Njiapanda was a pleasant, tree lined boulevard, but the road back, when the driver was laden with alcohol, was a whole different matter. It would narrow ever so much, and grow bumpy, twisty, and with rain, slippery. Twice Mabele planted his Peugeot in the ditch after a session in Njiapanda. Twice he appeared the worse for wear on Monday mornings, complete with knots and bruises about his head. But he was a fast learner and after these first two lessons he hired a driver to negotiate that chameleon-like, post pombe, road back to Malangali.

Whereas Kabati was a jovial pudge full of charm, good humor and cow droppings, Mabele was darker in color and mood, craggy faced, angular, and conscientious. He had a slow, purposeful gait coupled to a once athletic body with squared, if slightly age-stooped shoulders. He had graduated secondary school in 1939 when

Back to School

there were only two such schools in the territory: Tabora and Minake. He then went into teaching and Kabati was one of his students, somewhere along the line.

Mabele was politically active in his youth and was one of the founders of the precursor to TANU, before Nyerere moved in and changed a debating society into an independence movement. Rumor was that when Nyerere and his young lions moved in, the old lion was eased aside; too old in thought and too compliant in attitude. Mabele seldom mentioned this part of his life, but he was fairly sour towards TANU and Nyerere, and he took no guff from the local potentates. Politically he was a relic, but like an ancient warrior he had respect, and like an endangered species, he had protection. I shuddered to think what views he might have expressed at the pombe shop in Njiapanda, but whatever, if the grog loosened his tongue, and I suspect it did, the normally heavy handed regional and area commissioners lifted not a finger in admonition.

Mabele's modus operandi became apparent when some of the boys strayed beyond acceptable bounds. One evening while I was on duty word came to my house that there was a problem in the village. I rounded up the five inebriated students, escorted them to their dorms, and informed Mabele. There was no showy baraza, no loud proclamation of irate indignation, no canes applied to miscreant buttocks, no playing to the elders or other dignitaries. The five were immediately suspended and sent home, and the two who had propositioned some local women were never to return. The days of Kabati: "Heap big smoke but no fire,"[86] were gone. The effect on the school was immediate and sobering. Discipline and accountability had returned.

During this time I was trying to tie up several loose ends. I was applying for a scholarship at Northwestern University in Evanston, Illinois, but at the same time trying to make sure I could get back into the TEA program after I got my degree. I also had an elephant license to fill before leaving, one gun to somehow get licensed, one gun and a car to sell, travel plans to make, and storage to arrange for my goods and gun while I was gone.

The tuition scholarship came through in April, and even though TEA was being phased out, I did get in just under the wire and could return in 1965. The elephant license did not go to waste, though it took two safaris to fill, and eventually I sold the .500 for what I paid, and sold the car for the price of a good hat. The .375 I managed to get transferred from Dave's name to mine, through deceit and lies, but more on this later.

---

[86] Taken from a popular song of the 1950's.

CHAPTER 34

Lake Rukwa, One Last Time

Excitement is hunting elephant in tall grass. To exponentially increase that excitement, do it solo, do it among cows and calves, and throw in a cranky old tusk-less cow for good measure. And how about those babies? Mama elephants are **very**, as in single-minded-stomp-you-to-jelly, protective of their young, so just how close can you get to a wild baby elephant and live to tell about it? No hunter in his right mind would intentionally inject himself into such a mess unless he had suicidal tendencies or was just plain stupid, and I was definitely not suicidal.

The long rains had been light, so as the April break approached I was optimistic about the roads to Lake Rukwa and eager to get another set of heavy tusks. However, I had a rifle in my possession that I wanted to use but since it was in Dave's name, and therefore under my roof illegally, I dare not. On the Saturday before school let out, I screwed up my courage, drove into Iringa, entered the police office in a manufactured huff, and excitedly proclaimed: "Look at this mess! Those idiots in Dar not only gave me a visitor's license for my Winchester .375, they even got my first name wrong. Can you fix this?" The officer in charge was very understanding, being colonial British while the 'idiots' in Dar were without doubt African. He said he would fix it posthaste. Of course there was no such thing as posthaste in Tanganyika. He did transfer the gun into my name, but the actual license would have to come from the capital. That would not be instantaneous, and this little technicality rendered the gun inoperable for the foreseeable future. The .500 would have to do.

Two weeks into April I loaded up the Simca and left for Luika, alone. The last part of March Harold and I had gone to Rujewa for a weekend hunt, and while he bagged a topi and an impala, the mosquitoes bagged him. He had fed them well, but the ingrates repaid his hospitality with a bad case of malaria and I had to take him to the hospital in Iringa.

My optimism about the roads proved to be misplaced. I did make it to Luika, but the road from Mbeya was terribly rutted and gouged; and wet. I hired two guides and at first hunted out of Luika. The grass was high and pretty much everywhere. Earlier, when Dave and I had hunted there, the grass was just getting started and was only

Lake Rukwa, One Last Time

about knee to thigh high, but now it was eight feet tall and thick as the green on a frog's back. I didn't like it, but here I was, and there were tembo mingi[87].

For two days, the guides and I picked our way through the vegetation, mostly using the paths tamped down by the elephants. There was plenty of fresh spoor: footprints, steaming dung, and foaming urine, but in this maze they had created we couldn't find the elephants themselves.

After two days of fruitless, but nevertheless nerve-wracking stalking, I drove down to the lakeshore to have a beer with Mr. Nell, the proprietor of the Outspan Hotel.[88] The water had invaded the hotel, and Nell said it could go at any time. Just then a brisk squall came up and I noticed a crack in one of the main pillars growing wider and wider. The walls went slightly off perpendicular, and in a blink, the hotel was gone. The roof caved in, the walls gave way, and in a cloud of dust and spray, the hotel slid into the lake.

The Outspan was built in 1934-35 and would have stood for decades, but for the lake reaching it and gnawing away the foundation. Missionaries told Nell that in the north the lake had pushed some twenty miles beyond its normal highs. Nell estimated that it had expanded two to three miles here at the south end, where the land was much steeper. Ten years ago the lake had been a gigantic mud hole, and now it was growing like an out of control cancer, devouring crops and villages, and the Outspan Hotel.

The next day the guides and I decided to get more remote, so we slithered as far as the Simca could take us up the southeast side of the lake, about twelve miles past Luika. On the way we had to abandon the car at one point, as we were inundated with tsetse flies. It seemed the diminished rains had done nothing to stunt this bumper crop. They were so thick inside the car that my eyes blurred out of focus and teared up. We bailed, but after treating this infestation with pyrethrum spray, we reclaimed the Simca and continued on our way. We set up camp near a stream and I took a long cool bath in a deep pool. It was a nice campsite, green and restful, with several tall trees for company. That night I fell asleep as a male lion at some distance lent melody to the dancing of the stars. One of the joys of Africa: a clear night void of civilized distractions, the stars brilliant overhead, a serenade floating out of the dark.

So far this hunt had been uneventful, but for the high tension of nosing around in tall, thick grass with fresh elephant sign, and therefore elephants, all over the place. The next day would make up for it. The guides and I left camp just after sun-up, immediately crossing more fresh droppings. We worked our way to the top of a small knoll, and off about a quarter of a mile we could see the gray, curved backs of several elephants, a flapping ear occasionally adding animation to an otherwise static scene. We checked the wind and planned our stalk. Using the elephant trails through the grass, we eventually got close enough to hear their stomachs rumbling and I scrambled up a small tree for a better look. Somehow, the two guides managed to secure a perch just below me, and though the elephants were only about thirty yards off, we were having a difficult time spotting any ivory through all the greenery. Then, just below us, on the other side of the tree, the greenery started to move. The guides took one astonished look and bolted, in instantaneous recognition that this was not a good thing. I stayed put, concentrating on the waving grass as the small, unseen pachyderm scampered toward the safety of the adults. When the little snitch was about half way, without an alarm being sounded that I could hear, the entire herd suddenly swung around and in a perfect semicircle charged in my direction, ears back, trunks held high. I wasn't too concerned, as I was downwind, and the tree trunk and branches effectively broke up my silhouette, but nevertheless it was a relief when they pulled up short, about fifteen yards off. They stood there cocking their heads back and forth, their dim eyes searching, their trunks raised for scent and ears spread for sound. I remained silent and still, only blinking a tsetse fly out of my eyes. He lit on my neck and settled in for a meal. He could have all he wanted. I could deal as easily with him as those elephants could deal with me, so I would take a pass on squashing him to keep the elephants from performing a schottische on me. After a few tense minutes the elephants lost interest and moved off, their hulks slowly swallowed by the sea of grass. I eased my way down and went to find my guides, but they were on their way back to me, and we met up less than a hundred yards from the baby elephant tree.

As best I could with my limited Swahili, I recounted the event. They just shook their heads and turned down a wide elephant boulevard, headed in the general direction of camp. We hadn't got far when an elephant to our right let out a piercing shriek. One of the guides jumped up a small tree and reported a tusk-less cow karibu sana.[89] The guide, every fiber in his body primed for flight, watched her intensely as she milled about, embroiled in a tantrum. "Here she comes," he said as he started down the tree. "No, no, she has stopped." The guide inched back up the tree, only to repeat this same performance. As he regained his position the second time, he watched her for a few seconds when a blood curdling scream from the old gal sent him flying, his partner close at heel.

They fled right down the middle of the ten-foot wide swath. If the irate elephant did break cover, she would certainly see them, so I ran a few yards in their direction and to the far side of the path, planting myself into the grass deep enough for concealment, but in position to intercept, .500 at my shoulder, should she make an appearance. She didn't. She did continue to complain about our presence, however, but she was just being surly, a common enough tendency among elephants when humans invade their sanctum. For most females, this attitude stems from their concern for the young, but this old gal was extra touchy, no doubt nursing a severe case of ivory envy.

It took me about five minutes to hunt up my guides, one of them up a tree having a careful look-see, the other semi-shoeless. One shoe had been sucked off his foot by the muck of the trail, but when I suggested we go find it, he demurred. That shoe was as valuable to him as the Simca was to me, so surrendering it out of hand was an indication of how scary, and perhaps foolish, he considered our exploits.

Lake Rukwa, One Last Time

While we were discussing our options, I was idly playing footsie with a piece of rotten log. Suddenly the guides got quite agitated. They pointed at the log, "Ngay, bwana, ngay." I didn't know what an ngay was and I wasn't paying much attention, but they got more and more excited and finally one of them grabbed me by the arm and pulled me away from my exercise. The other guide then pushed the slender log over with a stick, and then I knew what an ngay was: there were four of those almost translucent, shrimp colored scorpions under that rotted wood, and the more I rubbed it back and forth over them, the angrier they had become. When Mother Nature teaches you a new word, you don't forget it.

I suggested we try following up on another herd that we had seen that morning, but the man who had lost his shoe exclaimed, "Hapana, Bwana!"[90] He suggested we go back to camp and give up on the hunt as our luck was very bad: Bahati mbaya, kabisa.[91] The other guide was willing, but as we headed toward where we had seen this herd's tracks, old one-shoe convinced his partner to quit the hunt also. They headed us back toward camp and said they wouldn't even consider going out the following morning. They pointed out, correctly, that we hadn't seen a big print in four days, and cows and calves were nothing but trouble. The big bulls, according to them, were further up the lake, and this put them out of reach, as the Simca was at the end of her tether.

Hoping they might change their minds, I decided to stay over another night, and as a bonus I had this great campsite to enjoy: another dip in the stream, another night cocooned in a stand of stately trees under a black, sparkling sky, and, hopefully, another performance by the baritone.

Morning came, and minds had not changed. Hating to leave, I hunted a few miles up the road, hoping to get lucky, and lingered around camp, but toward nightfall we loaded up and glided back into Luika. I paid the guides, said goodbye to them and the game scouts, and left for Mbeya, just as the sun was going down. In sympathy with the setting sun, my generator let out its last spark also. To save the battery, I drove the final thirty miles to Mbeya by flashlight.

---

[87] Tembo mingi means many elephants, the opinion not only of my guides, but also of the two game scouts at Luika.

[88] Not to be confused with the Outspan Hotel/Aberdare Country Club, built in the late 1920's in Nyeri, Kenya, and still in business in the Kenya highlands, with Mt. Kenya to the northeast and the Aberdare Mountains to the west.

[89] Karibu sana means very close, in this case about twenty yards or so, judging from the sound.

[90] Hapana, Bwana = No, Sir.

[91] Bahati mbaya kabisa means, in order: luck; bad; totally, completely, irredeemably.

CHAPTER 35

The Rain Forest, Again

Whereas the hunt in the tall grasses edging Lake Rukwa was a matter of circumstance, returning to the rain forest around Dabaga was a conscious decision, a triumph of necessity and optimism over experience. The rains in the Malangali area had been sparse so I had assumed the same held for Lake Rukwa. The fact that I had been wrong didn't alter the situation. I was there, I had a license to fill, there were tembo mingi, and the less than ideal conditions left me with but two choices: turn around, or go hunting. The first option didn't even register. Hunting elephant is always difficult, but unlike Olympic diving, you don't get to choose the degree of difficulty. And so it was with this second go at the rain forest. I still had a license to fill, the forest was permanent home to plenty of elephant, and the degree of difficulty was a concern, but not negotiable.

Nicoderm was always eager to go on safari as it was a good break from the dorm life at school, plus Dabaga was home to many of his relatives. Also, Ray Cairncross, a Peace Corps teacher at the middle school, was excited about the prospect of going on an elephant hunt. Ray and his wife Mimi had arrived in Malangali a few months earlier. They were a welcome addition to our little American enclave, he a tall, handsome blond, and she a petite, pretty brunette. And, they were from Olympia, just thirty miles down the road from Tacoma, so we had lots to talk about.

We slept at the trade school in Ifunda Friday night and arrived in Dabaga about 8:30 on a mid-June Saturday morning. My frazzled Simca just barely made some of the hills. Not only was it worn and tired, but I had installed some heavy duty springs under the rear end, after busting the originals for the umpteenth time, and the car bounced along like a pogo stick, thus constantly losing traction.

By 9:30 we had guides et al and departed cross country for a certain house which was to be our base. We had porters to carry our blankets, food, water, and my Winchester, and after a brisk two-hour walk through this beautiful, green, lush country, we arrived at our destination. I had sold my .500, and the .375 was now my rifle of choice. The Winchester had one disadvantage: it was only about 60% as powerful as the bigger rifle, but even so, that wasn't all bad. At least when I pulled the trigger

The Rain Forest, Again

I got to keep the skin on the front sides of any fingers in the trigger housing. Though considered something of a peashooter in East Africa, to me the .375 had several advantages. First and foremost was accuracy: a bolt action with a scope, my favorite combination. The second advantage was that I could cram four rounds into the thing. I would much rather have four anemic rounds to offer up accurately, than two hand grenades to lob hopefully. Karamojo Bell, after all, used a .275! In addition, the Winchester was about six pounds lighter, well balanced and not at all barrel heavy, and I had cut my teeth on bolt action rifles. The double was beautiful, a work of art, and I was a sucker for any beauty with nice barrels. But beauty, even with a great looking set of barrels, is not everything.

Around noon we headed off into the forest. We didn't come across elephants until four hours later, and then it was another hour and a half before I shot one. There were about fifty in the herd, scattered all about, so it was tricky poking around in the dense cover trying to locate one with good tusks. At any moment an errant breeze could inform on us and send the herd charging through the brush, in one direction or another. After much tense stalking it was getting late on what I knew would be my last day of hunting on my first tour. I would have to settle for half a loaf. Two of the guides and I crept along a rock cliff and got close to a bull with average-minus ivory. I shot him once in the heart, and as he ran, cranked another into the head. The second shot toppled him and he skidded down the hill for about twenty yards before crashing over a fallen log and coming to a stop.

Curiously, the other elephants did nothing. They didn't panic, they didn't charge, they just sort of stood their ground, mulling over the situation. Finally, three elders trotted off to the right. I felt they were possibly going to flank us, so I hustled along the base of the cliff, to keep them in sight. After a short exploratory jaunt they got my scent, pulled up, and after some indecision, returned to the main body. The whole herd hung around, mostly in the short brush that coated the hill opposite us. We could see their backs and the tops of their heads, and occasionally a flash of ivory. It was decidedly eerie.

After thirty minutes or so of this unusual behavior, and just before dark, they started to leave. Ray and the others came up and we clambered over, under and through the tangle of vegetation to inspect the dead bull. The elephant had fallen into such thick brush, overhung by towering trees, that only a stick of white shows up in my photographs. The ivory would go about thirty pounds a tusk: not good, not bad.

It was too late to go back, so we would spend the night in the forest, while our blankets, food and water would spend it back in the house that had been set aside for our comfort. The Wahehe got a couple of fires going, and soon we were supping on roasted elephant meat: juicy, tasty, with a mouth-watering aroma; and tough.

Darkness set in. There was no moon. Stars aplenty, but no moon. Ray expressed some concern. Was this safe? How about lions? I assured him there were no lions in the forest, though there were elephants, obviously, and leopard, and buffalo, and a fine representation of snakes. Ray was not mollified by this encouraging news, so I

Hunting and Teaching in East Africa

knew I would sleep relatively well. I settled in for the evening, as close to the fire as I could get without being singed, and fell asleep listening to the elephants trumpeting in the distance as they slowly munched their way deeper into the forest. Their complaints grew fainter as the distance between us increased, but when I occasionally woke up during the night, I could still hear them, their sad chorus of loss carried gently by the still, cool air.

Just before daylight, the coldest part of the night, I awoke, shivering and stiff. Ray was sitting up, close to the fire, a little disgruntled. He said he hadn't slept a wink. I tried to suppress a grin, but the effort backfired, the pressure was just too much, and I broke into a fit of laughter. First-timers make such good sentries.

Unlike my first hunt in this area, I had accumulated enough experience to avoid stupid decisions, refuse bad advice, and take control of the tactical aspects of stalking and closing on the quarry. The hunt had gone well, with no complications, and I was very happy with the performance of the .375.

We were back at the car around noon, and back in Malangali a couple hours after dark. I delivered a tired, bedraggled Ray to his door and a relieved Mimi bounced out and gave him a big hug and a kiss. Well!!! When I got home, I too was greeted with bounding love and affection. By Mitzy. My tail-wagging wiener dog.

It was good that Ray had spent a miserable night in the damp, cold rain forest.

CHAPTER 36

Leaving Home

I was to leave Iringa for Dar es Salaam on July 17 and leave Dar on the 22nd, and Nairobi on the 23rd. I would spend a week in both London and New York City as I made my way to Tacoma.

But after my last hunt I still had a month of school to finish up. The rains in most of the country had been light to non-existent, so famine relief poured in from the U.S. For the school this came in the form of rich, deep-gold, made in the U.S.A. corn flour. This was much more nutritious than the African maize meal, but the students were not used to it and were always complaining of stomach troubles. Still, rampant digestive disorders were not enough to waylay the safari I had planned for my Economics Society.

Ian Thomas and I escorted twenty-eight boys on a field trip to the township of Tukuyu in the Rungwe area just southeast of Mbeya. Several of our students were Nyakyusa,[92] so for them this was also a visit home. We were to see a tea factory, a soda factory, the cooperative shop, and other local businesses.

The school lorry hauled 26 of the students in the open bin in the back, while two rode with us in Ian's Peugeot. On the way there we saw a lion and three puff adders, one of which I have written about already. Ian was never much interested in animals and had been in the country since 1960 and never seen a lion. The road was dusty and undulating but straight, in the stretch where he was about to see his first.

Ian was driving, presumably with his eyes on the road, but as we crested one short rise a lion came into view, plainly resting in the middle of the road a couple of undulations ahead. We descended into a trough and I noticed that nothing had registered with my good, but unobservant friend. I asked, with a bit of a smirk on my face, if it was true that he had been in the country for four years and had never seen a lion. "Yes, but why do you ask?" "Because, if you don't slow down we are going to run one over!"

As we topped the next hillock, the lion was again visible, and Ian, in his best effort at enthusiasm emitted a "jolly good," as he slowed to let the beast labor to his feet and amble off into the bush.

We visited a tea plantation and then the processing factory. Tea was one of the main cash crops in Tanzania, and the aroma in the factory reminded me of the sweet smell of the cedar shingle mills around Gray's Harbor. This was in stark contrast to a coffee factory I had visited near Dar, where the fetid smell of rotting pulp was almost over-whelming. A coffee berry is much like a pie cherry in size and color, except the pulp is waste and was flushed out the end of the building to pool in the hot sun and ferment and rot. The pits, or beans,[93] are then dried in the sun: millions of off-white, slightly fuzzy kernels spread one layer thick over woven reed mats. The beans are rotated in a rather desultory fashion by workers who shuffle through them in their bare feet, the general idea being to promote uniformity to the curing process. Perhaps it also adds a little to the flavor and bouquet.

Tea, on the other hand, is just a leaf. To get high grade tea, only the small leaves at the ends of the branches were picked: two leaves and a bud was the formula. The larger, more mature leaves made a poor brew as they were too tart for taste, and too tough to steep well.

Unlike the expatriate-run Brooke Bond Tea Plantation at Mufindi, the tea around Tukuyu was managed by the Rungwe Cooperative Union, a co-op formed in the 1920's by the Nyakyusa. They were justly proud of their success, and were one of the most prosperous tribes in Tanzania, not unlike the Chagga around Mount Kilimanjaro. They were very friendly, and happy to show us their operation, including the cooperative store where we bought a few things. They also treated us to lunch, and upon leaving presented us with a case of fine tea valued at 400/-, or about $56.

While the students spent the rest of the day visiting friends and relatives, and, we presumed, abstained from the traditional porridge thick millet beer, Ian and I took a jaunt south to the north end of Lake Nyasa,[94] as I had never seen it. Here the land slopes abruptly down to the lake, which fills the southern section of the Rift Valley fault system, and is thus a sister to the larger, Lake Tanganyika. Lake Nyasa is about 350 miles long, and as much as forty-seven miles across. In places, it is over four tenths of a mile deep, or about as deep as eight American football fields stacked on end. We descended the escarpment to Itungi, nosed about this pleasant, palm-treed port, and then headed back for the Poroto Mountains, and Tukuyu, where we pried our still sober students away from their reunions and trucked on to Mbeya. The following day we visited a small hydroelectric station, did some shopping, and headed home for Malangali.

Another safari ensued before my departure, and that was a photography excursion to Scotty's Camp. Almost immediately the trip got interesting, as I ran over a spitting cobra just out of Malangali. Since I had my cameras, I got out to get a few shots, but the snake was quicker on the draw than I was, and got in two quick shots of its own. The Simca had scrunched its head somewhat, however, so although it could still spit, accuracy was wanting. In any case, I usually wore sunglasses, or kept a camera in front of my eyes when approaching one of these slithering pests.

Once arrived, I bumped into the game warden, Williamson, and he was escorting Chief Adam Sape around the park area. Sape was the great grandson of the legendary

Leaving Home

Mkwawa, and also speaker of the National Assembly. He was a big gregarious man, dark and portly. I joined them and got some good pictures of warthog and elephant, and then we went to Scotty's for lunch. After our meal, Chief Sape retired for a nap, and Williamson and I hiked into the park to look up some elephant friends of his. Since we were unarmed, one would think caution would be the modus operandi, but one would be mistaken in that assumption. First we found a young bull, probably a teenager, in thick bush. Keeping track of the wind, we closed to within fifteen feet or so. The brush was thick, which gave us good cover, but made photography difficult. I took a few photographs of the partially visible head anyway, and then he moved forward just a bit, exposing his whole head in profile, his trunk up in the air. This was not a good sign as it meant the shifting breezes had given him our scent, and his sniffer was at work. I snapped a quick picture, and we left before he could get a fix on our position.

Next, right out in the open, in an area laid bare by fire, we approached a mature bull. Williamson evidently knew this one personally and started calling out his name: Gondor. He repeated the name several times as we crept to within about thirty yards. Gondor was not in a sociable mood, however. He stopped, stood like a statue, and eyed us with interest. Then he emitted a rude blast and charged. We turned heel, fled through the blackened stubble, jumped down a four-foot bank, and scrambled as best we could across the loose sand of a dry riverbed. The game warden was slightly ahead of me, with his head turned to keep track of his friend, while I focused on Williamson's face. As soon as the warden's expression changed from one of concern to one of relief, I spun around and got a great picture of the bull standing on the edge of the drop-off, shaking his head and flapping his ears.

I was younger than the game warden, and certainly faster. I was trailing him so I'd be in position to get a good photograph if the situation allowed. But had that elephant come down the bank and continued his pursuit, I would have sprinted past Williamson like a gazelle passing an aardvark, leaving him to reason things out with Gondor. As it was, the beast was intent on giving us a warning, not a stomping, so he pulled up short, told us off, and left it at that.

When we got back to camp Chief Sape was having tea. We joined him, engaged in small talk over our chai,[95] and then I left for Iringa. To save the warden any further embarrassment, not a word was said about Gondor.

The school term was coming to a close and the newly instituted regional exams, practice for the Cambridge in December, were upon us. The exams were a mess. My input on the history test never got to the regional committee as the British teacher I had sent it to in Iringa, sat on it, and then forgot it. In addition, the English test was nothing like the Cambridge in format, so was not very useful. I didn't get a copy until six days before the tests were to start and consequently could make no suggestions. The copy was supposed to be in my hands over a month earlier, but, oh well, it was not as though these happenings were an abnormality.

We invigilated and marked our own exams, as they were only meant for internal consumption. I supervised the English test, and ended up grading the history tests:

my last official duties before I left my home of two years, in the outback of Tanzania.

------

92 Nyakyusa family names start with Mwa, as in Mwatujobe, Mwaikombo, Mwakangata, etc. Hence it was easy to know if a person was Nyakyusa.

93 Probably a marketing ploy: it sounds more appetizing to refer to coffee beans, rather than coffee pits!

94 Nyasaland became Malawi, upon independence in 1964, and Lake Nyasa was renamed Lake Malawi.

95 Words travel, and "chai" has been a world class traveler. It is Swahili for tea, and also Arabic, and also Russian! The word no doubt followed the product from its source, in China. Lately, the word has even shown up in the United States, though here it refers to a specific style: rich and creamy, in the Arab fashion, and spiced.

This is often all you see of an elephant in the bush. The Game Warden of the Ruaha Game Reserve and I saw this one while exploring the park unarmed.

Same elephant, but he has our scent. Time to leave!

CHAPTER 37

Going Home

Going home was easy. I would see friends and family, earn a master's degree, enjoy the conveniences of the modern world, and do some touring on the way. However, leaving Malangali was not so easy. I was leaving a place I had liked from day one. I was leaving good friends, and great students, and memories, and, as far as I knew, there were no elephants native to either Chicago or Tacoma.

Harold had already left, though we did receive the occasional letter from him. In one he related how he had almost got bunged in Rome by one of those little Italian cars. I couldn't help but wonder what it was like to get cussed out in a romance language, but it also brought home the fact that after two years in rural Africa, the pace of the West would take some getting used to.

Ian and Ceinwen would surely be missed, as many hours were spent with them over dinner and whist, picnics and safaris. Plus, just working with them at the school was a pleasure as they were not only wonderful teachers, but lent some stability to the fluidity of the staff. Both were popular with the students, first and foremost because they were excellent teachers who could get the kids through their Cambridge Exams, but also because they went the extra mile for them. They had small groups of students over for tea and biscuits and conversation, and they volunteered for all sorts of extra activities.

I particularly enjoyed watching Ceinwen teach the boys how to play field hockey. She would get right out there and take part in the scrimmage, and, I believe, could whack a shin with the best of them. Field hockey was a very popular game for men in India and Pakistan, and since we had many Asians in Iringa and Mbeya, there were teams the boys could compete against. They did quite well and when they won it was partly due to the skills they had been taught, and partly because the mostly middle-aged shopkeepers couldn't haul their growing guts at full pace through a whole match. The students weren't as skilled, being new to the game, but they were in athletic condition, as opposed to stand-behind-the-counter-selling-cloth condition.

When Ian and Ceinwen came back to Malangali, after having left on leave to have their first child, they were greeted by frond waving students who excitedly chased their Peugeot all the way to their house. Ian was embarrassed, Ceinwen loved it: English vs Welsh!

I would also miss our latest headmaster, Mr. Mabele. He was quiet, dedicated, reasonable, capable, and in control. He was a leader, a good role model for the students, and he took no guff from anybody. He was that kindly but sage older uncle most of us have tucked away somewhere in our family tree.

Driving up the dusty road from Malangali to Njiapanda, a trip I had taken dozens of times, felt very final. I would probably never pass this way again, a chapter closed.

I spent five days in Dar, a night in Nairobi, and left for London on July 23, 1964. Ian had connected me with his parents, Eric and Kit, so I spent most of a week with them, just as my brother Dave had done on his trip home. With Ian's parents showing me around I saw many of the historic places in a city steeped in history.

My second favorite was Hampton Court, built by Cardinal Thomas Wolsey, in the early 1500's. Wolsey lived a lavish lifestyle due to his positions as cardinal, Chancellor of England, and chief councilor to King Henry VIII. He started building Hampton Court in 1514, and it became his official residence. This all went away when he remained steadfast in his Catholicism and could not deliver Henry a divorce from Katherine of Aragon. Henry then founded his own national church, the Church of England, the only major religious body founded on the twin pillars of politics and divorce, and Wolsey died alone and in disgrace. Hampton Court remained, however, and ironically became the home for kings and queens to follow.

My favorite was the Tower of London, another buttress to royal power. The Tower has a menacing appearance and feel to it, like a Halloween caricature. This is only partly due to architecture. If a person knows next to naught about English history, it still vaguely registers that Britain has a monarchy and the Tower has a sinister reputation. The two are connected, like an umbilical cord connects a mother to her unborn, but in this day and age, the gore and glory of the Tower reflect only glory on the monarchy. The royal family, especially the queen, is very popular, and not just in Great Britain. A visit by Her Royal Majesty to North America creates a warm and fuzzy feeling among Americans. Grandma sailing across the snow to visit and charm the grand kids. Were she just to tour Canada, Americans would be greatly upset, not mad, just hugely disappointed. How could the Queen do that? How could she forget us? We love her! The monarch is more revered in the U.S. then she is, at times, in her own domain. Those with no knowledge or sense of history, i.e. Americans, do not tar the monarchy with the horrors of the past. Nor do today's Brits.

It was not always thus. Construction of the Tower was started in 1066, a fort for the Norman king William I, better known as The Conqueror. Over the centuries it grew from fort to castle to palace, but always it served as a jail, and not a jail for plebeians. It was a political jail, and you had to be powerful, rich, famous or infamous to lodge there. Hundreds checked in, few checked out, and a return stay, a la Sir Walter Raleigh, was almost certainly fatal. A slim representation of those Tower executions follows:[96]

Going Home

1305

In 1297 **William Wallace**, as in the movie **Braveheart**, a patriotic Scot of Welsh descent, rebelled against English rule in Scotland. He defeated the English at Stirling Bridge but he himself was defeated at Falkirk in 1298. For the next seven years he conducted a guerrilla campaign until 1305 when he was betrayed to the English and brought to London. It is said that he was carried from Westminster to the Tower, and from the Tower through the city and as an outlaw beheaded. It is also said that he was tied to horses' tails and hanged till nearly dead, his bowels torn out and burned, his head cut off and his body quartered (the customary penalty for treason).

1441

Eleanor, Duchess of Gloucester, wife of the king's uncle, she was charged with conspiring to kill the king by melting a wax image of him before a fire.

1465

Henry VI became a prisoner in his own Tower of London, his throne usurped by Edward IV. In 1470 he was restored as a puppet monarch but after a final victory at Tewkesbury a year later, when his only child, Edward, was killed, the deposed king's own turn came. He died in the Tower 18 days later.

1483

Before Richard, Duke of Gloucester could be crowned Richard III he had one obstacle to overcome, Edward IV's two sons **Prince Edward and Richard Duke of York**. The story of these two princes is perhaps the saddest tale from the Tower's long and bloody history. Edward IV died on 9th April 1483 and soon after Prince Edward was escorted to the Tower by Gloucester (Richard), who had assumed the role of Protector. Officially the prince was there to await his coronation however this would not happen. On the 13th June while the coronation was being planned, Richard rushed in with cries of treason and had Edward taken to Tower Hill and beheaded. His brother was also lured to the Tower to meet a similar fate. After this the Garden Tower was renamed The Bloody Tower. There were rumors regarding the fate of the two princes. One was that they were not killed but allowed to grow to maturity under assumed names thanks to a plan from Henry VII and Edward IV's widow Elizabeth Woodville. However in 1674, when workmen were demolishing a stone staircase on the south side of the White Tower, they found a chest containing two child-size skeletons. None doubted that these were the bodies of the two princes and Charles II ordered that the remains be taken to Innocents' Corner in Westminster Abbey.

1534

John Fisher Bishop of Rochester was committed to the Tower with Sir Thomas More, as both had refused to take an oath recognizing Henry VIII as the head of the English Church. Fisher was the first to die. King Henry had vowed, on hearing that the Pope meant to make Fisher a cardinal, that if a hat arrived there should be no head for it, and the bishop was executed on Tower Hill in 1535, Sir Thomas a fortnight later. Both were canonized in 1935.

1535

Sir Thomas More Statesman and scholar who served Henry VIII until the break with Rome. A Lord Chancellor, Sir Thomas More refused to acknowledge Henry VIII as supreme head of the English Church, and continued adamant when the king's subjects were required to subscribe to the oath. He also protested against the divorce of Catherine of Aragon, who had given Henry only one living child, the Princess Mary.

1536

Anne Boleyn, Henry VIIIs second wife, was taken to the Tower on a charge of adultery. She was sentenced to be burned or beheaded as pleased the King. In front of the chapel of St. Peter ad Vincula, her head was cut off and her remains were buried inside the chapel. Many were rewarded in this way.

1542

Catherine Howard, Henry VIII's fifth wife and according to him the very jewel of womanhood. He adored her and showered her with gifts and favors and pampered her in every way. In May 1541 Catherine appointed a former admirer as her private secretary. By September 1541 rumors were being whispered at court and early in November sufficient evidence of the Queen's misconduct had come to light to make Archbishop Cranmer feel he must inform the King. Henry's immediate reaction was one of total disbelief. However, he ordered an investigation and found that not only had Catherine been flirting behind his back, it was also alleged she had been promiscuously unchaste before he married her. For this he could show no mercy. Catherine went the way of her cousin Anne Boleyn. She was tried and condemned and on the 13th February 1542 she was beheaded on Tower Green, along with Lady Jane Rochford, who had been party to Catherine's infidelity.

1552

Edward Seymour, Duke of Somerset and protector lost his office to John Dudley, Duke of Northumberland, and was beheaded on Tower Hill, along with his wife with her gentlewomen and men servants. He was mainly guilty of betraying his class by trying to ameliorate the conditions of the poor.

1554

Lady Jane Grey, upon marrying Lord Guildford Dudley, the fourth son of John Dudley, Duke of Northumberland, was in line of succession. Northumberland persuaded the young Edward on his deathbed to transfer the rights of his sisters, Mary and Elizabeth. After the king's death on 6th July 1553, Lady Jane was publicly proclaimed at the Tower, but within eight days Mary's supporters rose in strength. On the 31st of July, Lady Jane's father, Henry Duke of Suffolk entered her chamber, tore down the canopy of state and told her she was no longer Queen. She begged to go home, but he turned her away. She was now a prisoner of the state, and Suffolk himself was soon to share her fate. In February 1554, Lady Jane watched her husband go from the Beauchamp Tower to his death on Tower Hill, a few hours before her own execution on the Green. They were buried in the chapel, which also holds the bones

Going Home

of the executed Northumberland and his old enemy Protector Somerset (Edward Seymour).

1571

John Store was a staunch Catholic who found favor with the queen, Mary I. As Chancellor of Oxford he earned a reputation for cruelty in dealing with Protestants. One account concerns his burning at the stake of a woman accused of heresy. As the flames rose, she bravely tried to sing a psalm. Store, unable to tolerate such heroism before a large crowd, rushed forward, grasped a piece of burning wood and thrust it into his victim's face. When Mary died in 1558, she was succeeded by her Protestant half-sister Elizabeth. Store was imprisoned but escaped to Flanders. He took a post in the local Customs House where his offensive behavior, to say nothing of his previous record, made him many enemies amongst visiting English seamen. Revenge was simple. He was required to inspect the hold of a ship, but as soon as he was below, the hatches were nailed down and Store next saw the light of day alongside the Tower. Found guilty of treason, he was drawn on a hurdle to Tyburn and there hanged, cut down and disemboweled.

1601

Robert Devereux (1566-1601), Earl of Essex was one of Elizabeth I's favorite courtiers, but rebelled against her and was executed on the Tower Green. He was beheaded on the 25th February 1601. The Essex Ring, now in Westminster Abbey, is said to have been given to him by the Queen, with the direction if ever he were in trouble he was to send it back to her and she would save him. From the Tower he tried to return it but either it did not reach her, or she ignored it.

1606

Guy Fawkes (1570-1606) was a Leading conspirator in the GUNPOWDER PLOT to blow up parliament. He was a Catholic convert who had served in the Spanish army before becoming involved in the plot. Fawkes and his fellow conspirators were taken to the Tower and interrogated in the Queen's House. He himself was racked, perhaps in the basement of the Wakefield Tower, where the instruments of torture are believed to have been kept. In January 1606 with three others, he was drawn on a hurdle from the Tower to the Houses of Parliament and there hanged, beheaded and quartered. Today the British celebrate Guy Fawkes Day, though why anyone would glorify a person who failed to blow up a gathering of politicians is beyond me.

1606

Nicholas Owen was a Jesuit builder, expert in the construction of secret cupboards and passages within the houses of wealthy Catholics where priests could hide from King James's men. Thus he saved the lives of many Jesuits, but was eventually captured and taken to the Tower. To make him implicate a fellow Jesuit in the Gunpowder plot, he was suspended by his thumbs and threatened with the rack, but gave little away. The official report says that he committed suicide with a blunt knife.

Hunting and Teaching in East Africa

1613

Thomas Overbury, the poet, was flung into the Tower at the behest of Frances, Countess of Essex, whose marriage to his friend, Robert Ker, Viscount Rochester, he opposed. Overbury was systematically poisoned and finally destroyed by the administration of an internal corrosive. His body all disfigured with sores and ulcers, was instantly wrapped in a sheet and hurried to a grave in the chapel. Two years passed before his murderers were brought to justice. The accomplices, who included the Lieutenant of the Tower, were hanged, but Ker and his infamous wife were pardoned.

1618

Sir Walter Raleigh (1552-1618) was an explorer known for his expeditions to the Americas, and for allegedly bringing tobacco and the potato from the New World to the British Isles. A favorite of Elizabeth I, he fell thoroughly out of favour and spent 12 years in the Tower on a charge of plotting against Elizabeth's successor, King James I. He was released in 1616, only to find himself back in 1618. This time he was kept in one of the most cold and direful dungeons before being beheaded six weeks later. In his speech from the scaffold he thanked God that he would die in the light, and not in the dark prison of the Tower.

This brief account of the sordid side of British history presses darkly against the stated agenda of the Christian West to 'civilize' Africa. These kinds of practices were common throughout Europe, and modern practitioners, without regard to race, creed or degree of enlightenment, abound also, from Stalin and Hitler in Europe, to Mao Tse Tung in China, Pol Pot in Cambodia, and Idi Amin in Uganda. It would seem a deep vein of cruelty runs through our genes, usually suppressed, but often enough expressed.

Once inside the Tower, the glory takes over. The Crown Jewels are there. When I visited, they were under glass, but well within reach, and only one unarmed bobby patrolled the vicinity. There are 8000 pieces of armor, 12,000 firearms and accessories, 900 pieces of artillary, 7500 swords, 6300 daggers and bayonets, 4200 staff weapons like pikes and lances, and 50 instruments of torture.

I was fascinated by the firearms collection. There were medieval handguns, matchlocks, wheellocks, flintlocks, and the more modern military issue of recent centuries. I developed an unhealthy desire to acquire, but the sight of the chopping block, and the ax for doing the deed, cooled my ardor.

My last tourist venture was to take a bus to the southern coast and Brighton, with its peculiarly out of place oriental palace, complete with minarets, but with a cross atop one of the spires. Brighton didn't appeal to me in any special way, but the openness of the countryside between London and there was a surprise. I guess I expected wall-to-wall settlement, like from Seattle to Tacoma. Beautiful country, and of course they do get their share of rain to keep it so!

One evening Ian's sister Ann and I went to dinner at a jazz club where a talented American pianist entertained, and the evening before leaving I treated Eric, Kit, and Ann to dinner at a posh restaurant complete with dance floor and a twenty piece

Going Home

swing band. Eric and Kit appreciated my intent, but were a bit embarrassed by the extravagance of it all. I assured them that compared to such a banquet in the U.S., the cost was very reasonable, and we proceeded to have a great time enjoying the meal, the music, and the dance floor.

The Thomases had been so helpful and gracious that leaving was a real downer. Home beckoned, however, and New York City was on the horizon. I spent some time there with Ardene and her fellow nurse roommates, checked in at Columbia University, and made one of the stupidest deals of my life: I bought a Jaguar sedan. I was and am an Anglophile, but my stay in London must have clouded my judgment because while there is much to admire in the British, the production of automobiles isn't their forte. They build beautiful, sensuous cars, but unlike the British themselves, these vehicles are not steadfast or reliable. Instead they are fickle, prone to fits of malfunction, and devilishly clever about choosing the perfect time to quit.

I left New York about 8 a.m., in other words, during the rush hour. Upon entering the Holland Tunnel in bumper to bumper traffic, the brakes gave out. I somehow managed to cram the transmission into reverse to stop, and then judiciously crept along, using the hand brake when necessary. After what seemed like hours, but in reality was only a few minutes the Jag and I emerged out the other side, and I pulled into a gas station wondering what to do. A mechanic wandered over, toweling off his grimy hands, and I explained my predicament. He fixed it!

I drove from New York to Tacoma in three and a half days, grabbing small blocks of sleep on the verge of the road when too tired to keep my eyes open. The U.S. is a wide country and I was eager to get home, but even at ninety miles an hour, eastern Montana seemed to go on forever, with little to recommend it. From the start I had noticed that the generator was constantly charging, the needle positioned at full charge. I ran my lights in an effort to burn up some of the wattage being produced, but when I pulled into Ellensburg to get gas, only a couple hours from home, the Jag refused to start, the battery and generator pretty much fried. Again a mechanic came to the rescue. He got me jump-started, but advised that I keep it running till I got home. This I fully intended to do, but there was no guarantee that the car would give me any choice in the matter. I pushed on over Snoqualmie Pass and gritted my teeth for home. As I pulled into the driveway, my brother came out, scratched his head, and said: "What in heaven's name did you do?" I replied: "Something stupid, can you fix it?" Dave couldn't believe I had bought a British car, and the most notorious brand at that. Fortunately he liked a challenge, and fortunately for him, his brother was considerate enough to provide one.

So I spent the summer of 64 at home with my parents, Dave got the Jaguar squared away as much as that is humanly possible short of a case of dynamite, and I prepared to go back to school.

---

[96] Taken from the internet site: <u>Camelot Village: Britain's Heritage and History,</u> with some editing and additions on my part.

CHAPTER 38

NU

From Malangali to Chicago, from friendly to couldn't care less, it was an adjustment of more than just geography, climate and pace. Tanzania was more like one large neighborhood. People nodded, said "Jambo", smiled. Acknowledge a stranger on the streets of Chicago[97] with an unsolicited smile or greeting and suspicion would immediately cloak his face. Welcome to the impersonal world of the big city.

Technically, I was in Evanston, a high class bump on Chicago's upper rump. The campus of Northwestern University edged Lake Michigan's western shore. I was here to work on my master's degree and then, never to look back, return to my old neighborhood. The university sprawls on what passes for a beautiful campus when you can see it, that is when it isn't covered with ice and snow, and when your eyes aren't teary from the wind.

Classes were brutal, and your comrades were competitive, like boxers. Make a mistake, an ill informed comment, and pow, right in the kisser. One roundtable seminar on anthropology met twice a week, with three lengthy, arcane books to be digested and discussed each week. I learned to skim, and to speak only when certain of my footing.

The professors were mostly brilliant, and always demanding. All but one were also sympathetic and willing to interact with and help students. That one was a man in his thirties, an ex-military officer, built like a wrestler, with a mustache on his lip and a two-by-four on his shoulder. He was abrasive, arrogant, abusive, and I'm sure had never visited Tanzania as his ego would not have fit. Still, even he was effective. We learned his lessons well. We dared not do otherwise. The Tower of London with its fifty machines of torture came to mind.

So classes were tough, big deal. There were a few aspects of Northwestern and Chicago that were actually impressive, or at least enjoyable. First came the library. The university had a tremendous Africana Library, reputed to be the best in the States. I spent hours there, even worked part time in its fusty recesses. When I did my thesis on Mkwawa, they had plenty of material on him, much of it in German manuscripts.

That covers the impressive side of things, but Chicago had a few (two) perks to offer. The first was a local tavern a couple blocks from my room. Evanston was dry, so when I got tired of nosing my books, I'd walk up to Howard Street, the dividing line between Evanston and Chicago, cross the street, go left for a couple of blocks, and enter a small, blue-collar bar for a Schlitz and a hot pastrami sandwich. It was a cozy atmosphere, not particularly well lit, but comfy, and a welcome break from the sterility of graduate work.

The other perk was The Loop, a section of Chicago that was home to, among other attractions, a number of jazz clubs. I saw John Coltrane at the Plugged Nickel, and on another occasion went to see Thelonious Monk, though no big surprise, he didn't show up. From Evanston, I would take a bus to the El,[98] and then ride that on into the heart of Chicago. On one occasion, during the Indian Summer we had that fall, I noticed a man on a postage stamp of a balcony. He was white, working class, overweight, and hairy chested. He and his chair took up all the space on this rusty iron perch jutting out the back of a tenement. He had a beer in one hand. He sat there, his head cast down, inert, staring at the El, or perhaps at the ugly rear ends of other dull brick structures like his that parted so the El could pass. It brought to mind a conversation with my mother.

Dave had evidently confided to her that he had been upset by the poverty in Africa. This shook me a little, as I had never considered the Africans' lack of material goods or comforts as poverty. This man on the balcony was my idea of poverty. No doubt he had a television, a radio, a refrigerator, a soft bed, electric heat and light, and an endless and reliable source of food. Maybe even a car. The African might have a radio, or a bicycle, but generally not, and certainly not all that other stuff. But the African for all he didn't have, was generally buoyant. He was not weighed down by poverty of the spirit. The man on the balcony, in his rusty cage, looked the picture of utter dejection.

Father came to my graduation and we drove home together in the Jag. I had been invited to stay on and pursue my doctorate, but several more years in Chicago, versus two more in Tanzania was no contest. Carl Sandburg had it partly right: Chicago was the hog butcher of the world. It also did a pretty good job on people.

---

[97] Chicago could be considered as generic for any large city, I suppose.
[98] The El was Chicago's subway, but most of the way in from Evanston, it ran above ground and was called the Elevated, or El for short.

CHAPTER 39

Arusha

In August I was in the air, returning to Tanzania. I had spent most of the summer with my family, but the send off this time was wrenching. My parents couldn't understand why I was going back. They were extremely apprehensive, figuring I had defied the law of averages on my first tour, and would surely come home in a box at some point in the second one. Tears were shed, the waves goodbye more a plea to stay.

After this damp as a winter's day farewell, I spent a pleasant couple of weeks at Columbia University playing the role of the old Africa hand, offering the new recruits glimpses of their near future. I also met a kindred spirit in Hal Anderson. Most of the people in the TEA program were big-city liberals and therefore not inclined to shoulder a rifle and head into the bush, but Hal liked to hunt and fish, a prerequisite for admission to his state of choice, Montana. I also got my posting. I would spend the next two years in Arusha, a town I had passed through on occasion and knew I would enjoy.

The flight over, though surely exciting for the new teachers, was uneventful: no drive through the quaint streets of Paris, no stops in Tripoli for a dollar Coke or Fort Lamy (NDjamena) for a haggling session. Even the airplane lacked character, the wings totally composed, unflappable one might say. London, Algiers, Entebbe, Nairobi, and Dar es Salaam. Dar was hot and muggy and the dank, sweet, rotting smell of the tropics permeated our DC-9 as it descended. Welcome to Tanzania.

Getting through customs promised to be a slow, sweaty, exasperating welcome for most of our contingent. For me, however, it turned out to be a cool breeze in the form of Stafford, that Anglophile ex-student of mine from Malangali. He had gained employment as a customs agent, and when he saw me broke into a huge grin, came to greet me, and with a flourish marked my luggage with his chalk. Off we went for a cold beer. The bar was just outside the customs area and in plain view. We took a window seat and gazed benignly out at my struggling compatriots as their bags were opened, prodded and searched with all the urgency and passion of turtles making love. Waves of envy radiated in my direction, envy with perhaps a hint of animosity. I smiled, graced them with the condescending wave of a politician on parade, and

Arusha

generally made a show of enjoying that first beer, and then another.

We spent three days in Dar, time enough for me to mend fences with the less fortunate, and then we were off to our schools. I flew to Arusha via Moshi and my heart skipped a beat as we skirted the great mountain before descending over the banana trees.

Arusha also snugs into the base of a towering cone, Mount Meru, which stretches to 17,000 feet. Occasionally the peak is graced with a light dusting of snow, though it melts by late morning. At 4600 feet, a couple thousand feet higher than Moshi, Arusha has a perfect climate, less humid, and cooler than its sister city fifty miles to the east.

Arusha was the center of the tourist trade and the focus of some Hollywood attention as it sits central to many game parks. Most tourism starts in Nairobi and from there the small zebra striped Volkswagen vans wend a circuit through Amboseli to Arusha, and then either south for Lake Manyara, the Ngorongoro Crater, Olduvai Gorge, and the Serengetti, or east to Moshi and north through Tsavo and back onto the Mombasa road to Nairobi.

One evening after dark, as I crossed the dimly lit clock-tower roundabout in front of the post office, who should appear headed my way but Bing Crosby. I said, "Howdy, Bing," he nodded slightly and continued on his way. He and his friend Phil Harris would come to Tanzania every so often to hunt birds. Another more major Hollywood effort was the making of the adventure film **Hatari**, starring John Wayne. The town barber had a number of autographed pictures of 'The Duke' on his walls, and as you got clipped, he would unfold a never-ending series of vignettes about the making of the film, and the star himself. The only byte that stuck in my hard drive had to do with Big John sparking a tall, willowy Somali woman of striking beauty.

I was posted to Arusha Secondary School, a coed Aga Khan school that had been nationalized after independence. The Aga Khan was one of the wealthiest men in the world at that time, heading the very prosperous Ismaili community, a 20 million strong branch of Shia Islam. Prince Karim had become the 49th hereditary Imam in 1957, leapfrogging his more famous[99] father in a line of succession stretching back to Fatima,[100] the Prophet's youngest daughter. The Ismailis are business oriented, liberal in philosophy and philanthropy, and the building of schools was just one aspect of their support of not only their own community, but of the countries which contained large numbers of their faithful. I would have occasion to test their progressive bent by making off with one of their daughters, but more on that bado kidogo.[101]

The school was rapidly being Africanized, so the lower grades were almost wholly African, while the upper grades were equally Asian. We tended to get the best Asian kids, as this is one of the few schools they could still get into, and the worst African kids, as the best ones opted for the boarding schools. The result was a certain amount of friction, frustration and hostility as regards the African students. While the Africans were mostly Chagga and WaArusha, there were others, including a Masai and a Somali. Among the Indians, not all were Ismaili, and there were even a couple of European girls from the Seychelles.

Hunting and Teaching in East Africa

As the school was a town school, most of our students were not boarders, though we had housing for about sixty, all Africans. The staff also lived in the town, and not on school premises, so school spirit and cohesion weren't nearly as strong as at Malangali. The staff was as diverse as the student body, with African, American, British, and Indian teachers. Why, I have no idea, but most of the Indian staff were Sikhs.

The principal of the school had absolutely nothing to do with anything immoral, but she was nevertheless saddled with that English title of dubious distinction: 'Headmistress'. Her name was Sarah Materu, a Chagga educated in the United States, bright, dedicated, and devoted to the task of 'building the nation'. This last tendency would sometimes lead to minor strains between her and the staff; and the students. Her insistence on a school shamba was the source of some resentment as both staff and students had to spend time and effort to grow, nurture and harvest the vegetables planted on this plot of maybe a half acre. This undertaking was not just a whim on her part, however, as the government wanted to instill in the students the idea that manual labor was not beneath them, and they should not uniformly aspire to a cushy office job in one of the larger towns.

While there was some grumbling about gardening, the fertilizer really hit the fan when we were called out of class, loaded into police lorries, and hauled out to the government farm at Ol Joro to harvest beans. The National Service was supposed to do this job, but the troops declared it beneath **their** dignity: they were soldiers, not farm hands! So anyway, we spent the better part of a few days toiling in the fields, I think more to impress and shame the soldiers than really accomplish anything. The crop was much too large for us to dent unless school was to be suspended for days on end, and the government knew this would provoke a collective howl of some magnitude from the conscripts, scholars who had studies to pursue and in any case considered themselves several notches above the layabouts in the National Service.

These lessons in collective labor for the common good were in keeping with Nyerere's teaching that socialism was a natural fit for Africa, as tribal life was one of sharing and taking care of one another. Ujamaa[102] was the application of this native practice of extended family to the entire nation, and its economic structure. But the winds of change were gathering for a major blow, and when presented with an opportunity outside the confines of tradition,[103] the African could be as individualistic as anybody.

Our staff meetings were lively affairs, with Sarah presiding, though not always in total control. One of the Brits was Irish, noisy Irish, and he could sidetrack a meeting with the best of them, and the Sikhs: they would get off on some animated tangent of their own, in their own language, and the rest of us would subside in awe, as altogether, though not in unison, they would gesticulate and expound on some matter until somehow a consensus had been reached, and then Sarah would quietly continue with her agenda.

The Sikhs have a warrior reputation, sort of the Masai of India. Our younger

Arusha

Sikhs; Argawal, Acharya, and Jorginder, were thoroughly modern, clean shaven with cropped manes, but Bogal was another matter. He was older and looked every bit the fierce, traditional Sikh with his uncut locks wrapped in a turban and his face sprouting a fulsome and fearsome crop of whiskers. He was the leader of this group, at least vocally.

Before one of our staff meetings I ran up to Naz's Restaurant and got a big bag of bhajias: veggies, dals, and grains deep fried into Ping-Pong sized balls. These make delicious snacks. For some reason, to me the word bhajias sounded like the word Punjabis, so bag in hand I entered the staff room and loudly proclaimed, "Lets all have some Punjabis!" All was quiet. The Punjab is, after all, a state in northern India. It is the home state of the Sikhs. Sikhs are often called Punjabis, and Punjabis are fierce and known to take insults to heart. Nevertheless, I was an irrepressible American with a huge, silly grin on his face, so while the young bucks were mortified, Bogal broke into a huge fit of laughter. Thereafter, though his wife would give me a wary look, Bogal would throw his arm around my shoulders, give me a jolt, and suggest we go to Naz's for some Punjabis. At our school, in our little society, bhajias ceased to be called bhajias.

The two African staff were Cecil Magembe and Alisante Kilimba, both young men, slight of build, though Cecil was fit and athletic, while Kilimba was frail looking, less outgoing, but in the end, more sociable. Cecil was confident, with a ready smile, but difficult to get close to and something of a loner. Alisante had a shy, half-smile, and while he would not take the lead, he was open to conversation and contact. He was, in short, a very nice person.

The two Englishmen were Guy Hopson and Dave Morgan. Guy was slight of build, always encased in a brown sweater, always, it seemed, with a cup of tea caught up in his right hand. He had an outstanding crop of brown hair atop a rather bland and flat face. Morgan was sort of the opposite, tall and lanky with a booming voice, thinning hair, and a hooked nose that his sunken cheeks accentuated like the beak on a flamingo. He was built like Abe Lincoln, and like Abe, thought lanky, he was tough. Rugby was his game, and he played with a rock-em sock-em, full speed ahead style that belied his build.

The Irishman in our midst was Chris MacDermott. For some reason, probably no reason really, Sarah always added the Swahili "i" to his name. There was no McNickli, or Morgani or Hopsoni, but there was a MacDermotti. He was painfully Irish, a walking, singing, boozing, charm oozing lady's man. At parties he would play his guitar and sing Irish ballads, and as the night wore on and the grog took hold, the drift became progressively maudlin. He was handsome, bespectacled, and debonair, yet his wife could charitably be labeled plain. She was a redhead, pale of skin, round of face, stout. The word frumpy comes to mind. A nice person, but definitely in the shadow of her gregarious husband.

The school itself was a rectangle of single story, whitewashed buildings with red tile roofs, and enclosed a courtyard about twice the size of a tennis court. The dormitory was outside and detached, a three story structure about fifty yards from the main complex. Like Malangali, this was a four-stream school with two classes per grade level, thirty-five in each class, a total of 280 students Forms I-IV. On the whole, the students here were younger, less mature, and less studious than those in Malangali, but still, in most aspects, several notches above their American counterparts.

I would teach some English, but mostly history and government, both British and Tanzanian. I also taught some adult education classes, mostly history and related current events. A lecture on Southern Rhodesia was followed with interest and elicited many excellent questions, most of which exposed a serious mistrust of British intentions: Perfidious Albion.

By November I had a house, much like the one in Malangali but with electricity 24/7, though hot water still had to be manufactured in a Tanganyika boiler. Via the cook of my next door neighbor, a fortyish British nurse, I acquired Haji. He would be my mpishi for the next two years, a spindly little guy about a cantaloupe short of six feet tall with dark skin and Somali features. He had several children, and a good natured wife about three times his size. Given the disparity, it was a good thing she didn't have black widow tendencies.

Haji was a good cook, not afraid of hard work, and neat and clean. His previous bwana had taken him on many a safari, and Haji would often accompany me on my longer hunts. As his name would imply, he was Muslim, so liquor was not an issue, and he was a family man, devoted to his wife and kids. As with Valance, I had to deprogram him a bit as he would show up at the crack of dawn and leave well after dark, if left to his own devices. Also, I had to get him to cut back on the size of the meals he served. He evidently thought I was either an army or an orphanage and produced portions accordingly.

My house was a white stucco rambler with a tile roof. Across one end was a large bedroom and the hallway leading to the living room was flanked by a bath on one side, and a small bedroom on the other. The kitchen and pantry finished the house at the other end, and out the back door was a one-car garage. The chief of police, first a Scotsman, then an Indian, and then a Chagga, was my neighbor on one side, my spinster nurse friend on the other, and out back were the shambas and houses of the local WaArusha, from which the town got its name.

So, just before school let out in December, I was pretty well settled in. My sea freight had arrived, I had retrieved my .375 from Iringa Stores, and I had a home and a cook.

---

[99] Prince Karim's father, Aly Khan, was known for his lavish lifestyle, which included racehorses and Rita Hayworth.
[100] The Ismailis are a branch of the Fatimids. It was the Fatimids who brought North Africa, Syria, and Sicily under Islamic control. They founded Cairo in

the tenth century, and their 200 yearlong dynasty marked one of the great periods of Islamic growth, both geographically and culturally.

[101] Bado kidogo: a little bit later, as in a following chapter.

[102] Ujamaa translates to Familyhood and was one of the main TANU slogans, along with Uhuru na Umoja, Freedom and Unity.

[103] Even traditional society was not static, nor insufferably conformist.

My cook Haji, David the gardener, and one of Haji's totos.

Arusha staff - Front Row: Mehrun, Pathan, R.D. Patel, Sarah Materu, Mrs. Ahmed, Bogal, Alisante Kilimba. Back Row: Cecil Magembe, Dave Morgan, Mr. Ahmed, Guy Hopson, Acharia, Me, Chris MacDermott.

CHAPTER 40

Serengeti to Tsavo

As mentioned previously, Arusha was central to the great game parks of northern Tanzania and southern Kenya, and being stationed in Arusha gave me the opportunity to visit them all, and often.

I had been there barely a month, when Bob and Sue Rogers came by on their way to Tabora to pick up Sue's dachshund. Sue was also on her second tour with TEA, and like me, she had taken a year off to get her masters degree, and like me, she did it at Northwestern, in Evanston. I got to know both of them at NU, as Sue and I were taking the same classes and Sue and Bob were courting and would be married before going to the teachers training college at Marangu on the slopes of Kilimanjaro, just east of Moshi.

Sue had brown, shoulder length hair to match her brown eyes, and was of average height and build, above average looks, and decidedly above average intensity. She was a feminist to boot and many things bothered her, a contrast to her laid back husband. Bob was good looking in a mature sort of way, his shiny dome contributing to this effect. Nothing much got Bob excited, and even if he were internally agitated, his soft, low voice conveyed a sense of tranquillity and control.

They had bought a Volkswagen bug, and this was to be its maiden voyage. We drove to Tabora through the Serengeti plains, but miles out of Tabora the bug chugged to a halt. Bob hopped a passing truck to go for help, while Sue and I held the fort. Out of boredom I began to fiddle with the engine. I opened the distributor cap and blew out the accumulated debris as best I could, and then burnished the points with Sue's fingernail file. Mshangao![104] It fired up on the first crank, and off we went in a cloud of dust, hoping to find Bob. Fortunately, he spied us and we him, as he was coming to our rescue, visible in the cab of an oncoming lorry.

After retrieving Sue's wiener dog, we headed back through the Serengeti. At the park boundary, we buried the little rodent under a blanket, as dogs were not allowed in the park. Wieners are not always the most cooperative of mutts, but she kept still long enough for us to be on our way.

After a short drive, we stopped to let the dog out to stretch its stubby legs and

Serengeti to Tsavo

sprinkle Africa. There was a Thomson's Gazelle nearby. These are a cute little antelope. They can go three feet at the shoulder and weigh up to sixty pounds, or to wax poetic, a little short of, but about the same weight as a big bull elephant's penis. They have a perky face, twitchy ears and tail, and a distinctive black stripe running along the lower edge of the rib cage. The dachshund went into killer mode and tore through the grass intent on meat. The Tommie took an altogether different slant on things, however, and was evidently quite pleased to have a playmate. He bounded around in circles in front of the earnest hound, sproinging[105] in delight, leading the hunter ever deeper into the dry grass. Even a cheetah catches a Tommie only with difficulty, so our gallant little mutt was greatly overmatched. She tired quickly, stopped, eyed the prize, and reluctantly turned back to the car. The gazelle followed, tail flicking excitedly from side to side, disappointed that the game had ended so quickly. The show was over. The hunter humbled.

Of course, that is a human perspective. Dachshunds see themselves as a combination of rottweiler and borzoi rolled into a neat little package of pure cunning and ferocity, able to leap buffalo in a single bound. Dachshunds have delusions. They just aren't the smartest phylum in the canine folder.

Further on we came across several hyena lounging in mud puddles, and a solitary buffalo, an old male with an impressive spread of horn. He was broadside to us, chewing grass, and eyeing us. Nyati have that malevolent stare that sends shivers down your back. He was giving it to us and we kept our distance. As a dachshund is no match for a gazelle, a Volkswagen is equally ill suited for close encounters with buffalo.

The Serengeti can be boring: flat, monotonous, with only the occasional tree or animal for relief. It is not always, in all places, teeming with game. We were bouncing along the dirt track that passed for a road, Sue and Bob napping, when we came to a dry creek bed. I slowed the car, and noticed a pride of lion under and around a tree off to the left. I eased the Volks down into the creek bed, crossed slowly so as not to awaken Sue and Bob, pulled up the far bank and came to a halt, about ten yards from the cats. The male had a perfect mane, his battle-scarred ears poking up from the tangle. He lazily noticed us, as a young cub hunkered down, on the sneak, about to pounce on one of its siblings. Bob stirred, looked at me with sleep in his eyes, and asked why we had stopped. I just kept looking through his open window at the lions just beyond his shoulder. He swiveled his head, and with a start the sleep left, and he almost backed into my lap. The commotion awoke Sue and she immediately swallowed a large gulp of air, but at least she had the comfort of a pane of glass between her and the pride. I carefully opened the door and got out the driver's side, keeping the car between the lions and me. I shot over the roof, and got some terrific slides of both the male and the biggest female, she with her mouth wide open in a yawn, displaying teeth just begging for a dachshund. I suggested we play host and provide the hors d'oeuvre: wiener in a blanket. Sue fixed me with one of those squinty-eyed looks that only a woman can give, even if she is a feminist. The kind of look that says: "You touch my baby, you won't live long enough to regret it." After that, she didn't much trust me alone with her pet. She wouldn't even let me borrow it for leopard hunting, accusing me of just wanting her little precious for bait. She knew nothing of hunting. How could she leap to such a conclusion?

Sue had another occasion, or so, to question my trustworthiness. The three of us, sans the mutt, had gone to Tsavo, my favorite park. Tsavo had it all: huge herds of elephant; Mzima Springs with its hippo, crocs, and visiting fauna; and every type of game, from aardvarks to zebra. There were some open areas, but also vast stretches of thorn scrub, making game viewing akin to hunting. Not everything was just standing out in the open posing for the tourists, like in Amboseli.

We had spent a full day in the park, including taking four charges from an elephant I was photographing. We headed home just before sunset, but before we got to the park boundary another cranky elephant confronted us, standing in the middle of the road, waggling its head. He would scold us for maybe a minute, then dash into the bush only to reappear in a few seconds to continue the diatribe. He did this three times, putting Sue even more on edge than she already was over the earlier incident. The third dash into the bush was it for me. Enough! I floored the Volksie, grabbed second gear, and sped past the spot where tembo mkali[106] kept making his dramatic appearances. Sue was really agitated now, and chewing on my rump with enthusiasm. That elephant was just off the road! We just missed him! We could have been killed! That sort of stuff.

Fortunately for my cheeks, around the next corner was more excitement, enough to quiet things, temporarily. A large herd of zebra was stampeding across the road, probably spooked by lions. We had built up a good head of steam bypassing the elephant and I kept it up till almost on the zebra, then I slammed on the brakes and came to a sliding halt just short of the streaming herd. They were filling our headlights with a blur of black and white stripes, some almost grazing our bumper. It was certainly exciting while it lasted, but it didn't last nearly long enough.

Sue was back at it, shifting from high gear to overdrive: What if one of those zebra had run into the side of the car? Are you trying to wreck my car? Are you trying to kill us on purpose? That sort of stuff. Now there seemed no chance at all that Sue would let me train her wiener dog for leopard hunting.

Another of my favorite parks was Lake Manyara National Park, about seventy miles southwest of Arusha, an easy day-trip. Manyara was a small park, about 200 square miles, but with a great diversity of game, including over 380 species of birds, and at that time, hundreds of elephants. It was the only place I saw a live leopard in my four years, but by the time I turned back from locating my camera, it had simply vanished.

Manyara was most famous for another cat, however: a cat with an unorthodox habit. There were a number of lions in the park, and they had learned to lounge in the lower branches of large trees, surely a cooler spot than on the ground, and no doubt one with fewer annoyances like ticks and flies. I have seen post cards, and pictures in magazines, but in person, despite several tries, I came up empty. Lions will go up a tree after a leopard's kill, if the leopard has been careless enough to bed it too low, but the lion is not a natural climber like his smaller, more agile competitor. This behavior on the part of the Manyara lions was therefore considered quite novel.

Manyara lies at the base of the Great Rift Valley escarpment and a narrow winding road works its way up this cliff to Ngorongoro Crater, the remnants of a once massive volcano. The crater is the largest intact unflooded caldera in the world, almost twelve miles across, with a rim that tops out at about 7500 feet and in the mornings is usually shrouded in mist.

The crater floor is some 650 yards below the point where a precipitous road starts to descend. The floor is not heavily forested like the eastern rim, but is savanna, with scattered thorn trees and a marshy lake. The lake has hippo, waterbuck, and an enormous variety and number of birds, while the plain is heavily populated with gnu, zebra, impala, buffalo, lion and rhino. And Masai cattle. The rim to the west has a low saddle that the Masai pass through, and towards the end of the dry season, October hereabouts, they burn off the grasses in the crater, thus stimulating the growth of fresh green fodder for their stock.

I visited Ngorongoro on a number of occasions, usually with students or visiting friends. Our usual transport was in the bed of a lorry, open at the top, but enclosed by three-foot sides. I suppose a lion could have climbed into our little kraal, but with all the other types of meat available, they were pretty well fed and as far as I knew, never dined on tourist.

On one trip we came across an adult male hippo laying at water's edge, alive, but obviously sick. I approached on foot to within twenty yards, and he just barely noticed. His thick skin was crisscrossed with deep, bleeding cracks, probably from being too long in the sun, an inert mass of protein. The scavengers would have a feast.

I got some excellent photographs of lion at Ngorongoro, but the beauties that most occupied my camera were rhino. They seemed used to tourist vehicles, and we could get fairly close. For lion, ten feet is fairly close, but for rhino, even those exhibiting no aggressive signs, twenty yards is really close. One pair was a female and her young offspring, about a four hundred pounder: momma and baby tank. The mom was broadside, while the mtoto[107] swung around to face us, his little brain and weak eyes trying to make sense of this large, multi-headed critter in front of him. Ah well, a mystery too difficult to fathom, and off he trotted, a miniature of his mother, stubby and powerful.

If you continued westward from Ngorongoro, you would drop down into Olduvai Gorge, the site of old bones and early history on the eastern edge of the Serengeti Plains. Here the Leakeys had been excavating for years, and here Mary Leakey had found a two million year old human skull in 1959. From this and other evidence found up and down the eastern part of Africa, archaeologists have concluded that modern man, that most exotic of beasts, got his start here.

Coming back off the escarpment, past Manyara, through the little village of Mto wa Mbu (River of Mosquitoes), and to Makuyuni on the Great North Road, a right turn would head you for the Tarangire Game Reserve. I never spent much time exploring this park, due to the fly,[108] but I did spend several days just outside the northwest edge of the park over the next two years. The attraction? Elephants.

[104] Mshangao has many meanings, including amazement and wonder.
[105] When an antelope sproings, it bounces up into the air, stiff legged, using all four legs to spring.
[106] Tembo mkali: fierce elephant.
[107] Mtoto means child. In English it is often shortened to toto, or totos (pl).
[108] In East Africa, "fly" is short for tsetse fly.

Lone buff in Sergenti.

Mama just begging for an hors d'oeuvre.

Papa - unruffled by our presence.

Large impala in Tsavo, a thorn scrub park with plenty of scrub brush. Best park in Africa.

Mama and baby tank in Ngorongoro Crater.

Kifaru - Ngorongoro.

CHAPTER 41

Kwa Kuchinja

Southwest of Arusha about seventy miles, just to the east of the Great North Road, lay the little village of Kwa Kuchinja (Cut Throat), Tanzania. The villagers were subsistence farmers, and they also made a little charcoal to sell. As near as I could tell, cutting throats was not one of their hobbies, though guzzling pombe was.

The village was within a couple miles of the Tarangire Game Reserve, and owing more to accidental timing than shrewd observation, I found this area to be fertile hunting grounds, especially after the short rains. Over the two years I hunted this area, it would yield three elephants, a fringed-eared oryx, and a buffalo.

During the dry season, the game bunches around the Tarangire River, which runs through the reserve, but when the short rains come the animals disperse from this overgrazed river habitat, and spill out of the reserve following the abundance of fresh grass and recharged trees and shrubs. As it happened, I was outfitted and ready for my first hunt as the short rains slackened. I had got my .375 back from Iringa Stores, bought an old Holland and Holland .577 for a back-up gun, and had purchased another Simca, a red and gray 1960 powered (?) by a small V-8, and with tail fins like a 1957 Plymouth.

Another Simca? I should have had the phrase "Slow Learner" stenciled on my forehead. This one was larger, roomier, heavier, but alas, no less fragile. Still, it was cheap, only $400. And the engine and transmission had been rebuilt, and the suspension strengthened, or so I was told. Rebuilt or new, the V-8 was the notorious Ford 60, and I suspect the '60' meant it would go approximately sixty miles before it started to burn oil. Towards the end of my tour I tried to hire a Pygmy to live under the hood and continuously pour oil down its throat, but Pygmys were hard to come by.

But the Holland and Holland was a jewel, albeit in the rough. It weighed four pounds less than my .500, but had 1000 pounds more muzzle energy: in other words it kicked like a Clydesdale. Every time I shot it, the trigger guard or the front trigger, depending on which lever I pulled, would tear the skin off my index finger. Fortunately, for more than one reason, I didn't shoot it often. I would later learn that the rifle had been built in the 1890's, and was meant for black powder. I was running

Hunting and Teaching in East Africa

nitro express ammo through the gun, and I'm sure the chamber pressures were well above the manufacturer's recommended tolerances. Still, it was sturdy; and it didn't come apart.

An Indian student at the school, Abdullatif Suliman, somehow learned I was interested in hunting. I think it probably had to do with my prolonged negotiations for the .577. Arusha was a small town, and news of unusual business dealings got around. I had stumbled onto this old rifle while hunting for forbidden fruit, namely South African liqueurs, illegal refreshments due to Tanzania's opposition to the apartheid regime.

While exploring the shops of Arusha I did find one with a supply of the contraband fluids, but the shopkeeper also had this old double leaning against the wall amongst a clutter of odds and ends. I inquired. $300. I examined. The gun was old and beat up. The bluing was mostly worn off the metal parts, the stock was a series of scrapes and bruises, the butt pad looked like it had been chewed on by rats, and though the exposed hammers both worked, one firing pin was broken. Still, the old thing was tight. There was no slack, no wiggle, when the barrel locked up to the receiver. I offered $50. The engagement commenced, and would take the better part of three months to consummate. Eventually I bought this beautiful old wreck for $100, with forty rounds of ammunition included. Holding it in my hands, I could only wonder at its history. If only it could talk: actually, it did talk, but with a vocabulary of only one word: **BOOM**.

Latif suggested I try Kwa Kuchinja. He also suggested I take him along, to which I readily agreed. Latif was a character: engaging, witty, and full of life; one of the most optimistic people I've ever met. He had a wild shock of jet-black hair, and busy, sparkling eyes. He was a hustler, always up to something. He would become a lifelong friend, go to college in Lawrence, Kansas, on my advice, and with his bride, the beautiful Anisa Musa, also a student at Arusha Secondary School, would move to Seattle, where he would live for a number of years before returning to Tanzania for good.

The last weekend before school was out, I decided to go have a look. Latif and I pitched our tent about a quarter mile from the few scattered huts that represented Kwa Kuchinja. My intention was basically to explore the area and get to know the kiongozi. Three of the locals volunteered to guide us into the bush, and within the hour we found ourselves in the midst of a couple hundred buffalo.

At first we saw a few here and then a few there, but no trophy horns. We cautiously proceeded and before long found ourselves in a sea of buffalo. Everywhere I looked, occupying every point of the compass, mbogo.

Fortunately this area was not one of dense thorn scrub. The thick vegetation was scattered, with clumps of trees and brush coming in patches. Our visibility was pretty good, though there were some tangles our eyes couldn't penetrate and one was never quite sure what lay around the next bushy corner. After a couple hours of this tense stalking, I concluded that there wasn't a decent horn in the lot. Northern Tanzania: that is where we were, and that is where the big heads were supposed to

Kwa Kuchinja

be, but not in this instance. The guides wanted meat, so we inched up on a lone female. I put her heart in the cross hairs and shot. She folded without complaint, but a set of horns flashed just behind her and disappeared into the brush. The quick glimpse convinced me that this was a rack worth pursuing. I ran to where the buff had disappeared, plunged into the brush, and there he was, five feet in front of me, head on. He was probably a teenager, in human years, but he was very close and certainly big enough to sort me out. His horns were well short of trophy size, so I had no desire to shoot him, but I had no desire to be killed either. He stared, raised his nose to sniff, and took a step towards me. I intuitively felt that this youngster was just curious and was not going to be aggressive. I slowly lowered the rifle, took off my hat and started shooing him away by flapping the hat in his face, while in a comforting tone urging him to go away. Neither of us broke eye contact. He bobbed his head a couple of times, still working his nose, then he turned and galloped into the thicket, gone in a flash.

Well that was interesting. The guides thought I was maybe a little nuts, but after that they weren't afraid to escort me wherever, after whatever.

We worked our way back to the village to get pangas and knives and porters, but on our return, we found a group of about thirty buffalo directly in our path. I wasn't in the mood for a long detour, so I brought up the .375 and snapped a shot into a large branch over their heads. They ignored the noise and continued to stand in our way. We would just wait them out, but while waiting, I couldn't help thinking about that shot. The fact that it had not dispersed the buffalo was not my concern as animals do not always react as expected. What bothered me was that the shot, at a distance of only fifty yards or so, was eight inches high and right. That shouldn't be. I looked down at the rifle, like a tennis player looks accusingly at his racquet after making a bad shot. If all else fails, blame the equipment! As per usual, it wasn't the equipment. In haste I had quickly shouldered the rifle and snapped off the shot, but the scope covers were still on the scope and that doesn't make for precision shooting. Evidently I had centered the scope with my right eye and located the target with my left, and let fly. This trick, not the scope cover trick but the right eye, left eye trick, would come in handy at a later date, point blank to a passing wall of gray.

Eventually mbogo gave way and the locals got their meat. A feast of pombe and buffalo steaks followed, a hard combination to beat. Latif and I packed up camp, and headed for home, but not without further adieux. Before we got to the main road I managed to zero in on a pothole and nail it dead center, breaking a front spring. The fender settled onto the tire and we came to a grinding halt accentuated by the acrid smell of burning rubber. I seemed to remember that my spare was a different, smaller size than the tires on the car. I checked, and sure enough, it was. Hoping it would provide enough clearance to allow us to move, I switched tires. We got the clearance, but just barely, and every little irregularity in the road caused the tire to rub. Luckily, once out of the bush the road was paved all the way to Arusha, so seventy miles and over two careful hours later, we made it back to town.

Hunting and Teaching in East Africa

When school was out, Haji and I went on my first elephant safari of the second tour. Initially, we tried south Masailand, but the limitations of the Simca soon became apparent. After spending five hours stuck in a mud hole, we headed back to Arusha where we regrouped and decided to try Kwa Kuchinja again.

Haji set up camp while I gathered the guides. After just fifteen minutes of walking we came up on four elephants. My but this was easy! And big, I mean, huge tusks. I took a frontal brain shot on the one with the biggest teeth, hit him a little high, evidently, and put two hurried shots into his ribs as he and the others made a hasty break through the brush. We found them about a half-hour later, and I brought him down with a shoulder shot. After three more days with much walking but no sightings, we went back to Arusha.

The tusks weighed 74 and 67 pounds, much larger than any I'd shot down south, and with the 2603 shillingi ($372) I got for them I paid off the car, the .577, some other bills, and I could afford to eat for the rest of the month. Not a bad payday for such an easy time of it. The next two would prove more difficult and exciting, however.

The following August (1966) I tried Kwa Kuchinja again. I looked up the same guides I had used before, and while Haji made busy at camp, they and I went hunting. These kiongozi were not really hunters in the sense that they knew the game and knew how to track, but they didn't have to be trackers in this area, all they had to do was keep the Great White Hunter from getting lost. The elephant were there. We didn't have to track them from a water hole to where they were feeding, we just wandered about in the bush until we bumped into them, or they into us.

We had been gone about two hours when we came across a lone cow. Naturally, her ivory was small, but she had one elegant long tusk that I decided I wanted for a mantelpiece. I indicated to the guides that we should approach, but they rightly observed that the ivory was small. I agreed, but in my best Swahili could not explain my reason for wanting that one long, thin tusk. They were puzzled at my mangled communications, and while we argued, she gave us the slip. Now, with her out of earshot, I could explain my position more clearly, not with improved vocabulary, but with emphasis on what words I did command. They understood, sort of, and we eventually relocated our gal, but she had joined a small herd of about ten, all cows and young. I had had experience with herds like this in the Southern Highlands and knew it could be trouble, but we started after them anyway.

We were gaining on them from the rear, the wind in our favor, with plenty of brush for them to occasionally be out of sight. Abruptly they changed directions and headed right for us. We were momentarily puzzled, but the snarling of lions soon explained things. At first they were out of view, but soon enough we saw them about forty yards away and swinging a little to our left. We ducked behind a large termite mound and I scampered up as high as I could go and still maintain a solid shooting stance. They changed direction again, passing right in front of us in that shuffle elephants get into when in a hurry. They were mildly agitated, emitting a few squeals

Kwa Kuchinja

and trumpets, but they really became vocal when my first shot slammed into the cow. They dashed into the thick brush just to our right, in a riot of noise, and I put a second one into her ribs, just before she disappeared. She immediately spun on a shilling and charged back out of the thicket, right back into my sights. The third blast put her down, and then the most eerie scenario unfolded: the rest of the herd, having followed her, stopped in mid-step, like kids playing a game of statues. They went silent, like gray, concrete tomb guards. I put my index finger to my lips, cautioning the guides to be quiet and with raised eyebrows and nodding heads, they fully agreed. We backed off the termite mound, keeping its bulk between the alert elephants and ourselves until we could melt into the bush. They were testing the air for scent or sound. Any betrayal of our position would bring the herd down on us, so we crept off to a safe distance, about seventy or eighty yards, and sat down to wait them out. For forty-five minutes we waited; quietly, nervously; constantly watching the bush to make sure they didn't surprise us. The only sounds we heard were the chirps of birds, the humming of flying insects, and the frequent grunts of the lions around us. There seemed to be no shortage of cats, though we couldn't see them for the bush. Finally the kiongozi said the herd had left but I wasn't so sure as I had heard nothing to indicate they had moved off, not a sound.

We threaded our way through the brush, tentatively approached the termite mound, and peered around it. Only the dead cow with her fatal cargo was there. We surveyed the surrounding bush carefully, satisfying ourselves that this highly unpredictable herd had really gone, and then we headed back to camp for the axes, knives and the whetstone.

We stayed on for a few more days, saw two rhino, six of those pesky lions, three eland, and an assortment of the common stuff, but no more tembo. Most of the bulls were evidently still in the park. Once back in town, I sold the smaller, 18 pound tusk and kept the elegant one, and have it to this day.

There were three more safaris to this area, two of which did not involve elephant. On one occasion Alisante Kilimba came with me, as I had promised him some meat. I was also looking to check with the guides and see if the bulls were about, but we didn't get that far. On driving down the road to the Tarangire entrance, we noticed a herd of oryx scattered about in relatively open grassland. Oryx are substantial antelope and can go four feet at the shoulder, and four hundred pounds. Also called gemsbok, these handsome antelope have long, thin rapier like horns with which they have been known to kill lions. Kilimba and I, using what brush and tree cover there was, stalked to within a hundred yards of one and I got into a sitting position. The shot took him just behind and below the shoulder, so vital organs had been hit and he wouldn't go far. And he didn't, but what progress he made was toward the game reserve. Bahati siyo mzuri![109]

We knew we were close to the park's border and relatively sure we were not across it, but we were concerned, maybe even a little panicky. We hustled back to the car, drove up to the beast and tried to stuff it into the trunk. It was too heavy. We needed to gut it, but my knife was in Arusha. I rifled the glove box. Bahati mzuri! A razor blade! So here we were gutting a four hundred pound animal on the edge of a game reserve with a razor blade. Evidently I was not a Boy Scout! Even handicapped as we were, motivation spurred us to perform at high speed, and shortly we had the entrails on the ground, the oryx in the trunk, and the Simca pointed towards Arusha. Alisante got his meat, and I got a nice set of horns. And after I bought a license, I could even keep them!

The second non-elephant trip came about because of a rumor. There were professional hunters at the Gymkhana Club where I played tennis, and word was that a game scout at Kwa Kuchinja had wounded a buffalo with huge horns. Kilimba and George Deganhart, a Brit from Ilboro Secondary School, accompanied me to Kwa Kuchinja to look for this monster. Of course I knew the odds were slim to none that we would actually cross his path, but still, a trophy buffalo was a prize worth the gamble.

We talked to the local guides and they indicated that indeed an mbogo mkubwa[110] had been wounded, and they were willing to take us to the site. This got our blood churning. We hiked into the area, not far from the village, and started to probe the bush. As I had the only rifle, I took the lead, but everybody's nerves were on edge. Then it happened. The dense brush to our left exploded with the sound of a charging buffalo. We were all startled just short of a collective heart attack, but I managed to swing the .375 to port. Oddly, nyati wasn't coming at us at all, but was crashing to the right, still inside the cover of the brush. I followed the commotion until the beast broke cover: two frightened warthogs in full flight and full retreat. I briefly entertained the idea of shooting one of them in the butt for giving us such a start, but warthogs in flight, their tails straight up like radio antennae, are just too comical to be targets of pique.

We prowled the area for another couple of hours, trying to keep a little distance between ourselves and any really thick patches of potential buffalo cover, but in the end we had to settle for the excitement the warthogs had provided.

My last elephant hunt to this area came in early November. It was not neat and tidy. There would be hard feelings and loose ends. Haji and I set up camp as usual, but the guides showed up drunk. I was not amused and decided to take them for a walk in the heat of the day to burn the booze out of them. Haji didn't think this was such a good idea, but he didn't offer any opposition beyond arched eyebrows. Still, for Haji, even a small showing of disagreement meant he really, seriously, didn't like the idea. But I didn't figure we would come across elephant near the village in the heat of the day. After all, walking out of the village didn't mean you would automatically find elephant.

Ten minutes out we found elephant. One of the guides got agitated and started jumping around and being noisy. I couldn't get him to be quiet, so I gave him a shove for emphasis, and took off by myself, trying to get a better angle on both the wind and the elephants. I got within maybe fifty yards, when the elephants got wind of the

Kwa Kuchinja

guides and took off, but right towards me. I sat down and just when the largest one came across my line of sight, the noisy guide shows up, yapping in my ear. This was a major distraction, but I tried to concentrate on the bull in front of me. I put one shot into him, and then another. He dropped and the others fled. I was relieved to have the elephant down and nobody killed. But, as the elephant started kicking and as I headed in to finish it off, the guide ran in front of me. He was dancing around, shouting to the heavens: and the elephant got up. Even in his state of inebriated excitement, the guide did notice this and he came running terrified towards me, suddenly more sober. I raised the rifle, but the only way to shoot the elephant was to shoot through the guide, not that I wasn't tempted. I brushed the guide aside and got off a quick shot at the head, and then tried to hit the spine as the elephant spun to take off. I raced after it, loading on the run, and in a span of 300 yards, put two well-placed shot into his ribs, but he kept going. I was confident he would shortly be dead, but less confident that my trusty guides could or would find him for me. They came up and we started after the animal, but they weren't as sure as I was about him being dead, so we wandered hither and yon, with no apparent objective except to avoid any encounters with any elephants, under any circumstances.

Back at camp Haji received the news with just the hint of a wry grin. It wasn't so much an I told you so type look, but more the indulgent look of a parent whose child has once again ignored his sage advice, and now look at the mess he was in: bwanas will be bwanas.

The next morning the guides appeared all contrite and sober and eager to find the missing elephant, but we headed out in the wrong direction. This was not good. We saw another elephant, in fact we almost rear-ended it. The guides were moving slowly, the better to absorb the hours, making a show of looking for sign. Their eyes were on the ground, earnestly seeking clues as to the whereabouts of my phantom elephant. They were a few yards ahead of me as we were meandering between two thick patches of brush and trees. The guides briefly disappeared as we rounded the shoulder of the thicket, and when I pulled up behind them, there they were, faces down, looking for sign, and there it was, right in front of us, plenty of sign: on the hoof so to speak. The big bull was not twenty yards in front of the first guide, right out in the open but quartered away from us, foraging, with his head in a tree. I thought: "Sign? You guys are looking for sign? I'll show you sign!" The breeze was in our favor, and the bull continued to concentrate on his meal, so I let them close to within ten yards, and then I gave a low whistle. They lazily looked back at me and with a smirk on my face I cocked my hand and pointed a finger at the large gray hulk immediately to their right front. They did a quick head swivel and then reacted as if they had stepped on a snake. Shock quickly gave way to speed, however, as they put it in reverse and sped past me and out of sight. Fortunately their sprint was accomplished quietly. I backed up slowly, making sure the elephant hadn't been alerted, and then set out to find my intrepid guides. They had a bad case of the jitters, but before long were lobbying for me to go back and kill this elephant that had given them such a fright. They even volunteered to stay where they were while I did it. The bull did have nice tusks, but I declined, saying I wanted only the one I had shot the previous day. After a few more hours of aimless wandering we ended up back in camp. Haji and I folded the tent, but I told the kiongoze I would return the next weekend[111] to retrieve my ivory, and after that was accomplished, I would pay them their due.

Alisante agree to accompany Haji and me the following weekend. I needed him to communicate to the guides, in crystal clear Swahili, my desire to collect the ivory already down. In spite of our statement of intent, the first day we went on another wild tembo chase, randomly roaming the bush. We saw plenty of game, including several elephant, three rhino, a mama lion with a cub in her mouth, a number of lesser kudu, and lots of impala, giraffe and zebra. A couple of the elephant were shootable, in terms of ivory, and one of the lesser kudu would have been a world record, but I was single-minded. I wanted my elephant: not some other elephant, not a record kudu, just the elephant I was sure was out there, and dead.

The next morning we left camp in an entirely different direction, one I perceived likely to be correct. I nudged Kilimba and smiled, but said nothing. About twenty minutes from camp a cry of astonishment leapt from the lead guide: "Tembo, labda!" "Tembo amekufa!"[112] And sure enough, much to the surprise of no one, there was indeed an elephant, and he was indeed dead. I looked him over. The ivory was right; the bullet holes were right; he was in fact the right elephant. As he had been decaying for a week, we didn't have to cut out the tusks. A hard kick with the heel of my shoe broke first one and then the other loose from its moorings. The guides pulled them out of the head, removed the nerves, stuffed the cavities with bunches of green grass, and hauled them back to camp.

All was smiles and congratulations, but while I was relieved that there wasn't a wounded elephant out there somewhere, I was also still irritated that my guides had tried to scam me. Their intentions all along had been to get me to settle for another elephant, and then after I rode into the sunset, collect the ivory and sell it on the black-market. I played nice however, paid them their wages, and Haji, Kilimba and I broke camp and headed home.

The tusks were duly weighed and registered in Arusha, coming in at 66 and 64 pounds. Heavy ivory for the time, but bigger tusks and better guides lay in the future. That would be my last hunt at Kwa Kuchinja.

[109] Bahati siyo mzuri = luck not so good.
[110] Big buffalo. In northern Tanzania, the Masai word mbogo was often used instead of the Swahili word nyati.
[111] School was in session, so I couldn't hunt during the week
[112] Tembo labda means: "Elephant, maybe," Tembo amekufa means: "The elephant is dead."

Kwa Kuchinja

Tembo with 74 and 67 lb. tusks taken at Kwa Kuchinja, Nov. 1965.

Chopping the bone away from the ivory.

CHAPTER 42

Mombasa

Kenya's port city of Mombasa was one of my favorite destinations. It was a fascinating city with history, ambiance and geography to recommend it.

Mombasa sits on an island at the entrance to a natural harbor that attracted the attention of the Arabs in about the 8th Century. They established a trading colony there and for centuries controlled the harbor and the trade along the East African coast. Some 700 years later, the first Europeans entered the harbor, with Vasco da Gama sailing in under the Portuguese flag. The Portuguese were on an expansionist binge that would take them to India, China, and even Japan, and Mombasa became an important trade center and way station for their fleets.

Mombasa changed hands back and forth between the Arabs, Portuguese and native coastal peoples for the next four hundred years. In the 1500's the Portuguese and Arabs warred often over this strategic asset, until finally in the 1590's the Portuguese built Fort Jesus to defend themselves from both the Arabs and the locals. They managed to hang on for another hundred years before the Omani Arabs captured the fort. The Portuguese had a lot at stake, however, and they retook the fort once again, only to lose it for good in 1728 when an Afro-Arab siege drove them out.

In 1832 Sultan Seyyid Said of Muskat, in Oman, established his new capital on Zanzibar, the better to direct the burgeoning trade in spices, ivory, and slaves. In effect, Mombasa, as elsewhere, became an appendage of Zanzibar. The Arabs maintained their dominance until the arrival of the British during the scramble for Africa in the 1880's. Mombassa fell in 1887, and Britain took control of Kenya the following year.

There is much to see in Mombasa: the shops in Old Town, accessible by narrow streets and alleys; ornate Hindu temples, the waterfront and shipping, but most of all, Fort Jesus. The fort served as sanctuary for the occupying party, administrative center, and jail and barracoon.[113] The Portuguese came with two objectives, to spread Christianity and to trade. Mombasa was an outlet for spices, cotton, coffee, ivory, and slaves. How the slave trade squared with Christianity might be a conundrum for Christians in this day and age, but at the time it was the natural order of things. The slave traders on the West Coast of Africa were all from Christian countries, their manifests laden with the names of their 'cargo'. Besides, their cargo would be exposed to Christian influence and thus be civilized and saved. Without the benefit of slavery,

Mombasa

how could the African attain everlasting life?

Fort Jesus thus partially served as a slave depot, and though all is quiet now, at the time conditions were harsh, torture was not uncommon, and no doubt the slaves yearned for that day when their toil and sorrows would end and they could go to their reward: eternal bliss in that wonderful Fort Jesus in the sky.

While the Christian slavers were not saints, the Muslims were probably just as bad. There had been a slave trade along the East Coast since before the time of Christ. For centuries this trade carried on in dribs and drabs, until the 1800's. From the start of the 19th Century, while the English were strangling the trans-Atlantic trade, the trade rapidly expanded along the Indian Ocean. In the 1820's, there were reportedly 20,000 slaves present on Zanzibar[114] at one time, before the trade had really gathered momentum. The close interior was being depopulated, forcing the caravans into the core of Africa where they would disappear for years,[115] much to the nervous consternation of the investors in Zanzibar and Mombasa. The slaves were marched from ever more distant locations: Tabora, then Ujiji, then the eastern Congo, as the supply receded into the rain forest. Often they were chained, and usually they doubled as porters, carrying goods like ivory or copper, or caravan essentials. If they faltered along the way, they were shot: this to discourage others from feigning illness or injury.

One tours Fort Jesus with a sense of history heavy in the humid air. The fort itself is quite impressive in appearance and size. It commands the harbor, and the old cannons are in position here and there, though some just lay on the ground, rusting. It is inside, in the rooms and cells, that one gets a foreboding feeling, a sinking heart.

The city itself is lively, its energy undiminished by the brooding fort. Presently, the city harbors half a million people, but when I was there, probably one fifth of that. Old Town was home to many interesting shops, and I went looking for carvings. A slightly built vendor of mixed African/Arab pedigree showed me his wares, but when I didn't show any inclination to part with my shillingi, he suggested I follow him to another location. We wound our way through gloomy alleys overhung with balconies and clotheslines until I started to become a little concerned. We were well off the tourist trail, but finally he stopped at a low doorway and he gestured for me to enter. I could hear singing inside, so I bent over and entered a room. It was dark, but for the glow of several candles. I could make out a circle of men wielding knives, adzes, and chisels. They were sitting and carving on wood, which was a good sign as it probably meant they were not going to be carving on me. I was told these men were from the Congo and that was probably true as their work was not at all typical of East Africa. I bought a beautiful statue of a man, heavy, about thirty inches tall, with a vertical line of knobs on his back and front that looked like bonbons. His concave face was typical of West African figures, his arms were raised up along side his body, reaching to face level, with his palms open and facing forward: he was a Congolese 'Protector of Children'. The vendor told me so. I was dubious, but later I confirmed his assertion in a book on African art.

Hunting and Teaching in East Africa

Another attraction was the beaches; wide, white sand beaches uncluttered by people or their paraphernalia. Bob and Sue Rogers, Tom and Judy Wagner, and I would holiday at the Twiga Lodge on Tiwi Beach, about ten miles south of Mombasa. These were lazy days spent in large thatch-roofed cabins with the beach and surf right out the front door.

Not far inland was the Shimba Hills Game Reserve with plenty of elephant and the usual game animals, but also about the only place in East Africa you could see sable antelope. Sables are larger than oryx, going over four feet at the shoulder and up to 600 pounds. They are dark brown or black, except for white markings on their faces and underparts. They have a tufted tail, and a slight mane, but they are best known for their long, scimitar-shaped horns.

This combination of beaches and a passable game park nearby made for a restful, enjoyable getaway. I, however, managed to coax a memorable scare out of this idyllic setting. Mombasa Harbor was noted for an abundance of sharks, a reputation we were not unaware of. If there were sharks ten miles north, perhaps there were sharks at Tiwi Beach. When playing in the water we kept an eye out, as the Great White and his lesser cousins were common in the Indian Ocean.

One hot, stifling evening I couldn't sleep so I went for a walk in the ocean. To cool off, I wandered out quite a distance to get waist deep. I was enjoying the night sounds and smells, the darkness, the caress of gentle waves, when something besides seawater caressed me. Something solid bumped my right leg. One thought leapt to mind! What to do? I was out too far and in too deep to run, swimming would just cause a commotion and probably attract further unwanted attention, so I slowly started walking toward shore. Another bump. Keep calm, keep walking. Yet another bump. It seemed to be following me. I had to know. I lowered my hand into the black sea and felt my assailant. It was covered with large, smooth bumps. What a pleasure it was to fondle those large, smooth bumps. No, it was not a mermaid, it was a tortoise shell, waterlogged and floating just below the surface. Relieved, I towed it ashore and dragged it across the sand to our cabin. The bed felt really good, and safe.

By the light of day, the shell was beautiful. I briefly contemplated tying it to the roof of Sue's Volkswagen, which would have looked like mama turtle carrying baby on its back. However we figured it was a bit of a large baby for mama to handle, what with her other responsibilities, plus customs could have been a problem.

Reluctantly we left it for future tourists to admire.

---

[113] A barracoon was an enclosure or barracks used for the temporary confinement of slaves.

[114] Zanzibar, with this concentration of slaves kept in squalid conditions, was called "Stinkibar," by visiting Europeans.

[115] Tippo Tib was the most successful, famous and powerful of these Arab slavers. A precis of my masters degree thesis on him is presented in Appendix A.

CHAPTER 43

Safaris with Hal

Hal Anderson and I went on a number of safaris together, hunting and fishing. We had several memorable adventures, including almost burying his car, almost being buried by herds of elephant, experiencing a sonic boom at ground level, and hunting with a tribe of ear gatherers.

Hal looked every bit the man from Montana: cowboy hat and boots, and weathered face with deep creases. He also managed to look professorial, puffing thoughtfully on his pipe. Pipe smokers, my brother was one too, emit an aura of intelligence. While someone else is talking, they are puffing, considering. When it comes time to respond, they continue to suck on the pipe, either in a trance or still mulling over a response. This keeps them from spur of the moment stupid comments, which alone raises their estimated IQ considerably. Some just keep on puffing, finding that preferable to talking no matter what the provocation. Hal wasn't one of those. He would join the conversation, though in that slow Western way common to those who commune more with coyotes and cattle than people.

Hal was thin, his gaunt cheeks adding a misleading perception of frailty. His wife Meg was also slight of build, but quick and gregarious. In spite of his stature, Hal had a deep, sonorous voice, comforting, but commanding if need be. In contrast to Hal's slow, deliberate manner, Meg was busy, physically and vocally. Her voice seemed to radiate a positive joy in life and family. When Hal came to hunt, he usually brought Meg and their two young boys, Steve and David. They would stay at my place, while Hal and I went hunting. The cool air of Arusha was no doubt a nice break from the humidity and heat of the coast.

Our first safari was to Kwa Kuchinja, just a day trip as Hal was passing through from observing teachers at Mwanza.[116] Forty miles out, we lost our windshield but carried on and before the trip was over had collected a Volkswagen full of grass and bugs. We didn't shoot anything, but almost stepped on a rhino in the tall grass, scared off another one, saw a cheetah, three kudu, some impala, and about twenty elephants. We gave chase to the tembo as there was one in the bunch with five feet of ivory sticking out of his head. The wind was tricky, however, as it was mid-afternoon, and they got our scent and fled toward the game reserve. We persisted for some time, and I could have snapped off a shot at the old boy on three occasions, but being near the Tarangire, I didn't want to chance a wounded one. They kept moving at a brisk pace until they came to a tree with a Tarangire Game Reserve sign on it. There they quit running, milled about the tree, showed us their backsides, and sauntered into the park. Had I been British, I quite possibly would have said, with just a hint of indignation: "By Jove, old chap, I do believe those cheeky blighters just mooned us!"Being American, I just said, approximately: "Aw, shucks."

Hal had to be back in Dar the following day, so we headed for Arusha, taking a short cut through grass that dwarfed his Volks. I knew there were washes in this area, so when the grass suddenly thinned, I yelled: "Stop!" Fortunately we were going at herding speed, and also fortunately, Hal didn't ask Why? like a spouse might do. He immediately slammed on the brakes just as a gap opened in front of us: a gap in the grass, and in the earth. Forget the windshield, here we almost lost the entire vehicle. The left front tire was suspended over the sheer side of a gully six feet deep and eight to ten feet wide. A split second more and we could have held a Bug funeral.

Hal put it in reverse and tried to back out, but the Volkswagen was teetering ever so slightly, and he couldn't get the traction needed. I had to climb down into the crevasse, stand in a sea of fresh spoor on the edge of what seemed a well and recently used buffalo trough, put my shoulder to the underside of the suspended tire and push upwards. I was no Hercules, but then I wasn't Audrey Hepburn either. The car got just enough extra traction to move, and taking discretion as the better course, we retraced our print through the grass and made for home.

Our next trip would be to the Yaida Valley, a remote and truly wild area about eighty miles west and then several miles, and hours, south of Arusha. I could find nobody who had been there, not at the school or the Gymkhana Club, not among the shopkeepers or government officials, not even among the resident professional hunters. From reading I did know that there was a pocket of Bushmen living there, much as they had since the Pleistocene Era, hunting and gathering. The Tindiga were a band of a larger grouping called the Hadazabe. These bands lived south of Ngorongoro and east of Lake Eyasi, throughout the Yaida Valley. All of these Hadazabe bands spoke a 'click'[117] language as did their more numerous brethren in the Kalahari. They had six-foot long bows strung with giraffe tendon, and used arrows tipped with poison on the front and stabilized with guinea hen feathers bound to the tail with antelope tendon. Their main prey was antelope, birds, baboons and monkeys. They wasted nothing, even using the marrow from monkey bones as a skin moisturizer.

The Bushmen are reputed to be the most inoffensive people on earth. But their neighbors were not so nice. Of them I knew nothing, but lessons were forthcoming.

Hal arrived on a Wednesday and we left early the next day. We got out of Arusha before the parades started, but at Mbulu we were stalled. It was Saba Saba Day, the national holiday celebrating the founding of Nyerere's politocal party,TANU, twelve years before. We met an ex-student of mine from Arusha, an Asian girl, got petrol from

Safaris with Hal

her aunt's duka, and had a nice visit, replete with tea and cakes. Indian hospitality is not escaped easily, but an hour later, tea flowing from every pore and cake oozing out our ears, we waddled out to Hal's newly acquired Rover and went looking for a Baptist missionary they had told us about.

The Baptist decided to guide us into the Yaida Valley, as one of his projects was to improve the lives of the Tindiga by settling them into an agricultural lifestyle and he was about due to pay them a visit. To be sociable, and get as much information as I could on the mysterious Yaida area, I rode with him while Hal followed. The missionary had been in the country fifteen years at that point, and as we bounced along, I absorbed a steady stream of invective directed at every size, shape and shade of African, except the Tindiga. He liked them. Africans were lazy; Africans were stupid; Africans were ....; the list seemed without end. I thought that maybe he was in the wrong line of work, but with some effort managed to keep my counsel to myself.

After what seemed an interminable amount of time we pulled onto a narrow track overgrown with grass and small shrubs and headed down into the valley. We hadn't gone far when two human legs approached from the bush, presumably the lower end of a Tindiga. The hunter's upper body was almost entirely enveloped by a large antelope, with a long bow and several arrows evident on one side of the package, and part of a curly head visible on the other. The bushman walked up to the Rovers and with a nonchalant shrug dropped the hartebeest at his feet. It fell in a limp clump, obviously not long dead. He and the missionary were acquainted and passed the time of day briefly, then the little man shouldered his outsized prize and sauntered on down the road as if carrying a sack of feathers.

The missionary didn't want us hunters anywhere near his prized Tindiga as he was trying to wean them from hunting and we would perhaps set the wrong tone. He suggested we cross the valley towards the Yaida Swamp and contact the Wamangati for guides, indicating that if there were elephant, they would be over there.

The Yaida Valley sits in a broad plain between the Great Rift escarpment to the west and the elevated plateau of central Tanzania to the east. Much of the valley along the western edge is dominated by Lake Eyasi, a shallow lake some fifty miles long and eight to ten miles wide. The valley itself is grassland and bush dotted with kopjes. Hal, Haji and I entered this wilderness totally excited. The rampant optimism of the hunter took over. Things would be good; the elephants would be enormous.

We located a village, arranged for some guides the following morning, then drove some distance north to set up camp, as the Wamangati were cattle people and cattle settlements tend to be attractive only to cattle people. We got camp set up a couple hours after sunset. Haji fed us, then we settled in for the night, Hal and I in the tent, and Haji, as always, in the Rover. My cook displayed no enthusiasm at all for sleeping in the bush under such flimsy cover as a tent. If there were something as solid as a Land Rover available, why would anyone want to sleep under a mere piece of cloth? Of course to me, after a couple of years with only the stars for cover, the tent was a veritable fortress, and in any case, much more comfortable than the cramped seats of a Rover.

Hunting and Teaching in East Africa

The next morning we picked up two Wamangati guides and shoved off into the bush. Soon the unvarnished truth became self-evident: there were no elephant, and our guides were less than worthless. Worthless would imply that they were merely inept. Inept they were, but they had additional traits that made 'worthless' look like a compliment. They were shifty, gruff, and menacing.

Since they seemed to know nothing about hunting, we ended up on a large kopje, using this high spot to scan for game. The longer we were with these folks, the uneasier I became. They dressed like Masai and like Masai had long, heavy spears. Since their demeanor was almost belligerent, the fact that they were armed only added to the feeling of concern. I did not trust them as far as I could throw a new Buick, for I had heard rumors of their past penchant for murder and mutilation. I suggested to Hal that while one of us kept an eye out for game, the other should keep an eye on their surly carcasses. Hal was evidently picking up the same vibes, as he readily agreed.

Wamangati is what the Masai call these people. To themselves they are the Barabaig. But because the Masai tag is so apropos, all their neighbors use it. Wamangati: it means: "The Enemy!"

At the time I did not know this little dictionary detail, but there was more than just an explanation of the meaning and origin of the name Wamangati in an article in the **Tanganyika Standard** a few weeks later. In the past they had practiced ritual murder, but this practice was supposedly behind them. In the past a prospective father-in-law expected a pair of human ears as part of the dowry, but this practice was likewise presumed suspended, relegated to the dustbins of history. Nevertheless, the article in the Standard reported that the Wamangati had just killed two middle school teachers, ambushing them while they were riding their bikes along a remote trail. Why did the authorities suspect the Wamangati? Missing ears. The ears had been severed from the bodies, no doubt cementing some young lover's claim to a maiden.

There was no mistaking the waves of ambition radiating from our two guides. Harvesting two sets of white ears would make for great trophies, like bagging an albino bison in Montana. We decided to end the day's hunt and jettison these two on our way back to camp. With camp only a couple miles from the Wamangati village, I was becoming concerned for Haji's safety. At the cattle boma we rid ourselves of the guides and sped over the open plain to camp. Haji was there, nervous, but in one piece, all appendages still attached.

The next couple of days we hunted north of camp, taking Haji with us. First we came across an unusually large pack of wild dogs. These are not handsome critters. They are coated with random splotches of brown, white, black, orange and yellow; the whole mess topped with outsized ears and supported by spindly legs. They are perky and alert, almost fidgety. They normally run in groups of fifteen or twenty, but we were looking at seventy to eighty in this closely packed mass. Perhaps it was a social gathering of several clans.

I had often wondered if wild dogs would be a threat to a man on foot. I stopped the Rover and got out, the car sheilding me from the motley crowd. When I got to the back of the vehicle I leapt out, waving my hat and shouting. They instantly took a quick step forward, eyeing me with interest. This didn't totally answer my question, but it was close enough. I scampered back to the safety of the driver's seat and gave them another look. Evidently I hadn't impressed them much. They continued to stand their ground and stare at us.

Wild dogs in the game parks are used to vehicles and don't pay much attention to them, but in the Yaida Valley there was not much traffic so we were being intently scrutinized. But eventually, since, as a whole, we were too big to tackle, and since the bite-sized morsel had disappeared, they lost interest and drifted off at a slow trot.

Later, Hal got a Coke's Hartebeest on the plain, and in a stretch of bush running up the east side of the valley, we located some eland. Eland are the largest of antelope, going to seventy inches at the shoulder and over 1500 pounds. They may be large targets, but they are difficult to hunt, being very alert and very skittish. We tried, but didn't get within range.

We decided to head home the next day via the same bushy slope so as to have another go at the eland. We got turned around and lost, for four hours. This cost us daylight, but more importantly, petrol. We finally found a rocky road up to the plateau, but it took two hours to negotiate the eight miles to the rim, thus using even more petrol as we had to use four-wheel drive and low gear the whole way.

We held our collective breath, hoping we wouldn't have to walk twenty miles for fuel, but somehow the Rover managed. We arrived at Mbulu about two hours after dark, got gas and ate with the Hirji family again until an hour before midnight, then, as it had been a long day and we were tired, we took a short cut to Arusha.

This was one of my father's short cuts. When my brother and I were young, traveling the back roads on deer hunts, father always knew a short cut. These exercises always cost us gasoline and consternation, to the point that David and I would roll our eyes and implore Pop not to do it. We two young smart mouths would beg in mock horror: "Dad, not another long cut!" Well this little time saver from Mbulu to Arusha turned a two-hour jaunt into a four-hour tour; a tour of strange roads, at night, in the bush. Father would have been proud: his son extending the family tradition. We pulled into Arusha at three in the morning, a truly prodigious long cut. Probably a family record.

Our next hunt would be more fruitful and much more exciting: the kind of safari you live for, if you live through it. We had had enough of the Yaida Valley with its abundance of ear gatherers but paucity of elephant. I had visited Roger Hagler, he of the Peace Corps in the Southern Highlands, in Montana, between tours. Roger had come across a great guide named Lati, a Masai living at Kibaya. We decided to give him a try.

Kibaya is a small village in the Masai Steppe, straight south of Arusha; about a hundred and fifty miles in a straight line, but two hundred twenty by road. We followed the Great North Road to Kondoa and then drove east sixty-four miles into the

Hunting and Teaching in East Africa

bush to Lati's village. Lati wasn't immediately available, as he was busy escorting a professional and his client. We had planned a ten day safari so were in no big hurry, and a young Morani[118] volunteered to help while Lati was occupied. This young man would cause us some problems.

His first bit of help was to suggest a camping site, and a very comfortable site it was. We pitched the tent under a large acacia tree for shade, and had a nice view of a watering hole only another hundred yards down the elephant path we were camped upon. We had come to get up close and personal with the elephants, and this handy arrangement accomplished that on the very first night.

Hal and I were very pleased with our camp. Haji cooked the evening meal, Hal smoked his pipe in the moonlight, and we shot the breeze around a comforting campfire. When the fire had gone to embers we called it a night. Haji climbed into the Land Rover and Hal and I unfurled our sleeping bags and settled down to a sound night's sleep on the tent floor. And we were sound asleep, until the earth started to shake. I suddenly woke up in the middle of a thunderous, screaming elephant stampede. While this was a nightmare, it was no dream! There were elephants rushing by both sides of the tent, panicked by the scent of man where it shouldn't be. I fully expected to be crushed, as the ground shook and the herd rent the still evening air with frightening volleys. In a few seconds it was over, leaving me quivering with fear and excitement. I looked over at Hal. He was still asleep! I shook him, hard. He barely woke up, half listened to my excited jumble of words, and turned over. He had other priorities. I settled down and bunched up my pillow, but no sooner had my nerves partially uncoiled, than in the still of the night air I heard a twig snap. I was suddenly all ears, alert, on a knife's edge.

Nothing. Not a sound. For minutes. Then a light swishing noise right next to the tent. An elephant was pulling up grass within six feet of my head. Then a soft plunk, plunk, as fresh droppings hit the ground. I carefully slipped out of my sleeping bag, cocked the .577, and slowly unzipped the tent. Shivering from the cool night air, or perhaps the excitement, I took a peek, fully expecting to see big gray butts parked next to the tent. But once again they had moved so silently I hadn't heard even a rustle in the grass. The herd of half a dozen was standing in a grove of trees about thirty yards away. They didn't seem to have a care as they plucked a few leaves from the trees and then slowly padded on down for a drink.

The next morning I regaled Hal with the lurid details of the night. He exhaled a small stream of smoke, took another drag, and allowed that, knowing we were here, they probably wouldn't be back. Haji was more impressed. He had seen the whole thing from the Rover, a fact that was of absolutely no comfort to him. His eyes wide open, his brows perched high on his forehead, he said: "Bwana! Matata mbaya! Tembo mkali sana ndani ya campi!"[119] He was not a happy camper and suggested we move. Well, that seemed a bit extreme. Haji could be little old lady about some things.

This very day, however, he would have further reason to cluck. We had no sooner finished breakfast when there was a crashing in the brush nearby. Evidently some stragglers had come for a drink, got our scent, and charged off through the bush. We rounded up the young Masai and he agreed to follow up the elephant for us. He put on a good show, but we soon realized that, as regards hunting, he had only one talent: elephant avoidance. We wandered off for about an hour and the more we walked the more the elephant noises receded, at about a ninety degree angle to our general line of march.

When we got back to camp, Haji was highly agitated: "Tembo mkubwa sana nakuja hapa! Hapa!"[120] A big bull had come right into camp while we were out chasing our tails. Haji had holed up in the Rover, but he was plenty shaken. And we were plenty chagrined.

The rest of that day was spent in exercising our legs, knowing our guide had an elephant phobia, but hoping we might accidentally come across some. There certainly seemed to be plenty in the area. Dinnertime rolled around and Haji fidgeted around the fire preparing the meal, but not happy about another night in this hot spot. That night passed without serious incident, however, though elephant once again did come into camp.

The following two days were more of the same. We saw lots of bush, heard a few elephants, but they always seemed to elude us. However, the following day Lati would be available, though his arrival did not come without further travail.

I was sound asleep when I was roughly grabbed and shook like a rag doll. Hal was excited, and a lot stronger than he looked. His speech was rapid, highly agitated, as he recounted another stampede: They were everywhere. The earth was shaking. The elephants were in a frenzy, screaming and trumpeting as they rattled the tent in their headlong panic. Or words to that effect. I feigned disinterest and settled back into my cozy nest. However, it was some time before sleep returned.

In the morning, over breakfast, Hal and Haji had formed a team: TIME TO MOVE CAMP! Since Lati was coming that morning and I didn't want to waste any more time in non-productive activity, I hatched a plan. I felt we could solve the problem in an organic, environmentally friendly way and not waste half the day or have to vacate the premises.

What do people do after breakfast? They go to the bathroom. What do they do in there? They void wastes accumulated from the previous day. I suggested we void in the middle of the elephant autobahn, about a hundred yards from camp. We did, and the elephants made no more forays into our little settlement. All they needed was a little courtesy, a little polite notification of our presence.

After solving the stampede problem but before Lati arrived, I got to thinking about those stampedes. Why had we not been trampled? The moon had been bright since we had arrived, so my best guess was that, weak though elephants' eyes were, in the moonlight the tent must have looked like something solid, an anthill for instance. Elephants will crash through brush with abandon, but they don't run headlong into baobab trees, or any other large, solid objects. That flimsy tent probably saved us, but maybe they were just kindly elephants, panicked but not murderous. NBL.[121]

Hunting and Teaching in East Africa

Lati arrived, and now the hunting could begin, hopefully. He was an mzee, and a rarity. Mzee is a respectful term for an elder, and Masai are not usually hunters, as they have no use for most game. They have food taboos, like most tribes do. The Hehe and the Bena, for instance, will not eat duikers or moles. The Masai will eat only cattle, or animals kama ngombe,[122] such as eland or buffalo. So here he was, a Masai, an elder, and a hunter, a rare breed indeed.

Lati knew his stuff and before the sun was high we were on the trail of a small herd. A small herd is a good sign, as a large herd is usually cows and calves. These elephant had fed into thick thorn scrub. We could hear them up ahead, close, but we couldn't see them as visibility was almost nil. I reached for some dirt to sift through my fingers and track the breezes. The elephant were almost stationary, languidly browsing. Judging from the contented purring of their stomachs, they had no idea we were there. We inched closer, the heat and tension oppressive. Twenty yards; ten yards; ten feet. We could see them, but couldn't make out one end from the other, nor could we see any ivory. Big gray slabs of wrinkled hide was all that was discernible, and even that seemed to pulse and dance out of focus in the heat and thorn. Lati touched my shoulder, motioning to back off. At mid-day, the breeze was bound to shift and give us away. We backpedaled, guns ready, but there was no need as we went undetected.

Lati suggested we try something else for a while and return towards evening for this lot. We got out of the thick stuff and into an area of clearings and patchy brush. Before long, maybe a couple of hours, Hal spotted half a dozen eland about four hundred yards away, up a slight incline. He set out with Lati, as I stayed put. Eland are so alert to danger, the fewer bodies in pursuit, the better. I watched through the scope on the Winchester, first the eland, then the hunters, back and forth. The eland were getting nervous, the hunters were getting closer. The hunters were within range. The hunters kept stalking! What was going on? I was silently urging Hal to shoot, my muscles tight with anticipation. I could just taste the savory eland steaks we would roast that evening. The eland bolted and were gone. So was my taste of juicy eland steak. I was not happy. I double-timed down the grade and then back up to where Hal and Lati were standing. "What happened? You were within range." "Lati wanted to get closer." "Lati knows elephant, he doesn't know eland. You can't shoot eland at ten yards!" I was hot, while Hal was disconsolate, having missed a good chance at a great trophy. As I cooled off, I could see that Hal felt bad enough without me piling on. OK, he had just learned something the hard way, just as I had on occasion. It was not right for me to get on his case for something I had also done, more than once. Thoughts of those plump, fatty eland steaks, cooking and radiating a mouth-watering aroma had got the better of me.

I consoled Hal, relating my early elephant hunts: how I had let the guides dictate the program with almost disastrous results. There comes a point where the man with the rifle has to take over and make the decisions, not just pull the trigger. The guide is just that, a guide. He gets you in the vicinity of the animal, but it is up to the hunter

Safaris with Hal

to decide how to close out the proceedings. Hal was a good shot and a pleasure to hunt with as he knew guns and was cool in tight spots, like earlier in the day. Experience was necessary, in order to make better decisions. Hal had gained experience. Still, dinner was going to be bland.

As evening approached, Lati suggested we return to that small herd of tembo we had got so close to earlier. Our guide had a sixth sense about elephants and great knowledge of their habits. In this instance, we were not tracking them, he just headed off in a direction to intercept them, as if he had a spotter plane overhead and knew just where they would be. As we walked through the bush I watched and admired this rare old man, probably in his sixties, slightly bent with age, rheumy eyed from malaria and pombe, his elongated ear lobes flipped over the tops of his ears, minus their usual decorative, copper weights.

The ear thing is worth mentioning, as at one time there had been two experienced Masai kiongozi in Kibaya, Lati and his partner. The Masai pierce their ear lobes and attach copper or lead ornaments, some the tear shape of fishing weights. Over time the weight of these ornaments stretches the ear lobe, making for a very handsome loop dangling down to the shoulder. Problem is, out in the bush, the thorny bush, these lobes can get caught in the shrubbery. This is how Lati's partner came to grief.

They had been guiding a professional hunter and his clients and when shots were fired, the elephants charged. Everyone fled, but in retreat his friend's ear lob had flopped down and then tangled in a wait-a-bit thorn bush. When he stopped to free it, he was caught by an enraged elephant, gored, tossed, and then stomped beyond recognition. I heard this story from the professional hunter involved, as I knew he used Lati and I had remarked that the guide seemed a bit cautious in his old age. The pro gave me a disapproving look for my unwarranted remark and said Lati had good reason to be, and then related this story.

It was late afternoon, hot and still. The faint smoky smell of Lati was left trailing in his wake as we wound around the thickest patches towards the herd. We could hear branches breaking up ahead. Lati had located the herd in this sea of thorn scrub. MMBA, and Lati had pinpointed this small dot on the continent. Uncanny.

We climbed a small knoll overlooking a clearing. Lati thought the elephant would emerge into this open area, so we positioned ourselves for shooting, and waited. The elephant were in no hurry, but eventually, probably twenty minutes, one of them broke into the clearing. He had nice tusks, in the sixty-pound range, but the others held back. We were hoping another one would enter the glen, but instead one came down our left flank and we had to scurry back to avoid being caught between the two. He got our wind and took fright and the others followed him into the bush. The bull in the open heard them move off and turned to do likewise. He was broadside to us at thirty yards, a bit far for my taste, but close enough. As soon as he had spun around, Hal shot him in the heart, and I placed one in his lungs for insurance. Hal had hit him low and forward in the chest, a perfect shot, so we knew he wouldn't go far. He broke into the bush with a grunt, but amidst the general melee of fleeing elephant, we heard him go down.

Hunting and Teaching in East Africa

I scanned the bush with my scope. I thought I could make him out but wasn't sure, but more importantly, I wasn't sure that he was alone. We waited until dusk. Lati was also not certain that all of the other bulls had left, so we turned for camp. It was too late to extract the tusks anyway, so we would come get them the next day.

The walk back to camp was very pleasant. The moon was bright, the heat of the day was giving way to cooler evening temperatures, and the hunt had been successful, a perfect day, except for that eland. I was dragging up the rear enjoying the moment, when a flock of guinea hens were startled by our approach and flew into an acacia tree. That eland would be replaced! While the others kept walking, I sat down and drew a bead on a bird perfectly silhouetted by the moon. Some might think a .375 a bit large for bird hunting, but while a .270 with a soft-nosed bullet would absolutely explode a guinea hen, a .375 with a hard-nosed bullet will just put a neat little hole in it.

In the quiet of the bush night the sudden report of my rifle caused more than just a dead bird! The guys in front of me about came out of their shoes. Naturally they thought we were being attacked from the rear by vengeful elephants. However the shouting and commotion died down when they were informed that I had just been gathering dinner.

Of course I knew the shot would give them a good jolt, but on the other hand, what choice did I have? And, on the other hand, in my gut I still hadn't totally forgiven Hal for blowing the eland hunt and depriving one and all of a succulent evening meal. That he should have to jump a few inches off the ground seemed little enough penance.

Haji did a good job on the guinea hen, very tasty. What could be better than a warm beer and roast guinea hen on a beautiful night in the middle of thorn scrub, in the depths of the Masai Steppe? Not much.

The next day we were in no hurry, so after noon we gathered our dental tools and left camp for our fallen tembo. As usual it was hot, and a dead carcass creates quite a buzz, mostly flies and bees. The elephant had bloated in the heat, and while Lati and another man were working on the tusks, other Masai had come along to harvest meat to be sold to the WaGogo just south of them. One young Morani was on top of the beast, hacking at the rear quarters with a panga. Hal and I were sitting nearby when the lulling hum of the insects was suddenly interrupted by a loud blast. It sounded like a low flying jet plane had just broken the sound barrier, right there at ground level. We jumped up and looked to our left just in time to see the panga wielding Masai go cart wheeling off the rear flank of the elephant whose stomach he had just popped. He lit in a heap, his face coated in half-digested elephant muck. He smiled an embarrassed smile, a small slit of white in a coat of green, slimy goo. Everyone had a good laugh at his expense while he tried with little success to de-goo himself and reclaim his dignity.

We spent a few more days beating the bushes, but got no more volunteers; elephant, eland, or otherwise. We drove back to Arusha well pleased with ourselves. We

Safaris with Hal

had accomplished our main purpose, to get Hal an elephant, and one with fine ivory. Most of all, however, we had experienced a safari to remember and had thoroughly enjoyed the services and company of Lati, a man of dignity and courage.

Meg was happy to see us, her husband still in one piece, and the boys were ecstatic over the elephant their Dad had bagged. Haji got the night off as Meg took over the kitchen, and over a nice dinner, we planned another trip.

Next we went fishing, our destination being an island with the reassuring name of Mafia. The Indian Ocean is renowned for its big game fishing, up to and including marlin and great white shark. Hal booked a reservation on Mafia Island, one hundred sixty miles directly south of Zanzibar. We flew in on a small plane, in itself something of a thrill. The airstrip on the island was rough and narrow, situated between tall palm trees. The day we landed, there was a strong cross wind and the pilot had to pull up at the last minute to avoid a palm tree landing. On the second try he put her down right on the money.

The lodge was typical of the coast, rustic, airy, and thatched. The food was excellent, mostly the fish guests caught. My favorite was the fish stew. It was a mix of types, and most parts were used though I didn't see any eyeballs looking back at me. We spent twenty-two hours on the boat, over three days, and the results were also mixed. Hal caught a beautiful, thirty-nine pound sailfish, Steve hooked a sleek, fierce looking barracuda, and I battled a huge tuna. What a struggle. It was enormous, bigger than a whale shark, bigger than Godzilla! OK, it wasn't all that big, but it was definitely larger than most trout. What I did get was a monster sunburn. I blistered, and peeled for days. Give me the bush!

This was my last major safari with Hal. It was a comfort to have a companion who was level headed and in a pinch would not only back you up, but wouldn't shoot you in the breeches. I was happy he got his elephant, and later on he did get a fine eland.

After Africa Hal and Meg bought a ranch in Belt, Montana, twenty miles east of Great Falls. When I got married, my wife and I would take our two kids there to visit. Here I was settled in a city, but Hal was still enjoying life off the beaten track.

---

116 Hal trained teachers at University College in Dar es Salaam.

117 The Khoisan language of the Bushmen and Hottentots incorporates four clicks into its alphabet. These are used mostly as consonants. The Zulu and Xhosa, also use some clicks.

118 At about 15 years of age a Masai male goes through a coming-of-age ceremony. Headdresses are made, his head is shaved, and he is circumcised. He is now a warrior, a Morani.

119 Roughly: "Bwana. Bad trouble. Fierce elephants were right in camp."

120 "A very big elephant came right here! Here!"

121 NBL is my shorthand for "not bloody likely," an expression of some severity among the British. Mostly we Americans considered it a pretty comical way to cuss.

122 Kama ngombe means "like cattle."

Lati and I posing for the camera at Kibaya.

Me at Kibaya camp, August 1966.

Haji bringing firewood at Kibaya.

Tembo trail and droppings, Kibaya area.

Hal Anderson and son David with Hal's sailfish. Mafia Island.

Lati clearing brush around Hal's elephant, Kibaya. 60 lb. tusks.

CHAPTER 44

Socialism

Tom was in for a quick lesson. Not that he wasn't used to lessons, having just graduated from the University of Chicago School of Law. The degree completed, he had brought his comely wife Judy and his two very blond sons to Tanzania to help the fledgling government implement a transportation cooperative. Tom was a good and valiant man, but this job called for someone with a machine gun, and the urge to use it.

Nyerere was a socialist of the liberal school, but lately influenced by the Zanzibar crowd of Chinese educated radicals. Nyerere had tried to unify East Africa for reasons of viability, even offering to step aside and let Obote and Kenyatta sort out the governing arrangements. Getting no cooperation, however, he decided to set Tanzania on its own course, down the socialist road. Banks were nationalized. The East African currency of the colonial period was replaced with Tanzanian currency. Businesses were taken over, usually with little or no compensation. The bus and rail services within Tanzania were to be run by the government. This was where Tom Wagner entered, stage left. The title of the drama: The School of Hard Knocks.

The drama starts as a rose in full bloom and ends with the rose first crushed, and then entirely obliterated. A Chagga husband and wife team had started a bus company. They saw a need to ferry people back and forth between Moshi and Arusha and in the best capitalist tradition, not foreign to Africans at all it seems, they bought a Volkswagen van and began meeting this need. Before long they added more vans, and in time a number of full sized buses. As the business expanded the husband died, but the wife carried on, managing this flourishing enterprise. Enter 'Uhuru na Umoja'.

The problem with 'Freedom and Unity' is that there is an inherent conflict between the two, given human nature. And with socialist unity, the problem extends beyond the restraints in the political sphere[123] to almost total government direction and control in the economic sphere.

Thus, following the relentless logic of collective unity, even an African business, non-exploitative of the proletariat in any way, was subject to nationalization. The

Socialism

woman lost her business to the government. It was put under the Ministry of Transportation, which would run it for the benefit of the whole of society, thus bringing profit to all, not merely the greedy and selfish proprietor. The owner was elbowed aside, bereft of any reward or role. Of course she would be compensated in due course (see bado kidogo in the glossary), but for now, she was out, and one of her drivers was in.[124]

The driver knew of gear shifts and bus stops. Of running a business he knew nothing, though under socialism if you did have business expertise, you were at a minimum suspect, but mostly you were considered entirely unfit to conduct an enterprise aimed at the general welfare. No loaf being better than half a loaf.

Given the above, it doesn't seem logical that the government would look to a lawyer from the bastion of capitalism to come help them run a nationalized business. But a country like Tanzania, newly independent with a thin veneer of intellectuals at the top, cannot be held to logical consistency at ground level. So riding to the rescue was a Chicago lawyer devoid of business experience or any idea of what he was getting into. And, on his arrival the person in charge, the person he was supposed to train in procedures he had yet to learn himself, left on holiday.

For a month Tom had to manage the bus cooperative pretty much on his own. He spoke no Swahili, and he knew next to nothing about busses, schedules, or routes. He was in for a condensed course in business management, and to his credit, he was a quick study. Unfortunately, Al Capone not being available, the situation was beyond salvaging. Tom was not an Al Capone type. Instead he was a soft spoken, tenderhearted Midwest farm boy type, too considerate of others for his own good. This admirable tendency to empathize with others almost cost him his life, in fact.

He was driving on one of the main roads skirting Arusha when he hit an old man who had suddenly veered from the edge of the road into the side of his car. Tom stopped and got out. While trying to attend to the fallen figure a crowd gathered. An angry crowd. Tom felt the heat and escaped to the safety of his car, then he fled for the police station. The police were not impressed. They dithered about for twenty minutes, presumably to let the angry people disperse, but really for no reason at all, except that they didn't want to be bothered, again, by this old man and his act. Seems he made a habit of walking into the sides of passing vehicles, whether to get attention or because he was just plain nuts, was not clear.

Anyway, back to the subject at hand. While the theorists in Dar es Salaam were riding the clouds of utopian idealism, the men at the local level were riding the bus business into the ground. Their visions tended toward the more immediate and mundane, the ubiquitous, existential three: wine, women and song. The vehicle for the realization and immediate gratification of these local visions was the maintenance budget. Money meant for repairs, or even basics like oil and tires, was spent on the existential three. Before long, the fleet built over the years by the Chagga man and his wife was depleted. Parts were scavenged from downed busses to keep others running. One bus disappeared altogether, until it was located providing service to an equally inept cooperative in Dodoma. At the first opportunity, meaning a moonless night, it was promptly stolen back, one of the few successes of the Arusha cooperative.

Tom worked hard to keep the cooperative alive and while he was there it was still, though barely, a living organism. But when Tom's tour ended there was nobody left to keep even a small part of the maintenance budget out of the beer halls. The rose was plucked and each petal savored and enjoyed, but even a vibrant flower has a finite number of petals. Which brings me back to that ironic observation on socialism, the no heart no brain thing.

Though still in my twenties, my four years in Tanzania weaned me from any socialist tendencies I might have had, and I did have some. The concept of human equality and of a state and economic apparatus geared to promote that equality has a powerful pull on the idealist in some of us. In practice, however, socialism is an artificial, human invention, and subject to human frailties. In practice, the managers become the pigs in George Orwell's Animal Farm: some more equal than others. The best intentions of a few leaders with selfless visions cannot stay this tide. It seems that Utopia cannot be imposed. Perhaps when man is a better beast socialism will evolve naturally from capitalism and its ideals prevail. Perhaps, but doubtful in the extreme. As Dostoevsky observed, man is an animal that walks on two legs; and is ungrateful. Give him Utopia and he will smack it with a ball bat.

---

[123] See Appendix B for Nyerere's explanation of preventative detention.
[124] Ever notice how socialist countries are gender specific, that is, run entirely by men?!

CHAPTER 45

AR 384/66

In December of 1966 I had a safari that Walter Mitty might well have dreamed up. But unlike James Thurber's character, I would live the dream, and live to relate the events that transpired. I had three solid chances to get killed, by lion, snake, and elephant, and shot my two largest elephants

Haji and I left Arusha for Kibaya early in the month. I had rented a long wheel based Land Rover from a professional hunter who ran a safari company in Arusha. I didn't have the shillings to pay for it, at the time, but was counting on the hunt to cover the cost. I knew Lati would deliver.

Lati couldn't deliver, as it turned out. In Kibaya we inquired about him and were told he was with a professional hunter from Arusha. We drove out to their camp site and the Count, his German client, and Lati were there having a bite of late lunch. I knew the Count from the Gymkhana Club in Arusha, and had played some tennis with both he and his slim but attractive wife. Lati would be tied up for some time, and to get me out of their hair and out of their area, the Count suggested I push another fifty miles into the bush and look up the Wandarobo, a hunting people settled around Kijungu.

What initially started out as a stroke of bad luck would turn into the best hunt of my life. At Kijungu we found two guides, Kisenge and an older man I respectfully addressed only as Mzee. Kisenge was in his early twenties, about five foot six, and dressed in a Masai like red robe. As I would soon learn, he was a hunter par excellence. He knew the bush and the animals, he was fearless, and he could track an elephant through this dry thorn scrub as easily as I could track a deer in fresh snow.

The next morning the guides and I drove to a nearby water hole and examined the spoor from the previous night. Elephant had been there three or four hours before sunrise, so Kisenge started tracking. A good guide doesn't have his nose in the dirt all of the time. If he did, the hunting party would just be keeping pace with the elephants and probably never catch up. A skilled tracker can scan the area and see where the elephant have left markers, though they be ever so slight. When the direction becomes less discernible to his experienced eye, then the hunt slows to a temporary crawl as he sorts things out. Sometimes the soil and shrubbery don't broadcast the path the elephants have taken. Sometimes herds cross, leaving a confusing mix of signals. Sometimes there is simply an interruption, and the trail has to be picked up after a detour of some distance, as happened on this day.

We were moving fairly briskly, following a group of three bulls, when about a hundred yards to our front a stray appeared, headed towards us. He had nice ivory, but only one stick of it, so we needed to pass him by without alerting all the game for miles with the noise of a shot. This was easier said than done, however. If we zigged, he zigged. If we zagged, he zagged. He mirrored our every move, all the time getting closer and closer. We were in spotty brush and what little air movement there was was in our favor so he did not detect us, but he soon would as we were on a collision course. Finally we had no choice but to retreat and circle away from the spoor of the three bulls.

About a half-hour later we got back on the trail of our three bulls, but another delay was due up shortly. I heard what sounded like moaning, off to the right. I asked the guides to stop and listen. "Umesikia?" "Ndio." "Tembo?" "Labda."[125] We interrupted our tracking and wound through the bush towards the sound. We clung to the edge of a thick patch of brush as we closed in. It wasn't elephant at all, but a rhino. She held her head very low and was softly groaning. We crept forward for a better view until we were directly in front of her with the thicket behind us to break up our profiles. A narrow stretch of low dry grass bisecting the brush in front of us and led directly to the rhino. By now it was mid-morning and the temperature was climbing. We had been on the move for three hours, so we settled into the shadows to take a short break and observe the rhino. We weren't alone.

The rhino was swinging its head slowly back and forth, a mournful sight added to by its constant lament. A dead calf lay just below its nose, killed by lions my guides were guessing. It didn't occur to us that those lions might be right behind us, several pair of sparkling orange eyes intently watching us as we plunked our buns between them and their kill.

About ten minutes into our break we decided to get back on the hunt and, bent over for concealment, sneaked our way out of the rhino's field of vision and around to the far side of the thicket. Evidently the lions, unnerved by our presence, had retired to this side of the scrub also. Suddenly the air was split with the warning growls of lions close to port. The guides were startled, but before they could run[126] I snagged the nearest rifle and turned to face the source of the racket. We backed up slowly, the .375 held across my chest, ready to be shouldered if necessary. As we moved back, the snarls subsided. We never did see them, but the audio was quite sufficient.

With the sun straight overhead, the air motionless and stifling, we heard our elephants. They were in a very thick stretch of thorn scrub, impossible to see at first. We inched along a game trail, flanking them on the right. Judging from the occasional stomach rumble, the nearest of them was pretty close. I knelt down and looked under the brush, and there he was, a fine bull with enormous tusks. My heart started to race at the sight: only twenty yards to two hundred pounds of ivory!

Somehow he knew of our presence, as he stood head on, looking in our direction. I didn't want to try a frontal brain shot, so motioned the guides to move ahead. We went about thirty feet, and I knelt down again to have another look. He had turned his whole body and was still facing us head on. I whispered for the guides to stay put and I retraced my steps. I got down on my hands and knees. He had followed me with his head only, leaving his shoulder exposed. As deliberately as I could, I assumed a sitting position and touched off a shot at the exposed shoulder. He slumped slightly at the impact of the 300-grain bullet, then he came. There were no theatrics. No screaming or trumpeting. The charge was silent but for the smashing of everything in his way. I jumped to my feet and brought the rifle to my shoulder just as his head broke cover like a bulldozer pushing brush. I fired almost straight up, his head filling the telescope. The shot didn't kill him, fortunately, but it did turn him. He went by so close I could have poked him with the end of the barrel. Instead, centering the scope with the right eye but placing the shots with my left, I emptied the last two rounds into his heart area as he thundered past and disappeared into the bush on the other side of the narrow trail. The guides came up and we listened as he and the other two fled. Amidst all the bushwhacking we heard a crash and then the dying gurgles an elephant makes from heart and lung shots. He had gone down. We closed in, anxious to get to him, but mindful of his two companions.

He was on his side, his eyes blinking at our approach. The other two we could see about fifty yards off. I quickly put a bullet into the top of his head, and then turned to face the others. They moved off slowly, sorry to lose their friend, but not wanting to suffer the same fate. The guides suggested we pursue them, as one of them was even bigger than this one. I declined: "Moja natosha leo."[127]

And indeed one was enough for the day. Now that the action was over, the shakes settled in. I realized that I should not still be alive. If my brain shot had killed him, he would have killed me. His momentum would have deposited tons of dead weight on top of me. If I had hit even close to the brain, close enough to make him stumble or drop, the result would have been the same. The other part of this miraculous escape was how he had managed to change direction in a flick of time, just enough to avoid flattening me. To him I was no more than a twig, though a painful one. At the angle I was shooting, it was next to impossible to hit his brain, but the flash and blast, right in his face, and the searing pain of the bullet tearing up through his trunk and out the top of his head registered immediately and served to turn him just enough. Bahati mzuri.

We got back to camp about four in the afternoon and the first food and drink of the day settled my stomach somewhat. The next day was spent cutting out the ivory, which I fully expected to be over one hundred pounds per tusk. Once they were extracted, however, I knew they would be closer to seventy-five. They were thick and looked enormous in the tembo, but the elephant's body was on the smallish side, which as I later discovered was not uncommon for big tuskers in south Masailand.

The following day, December 9, Uhuru Day for Tanzania, we drove six miles north and two miles west through the bush to another water hole the guides knew about. We found a lone bull's tracks from the previous evening, so were not very optimistic, but decided to follow it up anyway. We got lucky. After only an hour of tracking, we came upon the fresh dung of another lone bull. The pace quickened, but in trying to puzzle out his direction in an open, grassy area, he was just off a bit and got our wind. The net result was a three-hour pursuit before we caught him, resting in a clearing under a tree. We closed to within thirty yards and I placed a heart shot. As he turned I put another into his ribs, and then a third into his shoulder, dropping him for a two count, or thereabouts. He got up quickly and I reloaded on the run, dodging through the scattered bushes and trees as I raced through the dry grass after him. I put two more shots into his chest and he pulled up at the edge of a grove of tall acacias and turned to face us, tusks held high in a dead-on-his-feet gesture of defiance. The sight so thrilled me that I ignored the guides urging for more lead and just stood admiring the old warrior's last stand. Finally, since we weren't coming to him and I doubt he could even see us, he turned and took a few uncertain steps before giving up his precious ivory to the billiard tables. His tusks went 77 and 68 pounds, while the tusks of the first one weighed 72 pounds each.

That afternoon we went into Kijungu for petrol and water, and people to help with the tusks. The petrol I got from the Catholic fathers at the mission near the village. This mission was manned by American priests so we struck up a conversation over a glass of red wine. When I asked what they hoped to accomplish way out there, they stated modest goals: make a few converts, hopefully; show the hunters how to farm; set a Christian example for the people to follow.

We got a boatload of people, as the Wanderobo were really fond of elephant meat. They came to my camp that evening and there was much joyful noise as they contemplated the next day. Several of the hunters gathered around my tent and presented me with a poison arrow. It was finely crafted, with a straight shaft and a thin, sharp metal arrowhead. The blade was three-quarters of an inch from barb to barb, and an inch long. How it was mounted into the shaft I couldn't tell, as that area was coated with the poison, a substance the color and consistency of caramel candy. As I examined my gift I noticed that some of the poison had stuck to the blade. Thinking this maybe not the safest arrangement, I took my knife to it, chipping the offending stuff off the edges of the arrowhead. Safety first. It never pays. A flake flew off the blade and into my left eye. As my eye watered heavily I went over to a circle of Wanderobo and explained my predicament. They just smiled and said it was not a problem. They explained that the poison reacted to blood, and a person could actually eat it with no ill effects. When they made the poison, one of the men would make a small cut on his arm, let the blood trickle down in a small stream, and then they would touch a drop of the poison to the man's blood. If the blood boiled and turned black, the poison was strong and acceptable. They would then wipe off the blood before the poison could bubble its way up to the cut and kill the volunteer.

Some statements you can rely on totally. If your stockbroker has a sure thing, you had best think it over. If your doctor gives a diagnosis, perhaps a second opinion is called for. If a man of the bush tells you his poison will cause you no harm, you can believe it. These people know their world. Haji rinsed out my eye, and I turned in for the night, confident that I would not only wake up in the morning but that my eye would also survive the night. In any case, it wasn't my shooting eye. I drifted off to the comforting sounds of kindred spirits gathered around a campfire.

The next morning the whole troop headed for the carcass. On the way we cut some fresh tracks, so Mzee and I left the main parade to investigate. After a brief walk we heard branches being broken over to the left. We investigated and found three bulls in a thicket of choice, thorny tidbits. There was an open space in front of us, with an anthill about half way across. We could see the backside of one of the elephants and decided to get closer, using the anthill for cover. We could now see two of the elephants, and the one with the better ivory moved up in the bush right to the edge of the clearing, about ten yards from us. I knelt down looking for a shot when he decided to cross the clearing for tastier snacks on the other side, the side directly behind us. I brought up the .375 for a frontal brain shot, the only choice under the circumstances, and he certainly filled the scope! Deciding that the tusks weren't that good after all, I tried to back up without startling him. The guide had already cleared off but the elephant saw my attempt to do so, almost under his nose, and jerked his head back and then charged off in the opposite direction, a wise choice for all concerned.

The guide and I stood there a bit and listened. There was no excessive noise, so they weren't too startled. We decided to follow them up again and try for a look at the third one. Within the hour we had found them and I took an easy kneeling shot at the best of the three, hitting him perfectly, low and forward in the chest. He let out a tremendous grunt, staggered forward, regrouped, and was off. Sure of my shot's effect, I violated my principal maxim to kill dangerous game twice. Instead of sending another bullet into him, I just turned to the guide and said: "Amekufa." Well he wasn't dead.

For the next minute or so we could hear his wild, aimless flight as he took down everything in his path while blasting the air with squeals and threats. Then all was silent. We followed his tracks for three and a half hours before Mzee lost them in a maze of other fresh tracks. We returned to where the second bull was being butchered, somewhat downcast. As with the first bull, the Wanderobo found another lead ball from a muzzle-loader imbedded in the elephant. That would explain why the elephant around Kijungu were so aggressive.

The following day we went all through that area, Kisenge in tow, but found no sign of the wounded tembo. Evidently the bullet had hit nothing vital, probably deflected by a rib. We did come across some excitement, however. Early on as we were walking along a game trail I suddenly heard some violent rustling in the grass about three feet to my right. I looked down and saw the twisting and thrashing in the grass and assumed a large snake was crawling all over itself to get away from us. The snake had evidently been napping. He hadn't felt the soft tread of the bare footed kiongozi, but he felt the vibrations I gave off. Once he got himself sorted out, we could see his wavy path through the thick, knee high grass. He came out onto a small clearing and glanced in our direction, giving us that cold-eyed snake look that cobras are so good at. My third giant forest cobra, not as big or black as the first two, but big enough. The guides looked disapprovingly at me, still standing three feet from where the snake had done his contorted dance and exclaimed, as though explaining the obvious to a child: "Nyoka mbaya sana, Bwana!" I hunched my shoulders in a defensive shrug and replied: "Ndio, Najua,"[128] agreeing with their assessment.

Haji and I broke camp the following day and went back to Arusha via a different route, straight north from Kijungu through Masailand, two hundred miles of dirt track, some of it muddy as the short rains were lingering into the middle of December. We were carrying a nice load of ivory, as well as two elephant feet for Don Morris. Along the way I shot a Grant's gazelle for Haji, but other than that the trip was just a long drive over back roads through MMBTS[129] and mbuga,[130] nothing exciting, but very enjoyable.

Several miles north of Kijungu we slowed to watch a short string of Masai. There were seven of them, a squad in single file and in step. They were a hundred yards to the west of the road, and running parallel to it. With the shimmering heat distorting the landscape behind them they looked like ghosts in red robes running through a dreamscape on a mission for Lengai.[131] The sun glanced off their long blades, sending sharp spears of light into us. Their knees hardly left the ground, more of a shuffle than a run, but they were moving rapidly, looking neither left nor right, in a collective trance. It looked like they could run forever. Perhaps they would run the length of the Masai Steppe. Perhaps they already had, and these were merely trailing apparitions.

Before cleaning up the Rover, I dropped by the rental agency to show off my ivory and the professional was duly impressed, or at least as impressed as a stiff-upper-lip type could be. I got the tusks weighed and registered at the game department and sold them the next day, except for the 77 pound one: AR384/66.[132] That one I kept.

About a week later I was playing (doubles that is) (**Tennis** that is) with the wife of the Austrian professional who had hogged Lati and redirected me from Kibaya to Kijungu. She offered that her husband had mentioned running into me down there and that he had got his client a wonderful maned lion and a very large elephant, fifty pounds per tusk. I replied that that was nice, but held back, waiting for her to ask. She did, with a sweet, condescending voice: "And how did you do?" I was burning to brag, but volunteered only that I had done well enough, bagging two nice bulls. She persisted: "How large were they?" I dropped the weights on her and she visably blanched. She managed to stammer a compliment, but was, in fact, properly smote on her smug little fanny.

AR 384/66

Two days later I went by to pay the rent on the Rover and the resident professional mentioned, with a slight grin on his face, that the Count had been by, casually inquiring about my ivory. The Count was something of a stuffed shirt, maybe a little arrogant, so the agency pro laid it on thick, extolling the beauty and size of the tusks I had shown him. The count about busted his buttons! Walter would have loved it.

Kisenge and Mzee with first elephant taken at Kijungu - tusks were 72 lbs. each.

Second tembo taken at Kijungu. Mzee standing and five other Wanderobo, come for meat, squatting across the shoulder. Top tusk was 77 lbs., bottom, 68.

125 "Did you hear that?" "Yes." "Elephant?" "Maybe."
126 The guides knew better than to run, but if there was going to be a race, they were not going to be dead last.
127 "One is enough for today."
128 "That's a very bad snake, Bwana." "Yes, I know."
129 My addition to British Africanisms like MMBA. MMBTS is therefore: Miles and Miles of Beautiful Thorn Scrub.
130 Mbuga is Swahili for steppe, or savanna.
131 Lengai is the Masai word for God.
132 AR384/66 was stamped into the tusk by the game department. This would mean that this tusk came from the one hundred and ninety second elephant killed on license in the Arusha District in 1966.

Chopping bone from tusk. Note size of man's leg for comparison.

Kisange took a pretty good picture for his first attempt with a camera. Me and 77-pounder. Kijungu, December 1966.

CHAPTER 46

Oldoinyo Lengai

Most gods are aloof and silent, though there are people who profess to speak to one or another of them with some frequency. Lengai, on the other hand, was quite a vocal god and like most other gods, not always pleased with his creations. During the 20th Century he was particularly outspoken, venting his wrath with multiple blasts from his mountain redoubt.

In fact, Lengai did inhabit a mountain, **Oldoinyo Lengai** to the Masai: The Mountain of God. It is a very interesting place to geologists also, as it is the only active volcano in the world that bleeds natrocarbonatite lava. This is a black or dull, dark brown flow that becomes liquid at only 540-590 degrees C, about half the temperature of molten basalt lava.

I never had the urge to climb Kilimanjaro, partly because I didn't want to invest the time, but also because Kili just sits there, inactive, satisfied and content in all its splendor. But Lengai could be climbed in one day, and there was the added attraction that it was not dormant. Eruptions had previously been reported in 1917, 1940/41, and 1954/57, and while I was in Arusha Lengai was once again extremely active. It started erupting in August of 1966 and continued on and off into December. Then on July 8-9, 1967, there was another major explosive eruption and ash fell on us in Arusha, seventy miles to the southeast. I got to climb it in February of '67', sneaking in a safari between the mountain's spasms.

The August eruptions were first noticed by airline pilots on the 14th and two geologists visited the volcano six days later and climbed to the rim on the 21st. The following is their description of the activity. They first sighted the volcano at 2:30 p.m. on 20th August 1966, when:

> A Vulcanian-type eruption was in progress. A thick column of black ash was rising for approximately 3000 feet above the volcano and, due to the dominantly southerly wind, was drifting away northwards towards Lake Natron; the ash fall was very heavy on the upper northern slopes of the volcano.

During the climb on 21st August, the lower slopes were covered with about half an inch of new, snow white ash which reached a thickness of about two inches closer to the summit. The active crater was full of swirling ash and dust. In it was a new ash cone in whose summit was a shallow bowl-shaped pit about 100 yards in diameter. In the centre of this pit was a small double vent from which there was a continuous discharge of gas and whitish-grey ash and dust. There was a continuous roaring noise and a strong smell of sulphur. Ash was scattered all over most of the inside of the crater and there was about 6 inches of new black ash on the outer slopes of the east rim. The crater was observed from 10:30 a.m. to 1:50 p.m., during which period no lava extrusion was seen, and the ejected material was not larger than ash size.

At 2:45 p.m. on 21st August there was a violent harsh explosion and a dense column of black ash rose vertically above the crater. A series of loud explosions occurred at intervals of less than 15 seconds, each one accompanied by the expulsion of more ash. This continued until about 4 p.m. when the explosions ceased, though the ejection of ash continued all that day and thoughout the night.

Various geologists visited Lengai over the following months, and in mid-October they reported that the wild animals and the Masai and their cattle had left the area because the water and grazing supplies had been contaminated by the ash.

A local scout leader, an African of Haji's tribe, the WaArusha, was going to take some of his senior scouts for a weekend trip to climb the volcano. Others were invited, and I was lucky enough to be one of them. We left late on Saturday morning, twelve of us plus our gear crammed into one long wheel base Land Rover. Lengai is only about seventy miles northwest of Arusha, but to get there by land, you have to go southwest to Makuyuni, turn west onto the road to Ngorongoro Crater, and then, just before Mto wa Mbu, swing north.

As we got closer to the volcano, the landscape became increasingly moon-like. The ground was covered with ash, vegetation was sparse, and here and there you could see the remains of dead animals that hadn't escaped in time. You hardly ever see an animal carcass in Africa unless it is fresh, as the vultures and other scavengers dispose of it quickly. Obviously even those rugged types no longer resided here.

After six uncomfortable hours and 132 miles we arrived at the base of the 10,000-foot mountain. We got there just before sunset and with the light fading, the dark, naked flanks of the volcano radiated a threatening aura. We slept on the ground. Wild animals wouldn't be a problem, but the feathery ash got into everything.

We started before sun up, as the lower slopes could be approached safely without much light. Lengai was not a technical climb so sturdy, long sticks sharpened at one end were the extent of our mountain gear. The sun came up about the time we had covered the gently sloping lower reaches. From there it got steep, and to add to the difficulty the ash on the slopes had been rained on, forming a smooth, beige colored[133] crust about a half-inch thick. There was nothing to hang on to so on the steeper stretches we dug footholds with our sticks. Six hours later, all of it up steep ridges a few feet wide and often almost straight down on both sides, we reached the top. The view was worth the effort. We could see beyond Lake Natron to the north. Maybe that

Oldoinyo Lengai

was Lake Magadi we saw, in southern Kenya? Maybe it was mirage.

None of us ventured down into the crater, but the view was enticing. A crack on the far side floor of the crater was venting a steady though wistful plume of steam, along with that sulfur smell that escapes the bowels of the earth when given an avenue. A smaller vent to the left was also active, but sporadic.

We spent an hour at the top, enjoying the view and resting up for the descent. The trip back down took only four hours, but it was more demanding than the ascent, and almost fatal to one of the boy scouts. The young man, wearing a jaunty dark red beret, was about seventeen or eighteen years old, full of beans, and in a playful mood. He was also showing off. We were part way down with him in the lead. When he came to a short, gently sloping section he started running and leaping, taking long strides and shouting what I took to be Hindi for "Geronimo!" He covered the short distance quickly, but then it dropped off precipitously. He slipped and started to skid on his butt down the smooth crust towards the deep crevasse that paralleled the ridge. We watched helplessly as he sped along, flailing and screaming. Fortuitously a small outcropping of solid rock, about the size of a big toe, presented itself just to his right. He managed to snag it with his foot, and there he hovered, too frozen in fear to move, a yard from certain death.

I was the closest one to him, but I was occupied on the very steep part of the ridge just above him. We had three women with us, two nurses and the doctor's wife from the hospital in Arusha. The nurses were burly women who could take care of themselves, but the doctor's wife was petite in the extreme. At maybe five feet in length and ninety pounds on a humid day, she was too small to reach the footholds the Indian lad had cut in front of us, so I was acting as her personal brake. I would drop down about ten feet, anchor myself with my climbing stick, then she would slide down and bump into me: very scientific!

I yelled at the boy to be patient, I would come get him. But first I had to get down there, and progress was slow, ten feet at a time. Once we got off the steep part, I started carefully working my way down the flank of the ridge towards the petrified young man. I dug deep steps through the crust and into the ash below. None of this was very stable, so I did my best to test each step, reassuring myself that it would hold. When I got within six feet, about the length of my climbing stick, I dug a shelf for a seat, and two holes to brace my feet. I extended the stick. I was hoping that he wasn't going to get excited and jerk us both over the edge, but he had calmed down, realizing his perch was pretty secure. Getting him turned around and away from the ledge was slow, nervous work, but finally we gained some distance, and then scrambled up to safety at the top of the ridge.

The remainder of our descent was mercifully uneventful, but the young rake in the red beret was the last one off the mountain.

---

133 The ash turns from white to tan, or versions thereof, shortly after escaping the volcano, as it reacts to moisture in the air.

Oldoinyo Lengai - the Mountain of God.

Atop Oldoinyo Lengai. Me in back right with the jaunty Aussie hat, and the young man we almost lost upfront with the ladies.

CHAPTER 47

A Hunt with the Professionals

One of the people I occasionally played tennis with was a professional hunter named Leo. Leo was a short, thin wiry guy with flaming red hair and handlebar mustache to match. He was in his early forties and balding, and on this bare patch of skull there were numerous dings and dents, caused, I presumed, by the hen pecking he was getting from his wife.

Though Leo had been a professional for some time and had shot a number of buffalo, he had never shot an elephant. His ambition was to do so, and to that end he had scavenged up the coin for a license. This he had done without the proper spousal input, and now that was about all he was getting: spousal input. Mostly this was verbal, in the form of constant encouragement to get off his dead butt and get out there and recover that 600/-.

So Leo approached me to see if I would accompany him on an elephant hunt. I readily agreed as I also had a license to fill, though we also agreed that removing his bald pate from the endangered list would be our primary goal.

The third week in March we drove south into Masailand, to an area Leo had hunted before. On the way we met up with two more professional hunters from Arusha, Hans and Willie, both Afrikaners. I knew them casually and didn't like them much, and this hunt wouldn't change my opinion.

There was an African lawyer in Arusha named James Mkolo. He was from South Africa, where the Afrikaners ran the show, and he had been politically active down there and paid the price. He had been thrown in jail, beaten daily with a rubber hose, almost starved to death on a menu of bread and water, and then exiled. He washed up in Arusha where there was just barely enough demand for lawyers to fill his belly, but the government of South Africa wouldn't let his wife and children join him. He was one of the few South African exiles allowed to loiter long in Tanzania, as this breed was considered a sophisticated nuisance, so political in nature that they just couldn't help but meddle in matters that were none of their business, namely the internal affairs of their host country.

He spoke fluent Afrikaans, and I would see him visiting with Hans and Willie

Hunting and Teaching in East Africa

every so often. This I couldn't understand. On a number of occasions I marveled that he could even converse with this pair, much less seem to enjoy it. He would don a wan sort of smile and say something to the effect that none of us was perfect, acts of cruelty must be forgiven. In fact, many Africans were this way. Holding a grudge was more a European trait.

In spite of my antipathy, we joined up with Hans and Willie. Leo was providing the transport, so we fell in behind their Rovers and I kept my feelings to myself. They had a number of Africans in their hire, some for camp and some for hunting. Evidently these were regular employees, as they seemed familiar with the two hunters and knew to hop to when Willie or Hans called them via their baboon imitation. I'd have slit their throats.

The first order of business was to sight in Leo's new .458 Winchester. The .458 is not a toy, and certainly a brute of a gun for somebody as lightly built as Leo. I was selected to do the honors, though I didn't know if this was meant to save Leo from punishment, or to check out the neophyte in their company. I leaned across the hood of one of the vehicles, settled the crosshairs on a tree knot about thirty yards distant, and squeezed the trigger. It roared back and planted the scope rim in my eyebrow, making a neat, half-moon incision. Since I was used to my mild mannered .375, the push from this rifle caught me off guard, plus, the stock had been shortened to fit the smaller Leo. The three pros looked a bit shocked, and maybe a little concerned, but as soon as I recovered from the blow I adjusted the elevation and windage and fired again, splattering the knot. I handed the gun to Leo, without comment.

Willie and Hans pretty much ran the show. After camp was established they set about building a blind for lion or leopard. First they shot some bait, anything would do. In this case it was a hartebeest. Then they tied the bait to the rear bumper of a Rover and dragged it a mile or so to either side of the tree they had selected. This done, the animal was hung by its rear feet from a branch, with the nose about four feet from the ground, making it accessible, but not conveniently so. This would make the cats reach for their meal thus making them better targets, and it also anchored the carcass so the cats couldn't drag it off. While this was being done, and while they spent their mornings and evenings in the blind, Leo and I beat the bush for elephant, without success.

As seemed a common practice with professional hunters, we spent a lot of time running around in the Rovers. The second day we came across a huge herd of eland, easily fifty in their number. We raced up toward them and they took flight. We were driving parallel to them off about a hundred yards and when we passed them Willie slammed on the brakes and I jumped out, ran a few steps from the vehicle, and zeroed in on the last one in the group. The bullet kicked up dust beyond and just behind him. I worked the bolt and sighted in on the animal in front of him, figuring I needed about a body's length lead. I aimed for the heart of the surrogate, and hit the intended target perfectly, one of the best shots on running game I had ever made. The pros were demonstrably impressed. Kudos flowed.

A Hunt with the Professionals

We drove up to the eland and the Afrikaners descended on it like starving vultures. They craved the fat in the shoulder hump and devoured some of it on the spot, raw. The rest they had for dinner, and they were welcome to it. Leo and I settled for less exotic cuts.

Two days later, while Leo and I were out with the trackers looking for something to track, Hans and Willie got a Leopard. It was gorgeous. The fur was dense, luxurious. It was soft to the touch and felt like a plush, high quality carpet. I was amazed at the thickness. Most tropical animals have just a fine coating of body hair, as seems fitting for the environment. This animal looked and felt like it was designed for the Himalayas, or Siberia. Like the Wanderobo, I was not generally sentimental about game. I respected it and loved to watch and photograph it, but the taking of animals was as natural for me as it was the hunters of necessity. Still, the sight of this leopard aroused feelings of remorse. So beautiful, yet so dead.

For Leo and me the last day of the safari had come, but we rode with Hans and Willie to check their blind as they were still after cats, hoping for a lion. On the way we spotted where a herd of elephant had crossed, their path exposed in the dew laden, knee high grass that bordered the road. We parked the Land Rover and got hot on their trail: too hot. We walked at a brisk pace, later measured with the Rover odometer at five miles an hour. Hans, with his long legs, led the way. I had to jog part of the time to keep up, not uncomfortable at the pace, but wary of its end result.

We walked right into the elephant. They heard and smelled and saw us, and off they went at full speed. Immediately Hans and Willie gave chase, rifles at high port. I ran along behind them in wonderment. What were they doing? Just as the fleeing elephants were disappearing into the brush, the two hunters stopped and fired three shots into their backsides. I was nonplused. Now I knew what they were doing, I just didn't believe they were doing it.

The rest of our pack pursued Hans and Willie, as they continued their chase, but I could see from the dust cloud the elephants were raising, that they had swung to the left. I ran hard to cut them off, but came in behind them, catching only a face full of settling dust. Shortly Leo and Willie, and the African trackers and gun-bearers caught up to me. We stood silently in the footprints of the elephant, none of us in a talkative mood, when suddenly there were two blasts from a double rifle, and a whole lot of swearing.

Hans had been nosing around when he almost bumped into an anchored elephant. He and Willie had evidently been successful in breaking one of the elephant's rear hips, thus leaving him immobile,[134] but Hans was so startled at his bumbling discovery at point blank range that he snapped off two poorly aimed shots and then realized his ammunition was with his gun-bearer, and his gun-bearer was nowhere to be seen. The rest of our tribe scampered towards Hans, the cavalry to the rescue, but again I cut diagonally through the bush hoping they would scare one towards me and I could get a shot. I hadn't gone thirty yards when I could see a lone elephant through the brush. I took aim but decided the tusks were too small and held my fire. Then the professionals opened up, and this elephant was their target. I watched in disbelief at first, not sure they were actually shooting at this one as the animal didn't even react, much less go down. Finally the elephant winced from one of the shots, and then after a few more he slumped to the ground. Ten shots, a stationary target at ten yards, three professional hunters, the two Boers with doubles: Hans a .475, Willie a .577; and Leo thrown into the mix with his .458, the smallest cannon of the lot. I couldn't believe it.

I decided to circle the bush by myself for a while. Partly I hoped to come across one of the elephants, perhaps wounded and calmly awaiting execution, but mostly to cool off what I knew would be my smart mouth. I wandered around for about an hour, then returned to the sight of the kill. I managed to contain my comments to: "Pretty small tusks, aren't they."

Of course, that is one of the problems with shooting elephants in the butt. The ivory is at the other end and thus not readily visible, which leaves the hunter in a grab bag situation. The other drawback to rear ending elephants is that it is a low percentage shot, and even more so in this case where the quarry was running, as were the hunters. Snap shooting elephants in the backside was not something I would have done, but then I wasn't a professional hunter either.

Be that as it may, we had achieved our primary goal: the tusks weighed thirty pounds each, so at least Leo would recover his license fee and remove himself from the endangered list. And I had had a good time. I saw some new country, got an eland, and learned a few things, (+ and -).

---

[134] An elephant cannot move on three legs. If a shoulder is broken, he is immobilized. Because of their weight, they also cannot gallop, so when they run it is more of a shuffle, with at least one foot always on the ground.

CHAPTER 48

Last Hunt, Last Elephant

Getting through the summer of 1967 was something of a chore. A prolonged battle with dysentery, acting the host to a roundworm, bleeding gums due to calcium and vitamin D deficiency, and a bout of malaria all conspired to slow me down.

The malaria was disappointing, since I had been faithful in taking the prophylactic medication. The doctor diagnosed it as a mild case, though soaring fevers interrupted by shaking chills seemed like the real deal to me. He prescribed shock treatment in the form of massive pill popping. I was to start with ten anti-malaria pills, a different brand than I had been taking, and then decrease the dosage every four hours by two pills per dose, until I got down to the last two: 10-8-6-4-2. He kept cautioning me that this would give me a terrific headache, and I kept assuring him that I already had a terrific headache: Just give me the pills! Anyway they worked, and quickly. The next day the symptoms were gone, but for several years the malaria would reemerge in the form of night sweats, soaking the bed and necessitating a flip of the mattress and a change of sheets, a small price to pay for four years in Africa.

Also, during this time, the tone in the country was changing for the worse. Europeans and Asians were leaving Tanzania in large numbers, fed up with the government's petty racism and red tape. We had quite a shauri[135] at the school over a government poster showing three Africans carrying heavy bags as an Asian overseer greedily counted his profits. During a roaring staff meeting, four of us European teachers refused to post them in our classrooms, and it was finally agreed that the posters would not appear in the rooms, though the headmistress did hang one outside her office. It was hypocrisy that the government would hype its ideals about a multi-racial society and yet print and distribute that poster. And the poster was just a small splotch on a much larger collage of government policy towards the Asian population, a policy of confiscation and expulsion.

The cure-all for me was the bush. I had a license burning a hole in my hip pocket, but no transportation as my Simca was definitely on its last legs, using two quarts of oil for every tank of gas. Fortunately there was a Peace Corps chap in Arusha named Cleve who wanted to hunt elephant, and he asked me to show him the ropes.

Hunting and Teaching in East Africa

I agreed to do so, but would demonstrate the process by getting the first shot.

In early August we left Arusha with two Rovers, Cleve drove one and Don Morris the other. For some time Don had wanted to get in on an elephant hunt, so when he volunteered his Rover I eagerly accepted, as this way I would not have to keep the ever talkative and opinionated Cleve company. Cleve's friend Dave, from Vancouver B.C., could pull that duty.

Our destination was Ngasumet, a village in the Masai Steppe, halfway between Moshi and Kijungu. We drove west out of Arusha and at fourteen miles turned left, pointing southeast. 120 miles into the bush we located the dusty village, secured some guides, and set up camp.

This country was amazing. The thorn scrub was interspersed with open spaces, but in places the bush was extra thick, sometimes impenetrable. The elephant trails were like freeways, six to ten feet wide, and so worn that they were often sunk like trenches, a foot or more below the surrounding table of land. In one place where a naked bank bordered one of these highways, the tusk marks could be seen in the bank's face, the elephants evidently digging for minerals and salts. Broken trees, torn shrubs, fresh dropping: all abounded. This was going to be interesting.

The next day after less than an hour's walk we stumbled into a single bull, and as Cleve and Dave watched, Don and I closed to within ten yards. He was in heavy brush, but I got sideways of him with a good look at his head. I took a brain shot as Don put one through the cover into his ribs. He crashed to earth, covering us in dust and twigs. The ivory would go just over sixty pounds, so I was elated: my license had been recouped, and the kill had been executed perfectly.

The following day was spent trying to locate a suitable bull for Cleve, but to no avail. We saw plenty of sign and a few small tuskers, but our guides were not trackers, they were just guides. Evidently there were so many elephants in the area, tracking skills weren't necessary. As at Kwa Kuchinja, the guides just headed into the bush, and sooner or later elephants would materialize.

We hunted hard all day, putting many miles underfoot, but as darkness approached we were back near the Rover. We had parked close to a large, heavily forested spring, and as we eased our way along the brush at the edge of the spring we surprised a small herd. As they scrambled to escape, a young bull suddenly appeared, startling both him and us. He let out a bellow and raised his trunk, waggling his head and fanning his ears. As he raised his head, Cleve raised his .458. I was right next to Cleve and managed to bring my hand up and push the rifle off line before he could fire. The elephant was gone as quickly as he had appeared, fortunate for all concerned. Though he was close, maybe fifteen yards, we were in no immediate danger so there was no need for anyone to shoot, and shooting at a water hole was seriously illegal. The elephant was correct to be startled, and scared. He was in much greater peril than we were, for if he had come, we would have had time to react, and he would have been charging into a heavily armed firing squad.

Once inside the Rover, we headed for camp, but it was dark. We came to a fork in

Last Hunt, Last Elephant

the road, and the guide pointed right, which was wrong. The trail soon petered out, but Cleve kept going. He was nothing if not persistent. We spent the next 30 minutes bashing through the bush, plowing through brush and knocking over trees up to three inches in diameter, raising much commotion, but getting no closer to camp. Finally I convinced Cleve to shut down the motor. We listened and could hear the Masai dogs at the village, their occasional barks and tinkling bells penetrating the darkness. The others were content to spend the night in the bush, but I wanted dinner and a bed, so I volunteered to go to camp and return with the other Rover.

It was dark. There was no moon that night, only starlight. I decided to take Cleve's .458, as there was no telling what I might bump into out there and I wanted something with authority in my hands. My .375 was adequate for elephant, though on the light side, and, in fact, not even legal for elephant in Kenya or Uganda. Its main advantage was accuracy. In the dark, if something developed, accuracy would be problematic. Knockdown power was preferable. I also took the old Masai guide as his reward for getting us lost. Understandably he wasn't eager to go, but I insisted, and he came.

The Africans do not spend their evenings idly wandering the bush. For one thing, this is not a healthy practice. For another, in the dark they can get as easily lost as the rest of us, as their reference points and the lay of the land are swallowed by the night. Even a Rover's headlights only provide a narrow tunnel of vision, so it was easy to see why the old guide had chosen the wrong fork. Still, at the time, I was not in an understanding or forgiving frame of mind. We set out.

The stars gave off just enough light that we could make our way. Of course if there were snakes or other small problems like lions or leopards, we would not be able to see them. But even elephants, our main concern in this elephant rich environment, would be hard to make out in the brush. When we came to thick patches, we would get as low to the ground as we could, trying to silhouette any elephant outline into the sky. We would listen intently, stopping frequently. The dogs were our intermittent guides, and the Milky Way was our constant.

It took two hours of slow, careful work to arrive back at the village. Once back, I relaxed and had a cool beer before going after the others. I found where the road forked and followed the dead end to its dead end. Not knowing how far Cleve's Rover was from my position, I fired a shot in the air. To my utter amazement voices answered. The rest of the crew were within shouting distance! Thirty minutes of bush bashing, evidently in circles, had put the first Rover only a couple hundred yards from the end of the track. We got to bed around one, but not before enjoying dinner around the campfire, with Cleve and the old guide being the targets of much lighthearted banter, laced with the occasional sharp jab. With but one dissenting vote it was agreed that Cleve's next vehicle should be a D8.[136]

The following day was more of the same, wandering around in that marvelous scrub. We saw plenty of fresh sign, but none of the tembo responsible. The day after that, Cleve would get his elephant. We heard him before we saw him, as he was pulling a tree apart to get to the leaves. We closed to within thirty yards and had a clear view of the top half of the beast. He was standing on the fringe of a very dense thicket, broadside to us and unaware of our approach. His ivory wasn't very big, maybe thirty-five pounds, but Cleve was eager and it would do. I suggested he try a brain shot: halfway between the ear hole and the eye. The .458 gave a thunderous account of itself, and the elephant folded away from us, into the tangle of thorn.

Because the bull had folded over and not dropped like a bucket of bolts, I knew he was not brain shot. I ran up to the animal, but since there was no direct access to his head to see where the bullet had hit, I scrambled onto his rump and made my way to his front shoulder. I lifted the ear. The shot had hit too high and merely knocked the animal out. He would be getting up shortly, but I hated to intrude on another man's kill, especially his first elephant. I called for Cleve to hustle over and join me atop the elephant. We scooted around each other on the elephant's stomach and as I stood on the hind hip, Cleve reached the front shoulder. Just then the elephant started to revive. Cleve brought up his rifle and fired. The elephant gave a tremendous convulsion, bucking me off the rear end and planting Cleve in the thorns, but he didn't get up.

Cleve remounted the elephant and did a little jig on its front shoulder, a display I thought somehow disrespectful, and then the arduous task of retrieving the tusks began. A whole lot of brush had to be cleared before we could even begin the three to four hour job of removing the ivory.

Don and I left for Arusha the next day, but Cleve and Dave stayed there to try for another, preferably one with larger tusks. They came back a few days later, their safari shrouded in mystery. Evidently they had bagged a bigger elephant, but they would not talk about the hunt beyond that. From the way they acted, something had gone terribly wrong. My guess was that somebody had been killed, but that was just a guess and I never did find out as I was at the end of my tour and after settling with Haji and selling the .375 (1300/-) and car (400/-),[137] homeward bound.

---

[135] A shauri is a discussion or a debate, sometimes heated.
[136] A D8 is a Catterpillar bulldozer, no doubt more suitable for plowing brush than a Land Rover.
[137] In other words, I got $186 for the gun, about what I paid Chet Paulson for it in Tacoma, and $57 for the car, which was approximately $56 more than it was worth.

CHAPTER 49

Another One Bites the Dust

In the fall of 1966 my life took an unexpected turn. I was sailing along just fine, when a young Ismaili woman hove into view. We had just lost our domestic science teacher and Arusha being a small town, the news of the opening percolated through the streets and alleys and into Mehrunissa Mohamedali's apartment. She had been in England for a number of years, studying in the Midlands for her degree, and later teaching in London.

Some of the staff were idly standing around in the commons sipping tea between classes when she came down the steps on the far side of the commons, dressed in a yellow knit dress that highlighted her pleasantly female form. Dave Morgan, being a rugby player and therefore an overt admirer of the female figure, blurted an enthusiastic "U la la!" I had to agree.

Anyway, Mehrun entered our little circle and she and I became friends pretty quickly. Soon we were dating and, in the close Asian community of Arusha, the subject of much interest, and no doubt gossip. Haji was amused, and every time she came over for dinner, or just to visit, a small, silly grin would crease his face.

Others were not so amused, namely her family. She was living with her brother Nurali and his wife Rosie, and her mother and another brother, Nazir, were visiting. They were naturally concerned, since our romance was unusual, maybe even unnatural. I was a foreigner, a non-Muslim, certainly not an Ismaili. What could I be up to? What were my intentions? Did I already have a wife or two back in the United States? Certainly her family had never contemplated the addition of an American to their homogeneous little clan. This was indeed an unsettling development.

But Mehrun was not one to be cowed by family or tradition. Her parents were quite conventional and had tried to push her into an arranged marriage on one of their trips to India. She had arched her back, scuttled the offer, and with the reluctant intercession of a couple of her brothers, had maneuvered her father into granting her permission to attend university in England. Another brother, Amir, would accompany her as part of the bargain and they both completed their degrees there.

So here she was, confounding the family once again. She also confounded me

Hunting and Teaching in East Africa

somewhat. I had assumed there wasn't much a person could do that was more dangerous than hunting elephants, often alone, and always without useful professional backup. Well I was wrong. Mehrun bought a car. She wanted to learn how to drive it. Evidently those closest to her knew the risk, but love is blind, as they say. The honor fell to me, and looking back, it wasn't all that bad, kind of like when one looks back fondly on his tour of duty in the Army.

She had purchased a teal-green Ford Anglia, with a manual transmission.[138] At first, whiplash was a definite possibility, but the severity of initiating motion gradually dropped below the level of life threatening. Once this starting and lurching thing was under control, the next challenge was concentration in the face of distractions. As in: on one occasion an owl swooped down and almost hit the windshield. Mehrun dove for cover, taking the steering wheel with her. I just did manage to get us righted before we disappeared into the maw of a ten-foot ditch.

After mastering the rudiments around town, the open road beckoned. We decided to visit Bob and Sue Rogers at Marangu, on the lower slopes of Kilimanjaro just east of Moshi. By now she was getting the hang of it, and I wasn't hanging on with white knuckles. Bob and Sue taught at the Teachers Training College in Marangu, a school situated at 5000 feet. The drive up the slope was always pleasant, as the vegetation got heavier with altitude, and the climate cooler.

Before heading home Mehrun and I took a stroll in the cool and fragrant evening air. Here we had our first kiss, in the moonlight on the slopes of Kilimanjaro, with the snow of Kibo peeking down at us through the banana and coffee trees.

We continued to date, with a certain amount of policing by Nazir, but my tour was coming to an end and I was too unsettled in plans and health to make a decision. Once I got back to Tacoma things started to clear up in all aspects, and once the roundworm was passed, my energy returned and the future looked more promising. I telegrammed Mehrun asking her to marry me, and my future wife, ever the cool customer, drove all the way home from the post office with her emergency brake on. Smokin!

My parents were curious about the letters floating to and from Tanzania, and one day mother said to say hello to Mehrun. I replied: "Tell her yourself, she will be here in three days." She dropped into Sea-Tac a few days later, after thirty-six hours of sleepless travel. Though tired and excited at the same time, she was a little anxious about meeting my side of the equation.

On the way home from the airport, feeling a little guilty, she explained her situation. While her brothers couldn't stop her, her father could, and in their opinion, would. So she had flown to America, subrosa. We agreed that secrecy was not a good foundation for marriage and tired though she was, her first order of business after the 'hellos', was to pen a letter to her father in India.

As Mehrun settled in and got to know my parents, my sister Judy and my brother Dave and his new wife Joy, we waited anxiously for a response from her father, half expecting him to show up on the front porch with fire in his eyes. Instead, we got a

Another One Bites the Dust

letter, a very nice letter. Congratulations were in order, and he was even going to write the Aga Khan and have our marriage blessed.

The Muslim and the agnostic were married by a Methodist Minister on May 18, 1968. Another bachelor bit the dust, but our union has been long and fruitful, blessed with bahati mzuri and a son and daughter we are very proud of. Mehrun became a welcome addition to the McNickle clan and the Yank was warmly accepted into the Mohamedali clan.

So ends the saga. Kwaheri.

---

[138] Few cars in East Africa had automatic transmissions in the early 1960's.

Mehrun posing in my front yard aboard her Ford Anglia.

CHAPTER 50

FAQ

Though television documentaries on Africa proliferate these days, when I returned from Africa in the 1960's, the Dark Continent was still a deep shade of gray. People were curious and took the opportunity to ask questions of someone who had actually been there.

Q: What are Africans like?
A: Unfortunately they are pretty much like the rest of us, with all the positive and negative attributes of being human. What differences there are result from their economic situation and the long history of man on the continent. Being mostly subsistent peasants, they are more at one with nature, and living in the cradle of man, they have had extra time to develop a few exotic strains, like the seven-foot Watutsi and the four-foot Pygmy. But human they are, and the trunk of the family tree.

Q. Did you see any tigers while you were in Africa?
A. No, mostly because there are no tigers in Africa, though there are lions in India, limited these days to the Gir Forest in the state of Gujarat, just south of Pakistan.

Q. Do lions make good pets?
A. Yes, lions make excellent pets. Every Republican should have one.

Q. Were prices always negotiable, even in stores?
A. Yes, there was always room for bargaining. In fact it was expected. To give an example: Mehrun and I had gone to Nairobi to buy a few things, including a slide projector. We entered a top-drawer camera shop owned by an Indian merchant, but a sale was in progress. An American tourist was purchasing a Hasselblad, the finest camera in the world. These cameras were made in Sweden, had a wide selection of Carl Ziess lenses, took two and a quarter inch negatives, and had interchangeable backs. The large negatives allowed the photographer to develop sharply defined, expansive prints, and the removable backs meant that the photographer could carry

a different type of film in each back and change from one to the other as the lighting or subject matter dictated.

The American had selected a camera and a number of accoutrements, including some extra lenses and spare backs, and asked the price: $2800. That was more than half of what I made in a year. The vendor tilted his head back, thrust his jaw forward, hitched his pants, and was ready for battle. The contest would begin. But there was no battle. The tourist simply said O.K., pulled out a wad of traveler's checks, and started signing. The shop keep looked astonished, shocked, disappointed, even a little hurt. With a confused look on his face he glanced over at us, shrugging his shoulders, his palms out, as if to say: "What am I, a thief? Nothing but a cash register? A speck on the wall to be ignored?"

The transaction split him right down the middle. As a merchant he was delighted at his good fortune, but as a man he felt snubbed. Obviously the American was long on cash and short of class, but the warm feeling radiating from his wallet served to soothe the merchant's wounded ego. And after all, there were customers waiting, and the prospects for a good tussle looked promising.

We did not disappoint. I had my eye on a Zeiss Ikon projector that would handle the thick Agfa[139] mounts I used for my slides. As the name implied it was also fitted with a Zeiss lens and was therefore a top of the line product. We haggled for some time with the newly energized merchant, even leaving for lunch in the midst of hostilities. On our return the battle was rejoined, with both sides struggling for advantage.

In the end we got a good deal. We were rewarded for our efforts, no doubt, but also our adversary was flush with profit from his earlier transaction and maybe feeling a little guilty. In any case, I think that American tourist not only paid for his purchases, but, in effect, paid for a little on ours also.

Q. What do you think is the number one contribution Africans have made to America?

A. Three names: Art Tatum, Melodious Funk, and Bird. In other words, jazz. Tatum was technically the most phenomenal piano player ever, Thelonious Monk (his wife called him Melodious Funk) was the most innovative, and Charlie Parker soared like a bird, a swallow on a sax, darting unpredictably from note to note.

Q. What possessed you to go to Africa?

A. There were spurs: the books I read on Africa when I was young and impressionable; the visit from our Rhodesian relatives. But the primary influence was Pop. My father radiated energy and courage, traits that were channeled into activities we boys grew up with: hunting, shooting, camping, fishing. Outdoor stuff. Man stuff. A sense of adventure coursed through his actions and his genes, and therefore ours. The ultimate place for man stuff was Africa. When the door opened, I entered. "Navigare Necesse Est. Vivere Non Necesse."[140]

Hunting and Teaching in East Africa

Q. Just how dangerous was it out in the bush?

A. Obviously there were risks. Snakes, elephant, crocodiles, buffalo, rhino, lion, leopard, hyena, hippo, scorpions, tsetse, mosquitoes, and even the land and climate. All of the above, and many others that were unseen, microscopic, took their toll.

Shortly after I left three Peace Corps volunteers ventured into the Kujungu area to hunt. They carried two light rifles and were out for small game. They proceeded without guides to drive a thicket. The one without a gun, a former Green Beret in the Army, headed into the heart of the bush, hoping to drive something to one of the armed men flanking him along the outside edges. When the outer two met at the far end, the middle man did not show up. He never did. A few days later the police from Arusha rounded up a gang of locals, Masai and Wanderobo, formed them into a skirmish line, and combed the area. Nothing was found: not a boot, not a belt buckle. Perhaps he got bit by a snake and then dragged off and devoured by some scavenger. Perhaps he stumbled into a band of poachers. Lion, buffalo, elephant, rhino: the possibilities were many, but the answer was singular, and unknown.

In January of 2001, a young Peace Corps woman, Natalie Waldinger, was killed in another of my old haunts, the Ruaha Game Reserve. She left her vehicle to get a better photograph of an elephant. He charged. She ran for the car but didn't make it. A parks official said that it was probably the metalic clicking of the camera that set off the elephant. I suppose that could be, but she had no business being where she was. She knew nothing of approaching elephants and had no idea how unpredictable and deadly they could be. My guess is that she paid no attention to the direction of the wind and stood right out in the open. I would further guess that the pachyderm had been peppered by the muzzleloaders ubiquitous to the area and was not kindly predisposed towards hominids.

The article did not say how close she approached the elephant, but as a British lady in Kenya discovered, you don't have to be in an elephant's face to provoke him. Along with her husband Steve and their three children, Wendy Martin had been living in Nairobi for four and a half years. They were on their third visit to the Il Ngwesi Safari Lodge, a lodge that was owned and run by Masai and specialized in guided bush walks. One morning she and three others went for a jog:

> It was June 2, (2000), one of those glorious, cloudless African dawns when the whole world seems bathed in golden sunshine. Doves were calling, lulling the senses, and although Il Ngwesi lies deep in big-game country, there were no animals in sight.
>
> There were four joggers in the party: Wendy, two of her Nairobi friends, and Kipkorir Ntere, one of the Masai camp staff, who had volunteered to be their guide. If anyone questioned the wisdom of running through thick bush in elephant country, nobody mentioned it. Besides, says Wendy, who confesses to being a very cautious person, on previous visits, whenever we left the camp there were always armed rangers to look after us.
>
> On this fateful morning two armed rangers did indeed follow them down the lodge steps;

but none of the runners checked to make sure they were still with them as they set off. It was a mistake that nearly cost Wendy Martin her life.

They had been running for perhaps 20 minutes; but already the sun was hot and Wendy, who had begun to feel the pace, suggested they should turn and jog back to camp.

We were actually following our own tracks and joking about the small size of my footprints when this ear-splitting trumpet blast rang out, says Wendy. It was the most terrifying sound I have ever heard. Kip said, 'Stand still', and everybody stopped. I know exactly when it happened. Only a minute before I had looked at my watch and it was a quarter to eight.

Suddenly, maybe 200 yards away, an elephant's head appeared over the bushes. It was shaking its ears and thrashing around with its trunk and was clearly very angry. Kip clapped his hands, imitating the sound of a rifle shot, but it was no use. The elephant was charging. Kip yelled, 'Run, run', but I tripped and fell. According to Ian Craig, one of Il Ngwesi's mentors who lives on the neighbouring Lewa Conservancy ranch, it was Kip who helped Wendy to her feet when she fell. By now, says Craig, the elephant had targeted Wendy and, although Kip risked his own life by trying to capture its attention, the enraged animal was not deterred.

In desperation, she flung herself under a bush and curled up in a ball, thinking this might make it more difficult for the elephant to get her. But there was no escape. First it crushed her with its head, then drove its tusks into her torso. One went right through her - an injury that later necessitated the removal of her right kidney and twelfth rib. The other tusk went into her back and came out through her groin. Miraculously, her lungs were not touched, although her duodenum was torn.

I remember thinking, 'this can't be happening to me,' says Wendy. My only other thought was of my children. I have a vague memory of the elephant kneeling on me, and this must have been when my pelvis was crushed. Then it tusked me again, right through the flesh of my thigh and my calf.

People have said I must have been too shocked to feel anything, but the terror and the agony were only too real. At one point I was picked up - by tusks or trunk I cannot say - and hurled to the ground with devastating force. That was when my collarbone was dislocated and I just lay there, waiting for the elephant to finish me off.

Wendy didn't hear the rangers coming, or the shots they fired over the elephant's head to drive it off. That was the oddest thing of all, she says. I remember no sound. It was like watching a silent movie. I never heard the elephant go. All I could hear was my pounding heart. Then, as I lay there, waiting to die in the dust, I became aware of people screaming and shouting.

She was so covered with dirt and twigs that at first her friends could not find her. When they did see her, they could not believe she was still alive. It was then I looked down at my body and saw what had happened to it, says Wendy.

Hunting and Teaching in East Africa

Ironically, Wendy was the only person in camp with any medical knowledge, and luckily she was still conscious. I told them to tie my injured legs together, she says. By now I felt as cold as ice. I knew I was going into shock, so I told them to wrap me up and keep me warm.

Back in camp, a dining table was turned into a makeshift stretcher with a mattress on top, and the radio was crackling as Mayday messages winged over the airwaves. Within an hour, Craig, with a nurse, had flown in from Lewa Downs. By luck, the nurse, a senior trauma specialist, had been staying with the Craigs when news of the accident reached them.

Lying in Craig's plane on the way to Nairobi, Wendy heard somebody saying she would be dead before they arrived. But she clung to life by thinking about her children. By 11.30 am - less than four hours after her accident - Wendy was being wheeled into the operating theatre at Nairobi hospital for a six-hour operation.

Even before she arrived, the bush telegraph had been buzzing and friends were queuing to give blood. The surgeon at Nairobi hospital did a fantastic job, says Wendy. So much so, that just 10 days later she was flown to London and transferred to St George's Hospital in Tooting, where she has since undergone a further eight operations, with at least two more still to come.

Today, seeing her back home in Godalming, Surrey, it is hard to believe this 40-year-old woman could ever have been the victim of such a violent attack. Outwardly there is no sign of her injuries, although she is now classified as disabled and until recently was totally dependent on crutches. Then she shows me an album filled with photographs of her scars and tusk wounds, and an X-ray of her shattered pelvis (since restored by her surgeon at St George's).

But it is the invisible injuries that have left her traumatised. Her pelvis gives such constant pain that she is now living on painkillers, and the dreams are so bad she cannot sleep without sleeping pills. Otherwise, she says, every night that elephant comes back to get me.

One of the saddest consequences of what happened has been the effect on Wendy's children: Matthew, 10, Rosanna, eight, and Emily, who was four at the time of the accident. It has been devastating for them, she says. They saw the elephant. They heard the screams. They saw what it had done to me. I have tried to explain that it was not the elephant's fault, that it was in its own domain and we were the intruders. But now they all say they hate elephants.

Wendy herself has more ambivalent feelings. I always loved elephants, she says. Even now, there are elephant pictures and carvings all over the house; I would like to go back to Kenya to banish the ghosts. I want to be able to enjoy being with elephants again. But if I was in a vehicle and I was confronted by one, I don't know how I would react.

And yet, she says, she does not bear a grudge. I just want to tell my story so that others might be spared the nightmare I and my family have gone through. If you go on safari, you must always remember how dangerous Africa can be.[141]

FAQ

Such instances notwithstanding, driving on American roads is no doubt riskier business than a non-hunting stint in the African bush. The automobile is certainly a more deadly force than any beast in Africa.

All the time I logged in the bush, I could have done without a rifle at hand. The only animals that threatened me were the ones I gave reason, either by invading their comfort zone or shooting at them. In the three instances given above, none should have been serious. Ignorance is not bliss in the African bush. Even Wendy Martin could have avoided that charge by simply ducking into the bush and then changing course in the cover and running cross or downwind.

Q. Which subjects were the most difficult for your African students?

A. This has already been covered to some extent in Chapter 13. Subjects that required memorization or logic came the easiest: math, science, geography, Swahili, government, and to some extent, history.

History was something of a special case. The students had no trouble regurgitating what they were taught, and would do so to placate the teachers and pass the Cambridge Exam. But the western idea of cause and effect was not something they wholeheartedly subscribed to: this and this and this happened, therefore this resulted. They tended to look at it through the other end of the telescope: here is a result, how it came about is anybody's guess. We can postulate on the causes, we can invent a scenario, but no matter how logical our construct, it is nothing more than mental gymnastics.

To better understand their point of view, lets put it in the context of mathematics. The answer to a problem is 48. We know the answer, but what happened to arrive at 48? Was it an addition problem, and if so, what numbers were involved? Was it 24 plus 24, or maybe 47 plus 1? Perhaps it wasn't addition at all, but a subtraction, say 66 minus 18. 6 times 8 will work. How about 144 divided by 3?

I put their skepticism to work in a seminar discussion at Northwestern University. We were examining the Russian Revolution, running through all the causes to the inevitable conclusion. I questioned this inevitability. With hindsight we could see that the Bolsheviks under Lenin triumphed. But we were giving the stamp of certainty to something that at the time seemed highly improbable. I felt that given the complexity and uncertainty of the times any number of outcomes were possible and that luck and happenstance and individuals had as much to do with any outcome as economic determinism. Did I get stung! The king bee and all the drones set up such a buzz I fled screaming into the safety of Lake Michigan. So much for my African students and their silly reluctance to accept the obvious.

Their ambivalence towards western historical method they could live with however. What got them tied in knots was English. The long and the short of it: their languages were pretty straightforward and logical, Kiengreza wasn't. Again, refer back to Chapter 13 for a refresher course on the permutations of this language the British have foisted onto the world. The linguistic frustration of the African student is entirely their fault.

Hunting and Teaching in East Africa

And British responsibility doesn't stop there. A study of nutrition came up with the following:

The Japanese eat very little fat and suffer fewer heart attacks than the British or Americans.

The Mexicans eat a lot of fat and also suffer fewer heart attacks than the British or Americans.

The Japanese drink very little red wine and suffer fewer heart attacks than the British or Americans.

The Italians drink excessive amounts of red wine and also suffer fewer heart attacks than the British or Americans.

The Germans drink a lot of beer and eat lots of sausages and fats and suffer fewer heart attacks than the British or Americans.

Conclusion: Eat and drink what you like. Speaking English is apparently what kills you. Thanks a lot, Great Britain!

Q. What language did you teach in?
A. In spite of the health risk documented above, English, or British. British is a variant of English and is mostly confined to a small island off the coast of Europe.

Q. Did the pupils wear uniforms?
A. White shirts and khaki shorts were the norm, though the prefects (student body officers) wore white shorts, if they had them.

Q. How old were your students?
A. Somewhat older than those in an American high school. Many started elementary school late. Often there were interruptions in their attendance due to illnesses or family obligations, or other intrusions like being summoned to serve one or another man of prominence and power.

Q. Is Tanzania a good place to go for a holiday?
A. Definitely. Some of my relatives on my wife's side have been recently. The people are friendly and the game parks still have plenty of animals, though don't expect to see large herds of elephant or many rhino. One niece reported that the game parks she visited had more animals now than in the 1960's!

Q. Since you went to Africa for adventure, how do you define adventure?
A. If you can accumulate forty tsetse fly bites, that counts as an adventure. However tsetse, while always willing are not always available, so there are other criteria: if you get chased, bitten, stung, or battered, these count. If you get hissed at,

FAQ

growled at, trumpeted at, or snorted at, these also count. If you get killed, that also counts, although someone else will have to do the tabulating. If there is an element of risk, like climbing a mountain or swimming the Ruaha River around Scotty's Camp, that counts. Anything else is just an outing.

Q. What are the most dangerous things in Africa?
A. Microbes. Getting a disease isn't as dramatic as getting stomped or eaten by some large critter, but it is a whole lot more likely, and the results can be just as unpleasant.

Q. How do new concepts get incorporated into Swahili?
A. Via new vocabulary. Since Swahili is the language of a vast area still resident in the pre-industrial, pre-scientific world, additional words become necessary to describe the new machines, experiences, and ideas that flood in. Some words fit right in without audible alteration, like 'lorry', a British word for truck. In Swahili it becomes 'lori'. Many words that end in consonants just get a vowel added to the end; witness 'hotel' to 'hoteli' or the Arabic word 'salaam' to 'salama'. This sort of adaptation can be carried to amusing lengths, however, as when our headmistress, Sarah Materu, exhorted the kids to look for jobs that helped the country develop, not just desk jobs where the uniform would be a "longi, sleevdi, whiti, shirti."

Words such as 'bicycle' and 'English' are changed quite a bit in the spelling, but sound familiar enough when pronounced: 'baisikeli' (by-se(as in settle)-**kay**-lee) and 'Kiengreza' (key-**ngray**-za), the 'Ki' being the prefix for languages, as in 'Kihehe' or 'Kiswahili'.

Sometimes a Swahili word is adapted to a new reality, as with 'ndege' (n-**day**-gay), which means bird. 'Airplane' thus becomes 'ndege mkubwa', or 'big bird'. 'Eropleni' (a-ro-**play**- nee) is sometimes used instead of 'ndege mkubwa', as both 'gari' and 'motokaa' are used for car, motorcar, automobile.

Sometimes a new word is invented that reflects a new reality. In the 1960's a new tribe was born, named of all things, after a motorcar! This might seem capricious or arbitrary, at first glance, but in fact it was precisely, if comically, accurate.

The most expensive and prestigious car in East Africa was the Mercedes Benz. Until Uhuru, only wealthy Europeans or Asians owned these vehicles, but after independence a number of Africans started to show up behind the wheel, and not as chauffeurs. Who were these these suddenly affluent Benz owners? Politicians of course! Power begets wealth. Wealth whets appitites. Pretty soon a number of these newly minted power brokers were buying Benzes and driving them around, showing them off. The ever-observant locals decided a new tribe had emerged. Not one based on a common language and culture, but one based on power and priviledge. This new tribe was aptly called the WaBenzi.

Most of these additions make sense in one way or another, but some words defy logic and seem to have no association, one to the other. Such a word is 'pikipiki'. A 'piki' is a stick used for throwing to knock fruit out of a tree, but 'pikipiki' means not two such sticks, but motorcycle! The **Oxford Standard Swahili-English Dictionary** suggests that this name reflects the sound made by a motorcycle. Some might suggest that I have too much idle time on my hands, but be that as it may, I have given considerable thought to this puzzle.

Not only do I have a surefire explanation for this aberration; I even know the exact motorcycle that caused it. It was a Harley-Davidson. As usual, a brain-torturing riddle, once solved, seems so obvious.

This is what happened, kweli.[142] A few disgruntled engineers in Milwaukee were sitting around the drawing board grousing about management. How to shaft those guys in the longi, sleevdi, whiti, shirtis was the distilled essence of their discussions. Their solution was to fiddle with the exhaust system: tune it to produce an obnoxious sound, slip the new design through the manufacturing process, and watch sales plummet. They succeeded masterfully, except for the plummet part. The sound caught on, became popular, and in fact became the hallmark of owning a Harley.

Africans also recognized that sound, so somewhere in East Africa, when a Harley went chugging by, the local word for this sound was applied to the motorcycle, and, as it was so apropos, that word was incorporated into Swahili. It might require some linguistic detective work to find the exact origin of 'pikipiki', but I am certain that somewhere, in some local dialect, it refers to the sound escaping from a Harley: the passing of gas out the tailpipe.

Q. How did the races get along?

A. The different races and ethnic groups got along very well, especially on the surface and when in direct contact with one another. Of course, attitudes and actions varied among individuals, but there was a general atmosphere of cooperation and accomodation.

That having been said, there were undercurrents of emotions and prejudices that flowed through most everyone. On a 'Superiority Complex' scale, the pecking order would place the Masai at the top, followed by the Europeans, Arabs, Asians and the other Africans. But the intensity of such feelings varied greatly from person to person, and expressions of prejudice were usually uttered only in the comfort of one's own group.

A Hehe and a Bena, when speaking to each other, might make disparaging remarks about Whites or Asians, but when among their own, might make equally scathing remarks about the other's tribe. Europeans and Asians were of the same bent. A colonial Brit would speak his mind to a white American concerning the shortcomings of Africans, but might save his real venom until among his like minded colonials and then inject it into a discussion about those bloody Yanks. A Hindu and a Muslim could agree that the Whites were insufferable and the Africans stupid and lazy, but among their own, the Hindu would torch the Muslim, and vice versa. It was a complicated tangle, but one that was usually kept in the closet. Usually.

FAQ

Every once in a while something would bubble to the surface. In the school newspaper at Arusha Secondary, for instance, one of the boys wrote an article accusing the Headmistress of racism because, he said, she favored Chagga applicants and Chagga students, she of course being Chagga. At Malangali, during a speech in class to expound on the subject of colonialism, one of the students got really fired up and was laying it hot and heavy to the British in particular, and whites in general. The rest of the class was drawn into the flame and got pretty excited. When the speech was over I walked to the front of the class, feeling somewhat uncomfortable, and said that perhaps I should leave. The class was shocked. Not shocked that perhaps they had strayed out of bounds, but shocked that I would identify myself with the maligned party. I was not 'white', I was their teacher.

I dated an Africaans girl on one occasion. She was someone I played tennis with at the club and was blond, tall and slender, and attractive. She got going on the Africans, using typical Boer expressions: they had just come out of the trees; they had just lost their tails. Even a nice set of barrels and a great pair of legs couldn't compensate. Like I said, I dated her once.

Then there are the Africans along the coast of Kenya who insist they are Persian. They don't look Persian. They don't speak Farsi. But they insist. At first blush this seems comical, but it is in fact a sad reminder that the African has been relegated to the bottom rung of the scale and many have deep insecurities about their place in the order of things.

In the chapter about my last hunt I have already mentioned the government poster that was distributed to the schools. That was only the most concrete incident of official racism, but government policy towards the Asians drove most of them to other lands. There were problems.

Still, this is nothing that doesn't plague mankind generally, from China to Russia, from Europe to the United States. And like in most places, we muddle through. On the ground, in everyday life, the various peoples of East Africa got along well.

---

[139] I used the German film Agfa in my cameras and had it developed unmounted for easier shipping home. Once there, mother and our neighbor, Verona Gottschalk, would cut and mount the individual slides into the thick, blue and white Agfa frames I would send in bulk.

[140] Karen von Blixen's motto: "To set sail is necessary. To live is not necessary."

[141] This article appears on the **travel.telegraph.co.uk** web site, filed on 3/4/2001. A number of additional mishaps are also presented on this site.

[142] Kweli means "really", as akin to "without doubt", as in 100% guaranteed certain.

CHAPTER 51

FTQ

There is one question that many people might want to ask, but are too polite to broach. I call this a Frequently Thought Question.

Q. Why did you want to hunt elephant, or put more bluntly, why would anyone want to kill so majestic an animal?

A. My response is not meant to be an apologia to those for whom the hunting mentality is foreign. To them hunting is killing pure and simple, and born of a blood lust that should have disappeared in the Bronze Age. People who think along these lines will continue to do so and there is nothing I can say that will change their point of view. We are simply on different wavelengths.

Killing is integral to hunting. The object of hunting is to kill something, be it a pheasant, a deer, or an elephant. Hunting is visceral at its base: elemental and instinctive. Let a fly get loose in the house, the hunt begins. Most people think nothing of running for the swatter or the spray. To us, a fly is of no consequence, yet a fly is a form of life and the taking of any life is killing. We westerners tend to value some life forms above others, however, and when it comes to elephants, we see majesty. But the subsistence African sees vermin. To the people whose lives hang on what they can coax from the stingy soil, the elephant is nothing but a giant rodent, one that menaces their crops, stores, and lives. A rat would be more welcome.

We raise chickens but turn queasy if our fried egg shows any sign of fertilization, a necessary step to it becoming the meat we also crave. We raise pigs in crowded pens, slaughter them, and then call the meat 'pork', instead of 'dead pig'. The waiter asks: "How you would like your pork chops?" He doesn't say: "Sir, how would you like your dead pig?" We eat the product but we mentally distance ourselves from the process. The African makes no such separation. In Swahili the word for animal is the same as the word for meat: 'nyama'. Whether an elephant or a zebra, an animal is just that, meat.

From the beginning, animals have been a resource for humans and their antecedents. Modern man has sentimentalized some animals while farming or exterminating others. We still kill for meat, but only within artificial, accepted norms. Somehow killing a pest to remove an annoyance or killing a pig to put chops on our plate is acceptable, but, to some, the hunting kill is reprehensible.

However, if killing was it. If killing were the only reason to go hunting, there wouldn't be many hunters. The outdoors, the campfires, the unexpected, the weird and comical things that happen, the yarns that spin around the the hunt and linger for a life time, the friendships cemented and made, the thrill of the chase, the flow of adrenaline and the discipline learned to control it, all make hunting an experience worth while to those who indulge. It's back to basics, at least somewhat. The stresses of the job are left behind. The interruption of ordinary, predictable, everyday life with an adventure whose outcome is uncertain is something savored before, during, and long after the event itself.

Your bare, tired feet in an ice cold mountain stream. The chill of the early morning air. The first cup of coffee. The pancakes black around the edges but gooey in the middle. The anticipation. The unknown, uncharted rest of the day. The enjoyment of nature and her bounty. For those of us who love it, hunting is a breath of fresh air, a peak rising above the plateau of everyday life.

I grew up in a world of guns and hunters. Shooting and hunting were just part of the landscape. When you are a child, your world is pretty much restricted to your immediate family. Hunting was as natural to me as the theater might be to someone raised in New York City. My father's friends were like minded and many of my school chums were also, and once in a while one of them would show up on a Monday morning and brag on the deer he had bagged over the weekend.

I got my first deer at twelve, but that was not my first hunt. At that age I already had considerable hunting experience under my belt. A couple of years earlier Dave and I had received BB guns for Christmas. We lived on five acres, with a forest behind our property that covered a couple of square miles. I got very good at stalking birds and knocking them off their perches. Many of them were cute little sparrows, but the twinge of regret was fleeting, overcome by the satisfaction of a successful stalk. Shooting and hunting were not only admired skills, but from my father's point of view, something to keep young boys occupied and out of trouble. We learned patience and perseverance and how to handle not only a gun, but also failure and success.

Africa was different only in degree: there was more variety, in abundance, and some of it was large and fierce enough to fight back. Because of this, Africa was the Mecca of hunting. When I arrived in Tanganyika, I was only interested in the 'how'. The what, when, and where took care of themselves and the why didn't even register. In my very first week I located **Tanganyika Hunter,** the best outfitter in the country, and it was right in Moshi where those of us in TEA were doing our orientation. Kismet.

After I had shot a few elephants and continued to press for more, Don Adams, a fellow teacher in Malangali, asked what I was trying to prove. I thought this a singu-

Hunting and Teaching in East Africa

larly odd question, but I could see his point from his perspective. He had bagged two elephant on a safari to Scotty's Camp and like the other American in our program who tried his hand at elephant hunting, he was satisfied with that one success. Now he could say that he had shot elephant, and that was the extent of his reach. I had different goals, though I didn't look at it in those terms at the time.

Trying to analyze one's motivation in hindsight is a bit tricky. Certainly I didn't feel any guilt about killing elephants. There were probably about as many elephant in Tanganyika at the time as there were deer in the state of Washington. The government had run elephant control schemes for decades, trying to reduce their population and keep them out of peoples' crops and granaries. In Tsavo National Park the elephants were so numerous they were destroying the very vegetation that sustained them, and the Kenya Game Department was going into Tsavo East and exterminating whole herds, right down to and including the calves. When I was in Tanzania I don't think a person could have placed himself as far as fifty miles from the nearest elephant, not in Dar, and not on the top of Kilimanjaro.

There were basically two parts to the drive that kept me going into the bush after elephant: I enjoyed the hunt immensely; and I guess I was testing myself, for myself. I loved the bush, the walking, the people I met, the rituals involved in pursuing and shooting elephant; and I wanted to become good at it. I also wanted to prove to myself that I could take the tension, the queasy feeling in the pit of the stomach, the fear. Not once or twice, but over and over. Every hunt, as I closed on the elephant I would get that permeating, stomach knotting feeling. John Taylor, an ivory hunter who shot over 1500 elephant, put it this way:

> "If any man tries to tell you that he was not a mite scared when tackling his first elephant, and even more so his second and third, you can safely call him a liar or consider him a freak with no more imagination than a hen."[143]

It's the imagination thing that plays on your nerves and ties the knots in your innards.

When I got close and engaged the target and his herd mates, the tension was almost palpable, but once I raised the rifle the nerves left, replaced by a surreal calmness, like an old person facing death.

Most hunts were blanks in terms of ivory, but all hunts were experience gained and country and people enjoyed. Being out in the bush with the guides and in the evenings with their families and friends around a campfire was reward enough for the trials and discomforts of heat, thirst, thorn, and bugs. And as a hunter you were accepted as someone they could relate to, as someone who could bring something of value to the table. You were not a tourist clicking a camera in their faces and ogling them like exotic specimens in a great outdoor zoo, you were a man engaged with them in something they understood, something natural and useful.

Africa was indeed the apex of hunting, and at the top of the peak was the hunting of dangerous game, and at pinnacle were the elephant. At the time I was there the professional ivory hunters were either retired or escorting rich folks around in Land

Rovers looking for something to shoot. Few newcomers had the opportunity to learn their craft. Not many had the time or the skills (and luck) to do it repeatedly and stay alive. Hunting was steadily becoming more regulated and restricted. The last chapter was in the writing.

I sometimes think I was born fifty years too late. If I could come back for another life at another time, I would return as an African explorer and ivory hunter. Life might be short, but it would be interesting, and the sail must be set.

---

[143] John Taylor, <u>Pondoro-Last of the Ivory Hunters,</u> Frederick Muller LTD, London, 1956.

Appendix A

Tippo Tib

Hamed bin Mohammed, Tippo Tib, was a half-caste Arab, born in the early 1840's to wealthy Arab parents who were merchants in Zanzibar. He was a big man, about six feet two inches, with a fine, powerful, intelligent face,[144] according to one European who met him.

He built a great commercial empire founded upon trade in ivory and slaves in the area west of Lake Tanganyika. This country, called Manyema, was rich in ivory, but the spur to Arab entrance was the depopulation of those lands closer to Zanzibar due to years of heavy slave raiding. As early as 1821, 20,000 slaves were reported herded into Zanzibar for sale, mostly from the coast, and it was not until Sultan Seyyid Said left Oman and settled in Zanzibar (1832) that the inland trade became more intense and organized. He had moved to Zanzibar for economic reasons and his only source of revenue was a flat five percent import duty. For this reason he greatly encouraged and developed trade, both on Zanzibar itself and inland. About twenty five per cent of his total revenue came from the slave trade and the raids shifted further, steadily further, inland as tract after tract became worked out.

Tippo Tib spent his early years in and around Zanzibar, but at eighteen his father took him on a trading expedition to Tabora. By the early 1870's, TippoTib had become a rich man in his own right and at that time left on a trip to the interior with $30,000 worth of goods borrowed from twenty Zanzibar merchants. He left these twenty creditors behind oscillating between fear and hope, but he was so successful that his reputation was established and by the 1880's his caravans departed Zanzibar with $80,000 in goods.

Tippo Tib built his trading empire through family connections and his personal traits of ambition, audacity and ability. A quotation from his autobiography will illustrate his nerve. He had heard that a certain African chief called Samu (Nsama) had hoards of ivory, so he was determined to trade with him:

The porters tried to disuade us saying; 'Don't go to Samu, he's got plenty of ivory but he is treacherous.' Samu dispatched a servant to summon us to his village. We

Tippo Tib

were summoned to come and collect the tusks. He had posted all his warriors ready, a fact of which we were unaware. Twenty of us went, together with ten of our slaves. When we arrived and I was leading, I was suddenly hit by three arrows, two of which hit me squarely and one slightly. However, our guns were loaded with bullets and buckshot and the enemy were packed like sardines. One round and they died like birds! When the guns went off, 200 were killed instantly and others were trampled to death. They fled. In one hour more than 1000 died. Our casualties were only two slaves killed and two wounded. [145]

Tib then confiscated 1950 frasila (58,250 pounds) of ivory, 24,500 pounds of copper, and some salt. Afterwards Nsama made peace and thereafter carried on regular and peaceful trade with the Arabs.

Sharp dealing and audacious raiding made Tippo Tib not only rich but also well known. Soon the Sultan of Zanzibar, Barghash, was entertaining him and offering financial support. He directed the Indian and Arab merchants to give Tib credit up to any amount. Success led to more success and H. M. Stanley put it this way: **He had invested his hard-earned fortune in guns and powder. Adventurous Arabs have flocked to his standard, until he is now an uncrowned king of the region between Stanley Falls (now Boyoma Falls) and Tanganyika Lake, commanding many thousands of men inured to fighting and wild Equatorial life.**[146]

Tib held sway over these lands in the eastern Congo through force of arms and reputation. If someone crossed him, he took immediate and decisive action. On one occasion he had hired 200 porters from a certain tribe and after a few days on the march they deserted, to a man. Tippo Tib quickly returned to their country with: **eighty guns, and in the space of five days had seized 800 men. They called me Kingugwa, 'the Leopard', because the leopard attacks indiscriminately, here and there. I yoked the whole lot of them together and went back with them to Mkamba, where the craftsmen I had with me made chains. I put the whole lot of the porters in these chains and sent my brother to go ahead of them, while I followed behind so that I could seize anyone who tried to escape.**[147]

Yet he often befriended Europeans like Livingstone and Stanley, though initially he thought them weak and foolish. Livingstone he passed off as **a big fellow. He had neither goods nor rations.** Stanley reports the following conversation with Tib preparatory to his trip down the Lualaba: **But my friend, I said, think how it would be with me, with all the continent before me, and only protected by my little band.**

Ah, yes! If you wasungu are desirous of throwing away your lives, it is no reason we Arabs should. We travel little by little to get ivory and slaves, and are years about it. It is now nine years since I left Zanzibar, but you white men only look for rivers and lakes and mountains, and you spend your lives for no reason, and to no purpose. Look at that old man who died in Bisa (Livingstone)! What did he seek year after year, until he became so old that he could not travel? He had no money, for he never gave any of us anything, he bought no ivory or slaves, yet he traveled farther than any of us, and for what?[148]

Hunting and Teaching in East Africa

His opinion of Europeans would soon change, however. When Tib returned to Zanzibar, Barghash explained the facts of life to this man who knew power through the barrel of a gun: the British had bigger guns. So did the other European powers. Tib would see his empire disappear as quickly as it took Stanley to descend the Lualaba, discover it was the Congo River, and set off the scramble for Africa. The British would control Zanzibar and Kenya, the Germans, Tanganyika, and the Belgians, the Congo.

Tippo Tib watched from Zanzibar as these explorers of rivers and lakes and mountains gobbled up everything in sight. He took no part in the resulting wars and lost considerable wealth due to them. He lived out his life in Zanzibar, and died there in 1905.

---

144 Barttelot, Walter George, The Life of Edmund Musgrave Barttelot, Richard Bentley & Son, London, 1890, p. 63.

145 Muhammed, Hamed bin, Maisha ya Hamed bin Muhammed el Murjebi yaani Tippu Tip, translated by W.H. Whiteley, Supplement to the East African Swahili Committee Journal No. 28/2, July 1958 and No. 29/1, Jan. 1959, p.9. The original Life of Tippu Tip was in Swahili written in Arabic script.

146 Stanley, H.M., In Darkest Africa, Charles Scribner's Sons, New York, 1891, Vol.1, p. 63.

147 Muhammed, p. 15.

148 Stanley, H.M., Through the Dark Continent, Harper & Brothers, New York, 1878, Vol. II, pp. 192-193.

Appendix B

Preventive Detention

Julius Nyerere expressed his views on preventive detention in a speech opening the University College in Dar es Salaam on August 21, 1964.

If one person uses his freedom of speech and organization in a manner which will greatly reduce our prospect of economic development, or endanger our national security, what is the Government to do? Freedom of speech, freedom of movement and association, are valuable things which we want to secure for all our people. But at the same time we must secure, urgently, freedom from hunger, and from ignorance and disease, for everyone. Can we allow the abuse of one freedom to sabotage our national search for another freedom?

Take the question of detention without trial. This is a desperately serious matter. It means that you are imprisoning a man when he has not broken any written law, or when you cannot be sure of proving beyond reasonable doubt that he has done so. You are restricting his liberty, and making him suffer materially and spiritually, for what you think he intends to do, or is trying to do, or for what you believe he has done. Few things are more dangerous to the freedom of a society than that. For freedom is indivisible, and with such an opportunity open to the Government of the day, the freedom of every citizen is reduced. To suspend the Rule of Law under any circumstances is to leave open the possibility of the grossest injustices being perpetrated.

Yet, knowing these things, I have still supported the introduction of a law which gives the Government power to detain people without trial. I have myself signed Detention Orders. I have done these things as an inevitable part of my responsibilities as President of the Republic. For even on so important and fundamental an issue as this, other principles conflict. Our Union has neither the long tradition of nationhood, nor the strong physical means of national security, which older countries take for granted. While the vast mass of the people give full and active support to their country and its government, a handful of individuals can still put our nation into jeopardy, and reduce to ashes the effort of millions.

I agree that, in the idealistic sense of the word, it is 'better' that ninety-nine guilty men should go free rather than one innocent man being punished. But in the circumstances of a nation like ours other factors have to be taken into account. Here, in this Union, conditions may well arise in which it is better that ninety-nine innocent people should suffer temporary detention than that one possible traitor should wreck the nation. It would certainly be complete madness to let ninety-nine guilty men escape in order to avoid the risk of punishing one innocent person. Our ideals must guide us, not blind us.[149]

---

[149] Nyerere, Julius K., Freedom and Unity/Uhuru na Umoja, A selection of Speeches 1952-65, Oxford University Press, Dar es Salaam, 1966, pp. 312-313.

Glossary

Amekufa (ah-may-**koo**-fa) it is dead.
Amekwisha (ah-may-**kwee**-sha) it is over, finished.
Asante (ah-**sa**-ntay) thank you.
Asian - in East Africa this term refers to people from India and Pakistan.
Askari (a-**ska**-ree, short 'a' sound) soldier.
Bado Kidogo (**baa**-dough key-**dough**-go) means in a little while, which could be a half-hour, half a day, or some other indeterminate length of time, like when pigs fly.
Bahati (ba-**ha**-tee) luck. 'bahati mzuri sana' would mean 'very good luck'. 'Bahati mbaya sana' would mean 'very bad luck'.
Barafu (ba-**rah**-foo) ice.
Baraza (ba-**ra**-za) assembly, or meeting.
Baridi (ba-**ree**-dee) cold.
Bila Shaka (**bee**-la **sha**-ka) without doubt; for certain.
Bonnet - British for the hood of a car (or a woman).
Boot - British for the trunk of a car. Is this the origin of the current slang term for the human derriere: 'bootie'?
Bunduki (boo-**ndoo**-kee) gun; rifle.
Bwana (**bwa**-na) sir. Generally a reference to an important man, but is sometimes used in reference to women, especially in woman to woman conversations.
Chai (**cha**-ee, but in practice it comes out as 'chi', in rhyme with 'fly') tea.
Chakula (cha-**koo**-la) food.
Cheti (**cheh**-tee) note, ticket, passport, certificate, 'chit'.
Chui (**chu**-ee) 'chewy', a great name for a leopard!
Dawa (**dow**-wah) medicine.
Dobi (**dough**-bee) laundry; or a person who does laundry.
Dudu (**doo**-doo) insects. Like 'kuku' and 'chui', another Swahili word that segues nicely into English.
Duka (**doo**-kah) a shop or stall. Usually refers to a small store.
European - a general term that covers all white people.
Gari (**gah**-ree) any vehicle on wheels, but commonly used for automobile.
Groundnuts - peanuts; not a reference to people, though the author has heard it applied variously to Californians and Texans, obviously a reflection of petty, politically incorrect prejudices.

Hunting and Teaching in East Africa

Hakuna (ha-**koo**-na) there is/are no, as in: 'Hakuna matata.' 'There are no problems.' 'There is no trouble.' 'There is no mess.' 'All is well.'
Hamna (**ha**-mna) there is none, as in: 'There is no food.' 'Hamna chakula.'
Hapana (ha-***paw***-na, all 'a's' with a short sound like in papa) no, none.
Hella (**heh**-la) a word for money referring to a coin, the Heller, from the German period of colonial rule. Used by some older people.
Huko (**who**-ko) there; over there.
Jambo (**Ja**-mbow) hello.
Kahawa (ka-**how**-wa) coffee.
Kama (**ka**-ma) like, as in "Kama ngombe," "like cattle."
Kanga (**ka**-nga) guinea fowl. The 'a' here is like that in 'angry'.
Karibu (kah-**ree**-boo) close, also an invitation to come into a home.
Kibo (**key**-bow) snow, in Kichagga. From this Chagga word comes the name for the main peak of Kilimanjaro.
Kiboko (key-**bow**-ko) hippo.
KiEngreza (Key-**ngray**-za) the English language.
Kifaru (key-**fah**-roo) rhino.
Kilima (key-**lee**-ma) hill.
Kiongozi (key-en-**ngo**-zee) guide.
Kismet - Arabic for fate. Also the well-chosen brand name of the foot motivated tire pump ubiquitous in East Africa.
Kiswahili (Key-swa-**hee**-lee) is the lingua franca of eastern Africa, including Tanzania, Kenya, Uganda, Malawi, and the contiguous parts of Zambia and the Congo. In English it is usually just 'Swahili'.
KNCU - Kilimanjaro Native Cooperative Union the name of the Wachagga coffee cooperative. The Chagga live around the southern slopes of the mountain, and Moshi is their principal town.
Kufa (**koo**-fa) death.
Kuku (**koo**-koo) a chicken. A name so perfectly suited to its subject.
Kuni (**ku**-as in you-nee) wood.
Kwaheri (kwa-**heh**-ree) goodbye.
Kweli (**kway**-lee) really, as in "for certain." Often spoken with a question of doubt in the voice: 'That kudu jumped over my Land Rover.' 'Kweli?'
Labda (**la**-bda) maybe.
Lengai (leh-**nguy**-ee) Masai name for God.
Lorry - British for truck, particularly a truck with an open bed.
Mafuta (ma-**foo**-ta) fat.
Maji (**ma**-jee) water.
Mbali (m-**ba**-lee) far off; distant.
Mbaya (m-**by**-ya) bad.
Mbogo (m-**bo**-go) Masai for Cape Buffalo, often used in the north-central part of Tanzania in preference to the Swahili word 'nyati'.
Mbu (**m**-boo) mosquito.

Mbuga (m-**boo**-ga) steppe, savanna.
Mchawi (m-**cha**-wee) a wizzard, a witch, one who practices the black arts. A sorcerer, a magician. A person to be feared and respected.
Memsaab (**mem**-sob) important and/or white woman. Sometimes a 'u' is added to the end, in keeping with standard Swahili: all words ending with a vowel.
Mganga (m-**ga**-nga) - a native doctor, a medicine man. Also used by Europeans for wizzard or witch doctor. See 'mchawi'.
Mingi (**mee**-ngee) many.
Mkali (m-**kaa**-lee) fierce, sharp. 'Tembo mkali.' 'Fierce elephant.' 'Kisu mkali. "Sharp knife.' 'Watu wakali.' 'Warlike people.'
Mkubwa (m-**koo**-bwa) big, superior.
Mlima (m-**lee**-ma) mountain.
MMBA - Miles and Miles of Bloddy Africa.
MMBTS - Miles and Miles of Beautiful Thorn Scrub. My addition to British Africanisms like 'MMBA'.
Moja (**mow**-ja) one.
Moshi (**mow**-she) smoke, and also the name of the Chagga town at the foot of Mt. Kilimanjaro.
Motakaa (mow-ta-**ka**-a) automobile.
Mpishi (m-**pee**-she) cook.
Mshangoa (m-sha-**ngo**-a) astonishing, amazing.
Mto (**m**-toe) a river of any size.
Mtoto (m-**toe**-toe) child, though usually just 'toto' when mixed into English. Plural would be 'watoto', and when used in an English sentence, 'totos'.
Mungu (**moo**-ngoo) Swahili for God. 'Shauri ya Mungu' would mean the same as 'kismet': fate.
Mwalimu (mwa-**lee**-moo) teacher; or a respectful reference to Julius Nyerere who had been a classroom teacher and was also considered the head teacher for the nation.
Mzee (m-**zay**-ee) an elder. A term of respect.
Mzungu (m-**zoo**-ngoo) a European, a white person; something wonderful, surprising, startling; ingenuity, cleverness, a feat, a trick, a wonderful device; instinct in animals and insects. 'Kizungu' - a European language. 'Vaa Kizungu' - to wear European clothing.
Mzuri (m-**zoo**-ree) good.
Najua (na-**jew**-ah) I know, the root word being "jua."
Ndio (n-**dee**-oh) yes.
Ndogo (n-**dough**-go) small; 'ndogo sana' would be 'very small'.
Ngay (**n**-gay) scorpian.
Ngombe (n-**go**-mbay) cattle.

Hunting and Teaching in East Africa

Nyama Wote (**nya**-ma **whoa**-tee) 'nyama' means meat or animals. Adding 'wote' would mean 'all the animals' or 'all the meat'.
Nyati (n-**ya**-tee) Cape Buffalo.
Nyika (n-**yee**-ka) wilderness; the bush.
Nyoka (n-**yo**-kah) snake.
Panga (**pa**-nga) machete.
Piki Piki (**pee**-kee-**pee**-kee) motorcycle.
Pombe (**po** -as in pom pom-mbay) local beer. Can be made from most any grain, and many fruits, bananas being a common base.
Porini (po-**ree**-nee) the bush, wilderness, the uninhabited wilds.
Punda Milia (**poo**-nda me-**lee**-ah) donkey with stripes, in other words, a zebra.
Rafiki (ra-**fee**-key) friend.
Saba Saba (**Saa**-bah **Saa**-bah) literally: seven, seven. Actually: July 7, celebrating the founding of the Tanganyika African National Union, Nyerere's political party.
Safari (sah-**fah**-rhee) a journey, or trip.
Salama (sa-**la**-ma) peace; often a greeting meaning peace be with you.
Shauri (**shah**-rhee) a discussion, debate, or argument.
Tembo (**teh**-mbo) elephant.
Twende (**tway**-nday) let's go, let's get out of here.
Twiga (**twee**-gah) giraffe.
Uhuru (Ou-**hoo**-roo) All syllables rhyme with "who". Freedom.
Ujamaa (ou-ja-**ma**-a) familyhood; encompassing the whole, extended family.
Umoja (Ou-**mow**-jah) unity, coming from the root word for "one," "moja."
Wabenzi (Wa-**ben**-zee) a new tribe formed after independence and peopled by the newly minted Mercedes Benz owners who were also the newly minted political elite.(Footnotes)

ISBN 141201935-4